The Whig Ascendancy

Colloquies on Hanoverian England

The Whig Ascendancy

Colloquies on Hanoverian England

Edited by John Cannon

Edward Arnold

© 1981 Edward Arnold (Publishers) Ltd

First published 1981 by
Edward Arnold (Publishers) Ltd
41 Bedford Square, London WC1B 3DQ

British Library Cataloguing in Publication Data

The Whig Ascendancy.
1. Great Britain – Politics and government – 18th century
2. Great Britain – Politics and government – 1660–1714
3. Great Britain – Politics and government – 1800–1837
I. Cannon, John
320.9'41'07   JN210

ISBN 0–7131–6277–5

Printed by Richard Clay (The Chaucer Press) Ltd,
Bungay, Suffolk.

Contents

Acknowledgements

It is always a pleasure to have the opportunity of thanking the people who have helped in the production of a book. First we must express our gratitude to the staff of Derwent College, University of York, who made our stay at Easter 1979 most agreeable and provided us with excellent facilities for our recording sessions. We were delighted to find, when we played the tapes back, that our rather earnest discussions had been punctuated by the ducks on the lake, who achieved, at times, a distinctly satirical effect.

We would also like to thank Professor Norman Hampson and his wife for some welcome hospitality on our stay.

Among the many people in the University of Newcastle upon Tyne who have given assistance, we must mention Miss Pat Murrell, who read the drafts and saved us from many errors. Miss Joyce Perkins and Miss Maureen Kavanagh of the Department of History wrestled with the typescript and reduced it to some order. Lastly we have to thank several of our students in the Department for suggestions and help, and particularly Miss Jill Dryden for assistance in proof-reading and indexing.

The whole enterprise received financial assistance from the Research Committee of the University of Newcastle upon Tyne, whose help is most gratefully acknowledged.

Preface

This book calls for a little more explanation than most. In origin it was an attempt to exploit the fact that seven of us, known to each other and working in northern universities, share a particular interest in eighteenth-century English history. It was therefore planned as a collective enterprise of a rather novel kind. We agreed that each of us would write a chapter on a theme of his own choice and then defend it against the others, in what turned out to be an unusually gruelling form of *viva*, with six examiners instead of the normal two. In the final discussion, we intended to draw together some of the themes that had come to the surface.

Our immediate objective was therefore twofold. We believed that the study of eighteenth-century history was emerging from the shadow that had long covered it. In particular, since the criticism has often been voiced that historians have left the Hanoverian period shattered and splintered, hard for the non-specialist to make sense of, we wished to look at it again, in the light of recent work, to see whether we could perceive some general interpretative framework within which it could be discussed and understood. Our second aim was to demonstrate to students how an article may be criticized and assessed. It is easy enough to advise students that they must at all times be wide-awake and vigilant in their reading – that, in Bacon's phrase, they must chew and digest: it is less easy for them to practise. We thought that they might find it instructive and even entertaining to see their elders taken to task for overstating their case, neglecting important evidence, employing misleading vocabulary, or trailing their prejudices.

We are all primarily political historians and we accepted the fact that there were important aspects of the period which we were not competent to discuss. The contributions reflected our own personal interests and preoccupations, but were grouped around a common theme – the nature of the Hanoverian political régime. Hence we arrived at our title, *The Whig Ascendancy,* with the sub-title drawing attention to the element of discussion in the volume. The colloquies took place on neutral ground at the University of York during three days of Easter 1979. Each session was recorded. We took it in turns to act as chairman and each chairman was responsible for producing the summary printed at the end of the chapter. The final discussion is printed almost verbatim, with the minimum of editorial interference. I should perhaps add that the original tapes are preserved in the Department of History at the University of Newcastle, *intacta et inviolata*, with no 'expletives deleted'.

I have also to report that, after some fairly rigorous exchanges, the combatants remained indefatigably on speaking terms. Indeed, the colloquies overflowed the seminar room into the bar and proceeded, unrecorded, long into the night.

This preface may help to explain some features of the book that might strike readers as tiresome. The articles are not as polished as they might be, since we took an oath not to alter them in the face of criticism – otherwise the point of the objections would have been blunted. Instead, each author was permitted to add a short rejoinder if he wished. In the final chapter, the use of christian names may seem somewhat cosy, but it is an attempt to retain something of the spontaneity and mood of the discussion. Finally, we must ask the indulgence of the people I call in the last chapter our 'absent friends' – those historians, many in number, whose work and opinions were dragged into our deliberations. If we have misrepresented them in any way, it was inadvertent: our debt to them is gratefully acknowledged.

John Cannon
Newcastle upon Tyne, 1980.

Notes on contributors

Cannon, John Ashton; born Hertfordshire 1926 and educated at Peterhouse, Cambridge; PhD, University of Bristol; subsequently employed by History of Parliament Trust; appointed Lecturer at Bristol 1961; Senior Lecturer 1967; Reader 1970; has held the Chair of Modern History in the University of Newcastle upon Tyne since 1976; Dean of the Faculty of Arts since 1979; publications include *The Fox—North Coalition* (1969); *Parliamentary Reform, 1640—1832* (1973); *The Letters of Junius*, ed., (1978); *The Historian at Work*, ed., (1980).

Derry, John Wesley; born Gateshead 1933 and educated at Gateshead Grammar School and Emmanuel College, Cambridge; MA, 1958; PhD, 1961; Research Fellow, Emmanuel College, Cambridge 1959—61; lectured at London School of Economics 1961—5; Fellow, Downing College, Cambridge, 1965—70; Lecturer at University of Newcastle upon Tyne 1970; Senior Lecturer 1973; Reader 1977; publications include *William Pitt* (1962); *The Regency Crisis and the Whigs* (1963); *Reaction and Reform* (1963); *The Radical Tradition* (1967); *Charles James Fox* (1972); *Castlereagh* (1976); *English Politics and the American Revolution* (1976).

Dickinson, H. T.; born Gateshead 1939; Reader in History in the University of Edinburgh and, from October 1980, Richard Lodge Professor of British History at Edinburgh; BA and MA University of Durham; PhD University of Newcastle upon Tyne; author of *Bolingbroke* (1970); *Walpole and the Whig Supremacy* (1973); *Liberty and Property: Political Ideology in Eighteenth-Century Britain* (1977); editor of *The Correspondence of Sir James Clavering* (1967) and *Politics and Literature in the Eighteenth Century* (1974).

Holmes, Geoffrey; Professor of History in University of Lancaster; born in Sheffield 1928 and educated at Woodhouse Grammar School and Pembroke College, Oxford; Doctor of Letters of University of Oxford, Fellow of Royal Historical Society and a Visiting Fellow of All Souls' College, Oxford, in 1977—8; lectured in History Department at Glasgow 1952—69 and Reader at Lancaster 1969—72; much of his published work has been on politics and religion, including *British Politics in the Age of Anne* (1967), *The Trial of Doctor Sacheverell* (1973) and *Religion and Party in Late Stuart England* (1975).

McCord, Norman; born at Boldon, county Durham, in 1930; graduated in King's College, Newcastle, then part of the University of Durham, in 1951;

national service as RAF fighter controller; postgraduate research at Trinity College, Cambridge, which resulted in his first book on the Anti-Corn Law League in 1958; Research Fellow at Newcastle and then Lecturer at University College, Cardiff; returned to Newcastle in 1960 and was appointed to a personal chair in social history in 1975; recent publications include *North East England: the Region's Development 1760–1960* (1979).

O'Gorman, Frank; born 1940 in Manchester; educated St Bede's Grammar School, the University of Leeds and Corpus Christi College, Cambridge; joined Department of History in University of Manchester in 1965 and is now Senior Lecturer; publications include *The Whig Party and the French Revolution* (1967); *Edmund Burke: his Political Philosophy* (1973) and *The Rise of Party in England* (1975); at present completing a study of popular politics and electoral behaviour from the time of Walpole to the Great Reform Act.

Speck, William Arthur; born Bradford 1938 and educated at Bradford Grammar School and The Queen's College, Oxford; BA, 1960; D.Phil., 1966; Tutor at Exeter University 1962–3; Lecturer at University of Newcastle upon Tyne 1963; Reader 1974; his books include *The Divided Society: party conflict in England 1694–1716* (1967, with G. Holmes); *Tory and Whig, the struggle in the constituencies 1701–15* (1970) and *Stability and Strife: England 1714–60* (1977); at present working on a study of the Duke of Cumberland.

1

The achievement of stability: the social context of politics from the 1680s to the age of Walpole

Geoffrey Holmes

Few periods of domestic politics have been as comprehensively researched and reinterpreted over the past 25 years as the years between the accession of James II and the high summer of Walpole. Yet, by a strange paradox, no other tract of English political history has been surveyed with so little regard to its social and economic climate. For much of the 1950s and 60s research on England's economy and her pre-industrial society in the late seventeenth and early eighteenth centuries failed to keep pace with the surge of new interest in the politics of the age, and political historians were chary of attempting ambitious social perspectives from a rickety platform. Today we can offer no such excuse. The days of pioneer building by such scholars as J. D. Chambers, Edward Hughes and Ralph Davis are now well in the past, and where Laslett beckoned many have followed. Some admirable textbooks have become available, synthesizing much important work; so that the 'student of 1979 must wonder why the politics of England from the 1680s to the 1730s and the structure, mobility and wealth (or poverty) of her population should still have to be studied in compartments with so few points of contact.

There are, of course, exceptions. Close attention has been given, for instance, to the political ramifications of the hostility between the landed and 'monied' interests after the Revolution and Edward Thompson has made an enterprising foray into the territory of Walpolean Whiggery through his study of the Waltham Blacks.[1] Small beginnings are better than none; but this paper has been written in the conviction that it is high time we went much further. In a single essay I can only take one of the problems with which political historians have been concerned in recent years and discuss it within its social context. It is, however, an important problem and remains as intriguing today as when it was first posed by Dr J. H. Plumb in the Ford Lectures of 1965.[2] Why was it that the political stability which had deserted England for most of the seventeenth century, and which for at least four decades after the early 1680s continued to elude the determined search of her monarchs and statesmen, was at length restored under a Whig ascendancy during the 20 years in which Sir Robert Walpole dominated the arena?

On the theme which Plumb so skilfully developed certain variations have since been composed. Some have suggested that instability was not as chronic a condition, even in Anne's reign, as the banshee howls of the party men tend to suggest; nor was stability an entirely hopeless dream as early as the 1680s, despite the scarring of that decade's politics by plot, rising and revolution. Others would argue that the stability of the Whig oligarchy was neither so unshakeable, nor so 'profoundly inert' as Plumb suggests. But whatever their differences of emphasis, few historians have challenged the three essentials of the original thesis: that some of the raw materials of stability, for example the great resources of patronage at the Crown's disposal, had already become available under the later Stuarts; that until Anne's death there were crucial vitiating factors – major political and religious problems still unresolved – which made it exceptionally difficult in an age of party strife to put these materials to good use; and that the Whig achievement after 1714 was and remains a notable one, whether or not we are content to personalize it as much as Plumb does.

Walpole's rôle apart, attempts to explain the ultimate achievement of stability have concentrated heavily on two factors, the functional and the ideological. Much has been made, and rightly so, of the subjugation of the early Hanoverian electorate by manipulative and corruptive techniques, and of the scientific application of patronage to the control of parliament. It has also been shown how most of the toxic party issues which had kept both the electorate and parliament in a state of fever lost their potency between 1715 and 1725, and how the whole temperature of politics fell sharply in consequence.[3] Admittedly, it has also been argued that in the years which followed the end of the wars with France in 1713, and especially after the South Sea storm had abated in 1721, the marked easing of the so-called 'conflict of interests' did something to tranquillize both parties, and that Walpole's policies in the 1720s made no small contribution to the process.[4] But with this sole exception it would be true to say that in social or economic terms the subject of the achievement of political stability in England has never been seriously debated. It is an omission which may well seem strange to anyone carefully re-reading the 1965 Ford Lectures, since they offered us a number of significant leads in that very direction.[5]

In this essay I am concerned with two questions that were not raised by Plumb's original thesis and with one question that was. The two former concern aspects of the restoration of stability which have been almost entirely neglected. In the first place, why did England manage to confine her bitter political feuds after 1688 by and large within strictly constitutional channels, that is to say, within the framework of parliamentary elections and regular meetings of parliament? Why, indeed, neither from 1681 down to the summer of 1688 nor from 1689 down to the 1720s – not even in 1715 – was there any significant support in England from any section of the higher orders of society for any resort to desperate or violent political solutions? (It was symbolic that the one successful revolutionary *coup* of the whole period, that of 1688 itself, was so profoundly respectable that it made the election of a 'free parliament' – in which political divisions could be legitimized – its main agreed objective.) In the second place, why was it that at no stage after 1681, not excluding 1688, was there any serious pressure from below, from the sub-political nation,[6] to exploit the troubled conditions created, first by the Stuart reaction, then by the prolonged 'rage of party'? Why, in other words, did the great issues of the day, while sometimes arousing popular interest, so singularly lack any intrinsic popular dimension, by complete contrast with the divisive political issues of the mid seventeenth century and the late eighteenth? I suspect it is mainly because they can only be satisfactorily understood in the light of what was taking place in English society between the 1680s and the 1730s that these two questions have so often been begged. It is always easier to discuss what did happen in the past rather than what did not happen. And yet in both cases what did not occur plainly had the most vital bearing on the country's prospects of achieving political stability. Whatever contrivances, electoral or parliamentary, were devised to stabilize the political nation, they could easily have been rendered ineffective by forces determined to by-pass their conventions.

Our third questions concerns that part of English society which formed 'the political nation' of the day. Historians have not demurred from J. H. Plumb's view that by the end of George I's reign these groups had achieved a measure of fusion, through a recognition of common interests and 'common identity', which they had not experienced since before the seventeenth century. But we know surprisingly little about this process. What can social or economic development themselves tell us about why, and when, it came about?

A paper concerned with the achievement of stability inevitably sets out to identify and emphasize those elements which tended towards fusion rather than schism in society and politics. This in no way implies that the *Divided Society* which Dr Speck and I portrayed in the late 1960s was a chimera.[7] A society riven by the animosities of Whig and Tory unquestionably existed in England after the 1688 Revolution, especially in the reign of Anne. As I now see it, however, the reality was less stark than we then depicted it. Even between the mid 1690s and the early years of George I – when party strife was at its most acute – there were softer contours on the social terrain, among them features which few scholars a decade ago were aware of. These contours, which began as early as the 1680s continued even through the volcanic eruptions of

1701–15, to hold out sure promise of a very different political landscape ahead.

★　★　★

Of all the 'social interpretations' of England's acute political instability between the 1620s and the 1650s, two have always struck me as inherently plausible. One relates to the popular, radical dimension which politics acquired after 1640: namely the fact that for long before the outbreak of the Civil War far too many of the rapidly multiplying 'poorer sort' in England had been pressing on economic resources inadequate to sustain them, above all on food supplies. Equally credible is the argument that the politically active families in the country had for some decades before 1641 been producing more younger sons than could be settled independently on the land. For in a pre-industrial society, even a relatively mobile society, where inheritance within the élite was largely governed by primogeniture, where the traditional occupation, fighting, had become an archaism, but neither professional life nor the political system had yet developed sufficiently to provide an adequate alternative to it, an over-supply of educated but frustrated younger sons was a recipe for serious disturbance. However, when we look ahead to the situation between James II's reign and George I's a difference of the utmost importance emerges. England still experienced acute constitutional and political problems; but they were no longer subject to aggravation from either of those two quarters formerly so dangerous. This was essentially because a basic socio-economic equation which had defied solution in the first half of the seventeenth century had at last been worked out. The three crucial elements in this equation were population, economic resources and opportunities for respectable employment. In late Tudor and early Stuart England these elements had been irreconcilable. I shall argue, however, that between, roughly, 1680 and 1714 they were brought into balance, and that this balance was then maintained well into the Hanoverian period.

　The first two major questions posed in this essay can only be adequately answered in the light of this remarkable achievement. A decisive check to population growth, together with the expansion of the country's economic resources (in particular her food supplies) and an eleventh-hour victory of wages over prices, had major implications for popular politics, and above all for the disappearance of popular radicalism. The same demographic trend interacted both with an upsurge in the economy and with a dramatic expansion of the employment opportunities available to the gentry's sons to inhibit violent reactions from politically alienated sections of the governing class, either from 1680–87 or after 1714. In each part of the equation supply and demand were brought into a comfortable balance which had been unattainable before 1660. And without such balances, I would contend, the resolution of the complex political problems of the late seventeenth century would have been far more difficult and the achievement of stability longer delayed.

The most important key to the whole situation is population: yet it is one which political historians investigating the years 1660–1760 have left almost entirely unused. So much uncertainty persisted for so long about the demographic trends of this century that ambitious speculation about their political consequences was naturally discouraged. With the mists now beginning to clear, however, it is profitable for us to ponder the situation that is being revealed and its implications for the achievement of stability.

England's population had grown with great rapidity for much of the sixteenth century, to reach a figure that was probably very close to four million by 1600; and recent years of patient analysis of parish register evidence[8] has confirmed contemporary impressions that this upward trend continued into the Stuart age, so that between 1600 and 1640 a population rise of a further 25 per cent or thereabouts took place. Although it is well nigh certain that the brakes then went on, the registration of baptisms, burials and marriages was so severely disrupted by the mid-century traumas of the Church of England that their evidence for the period of the Civil Wars and the Interregnum can never be wholly satisfactory. By 1662, however, a settled Anglican ministry had been re-established, keeping for the most part reliable records; and their message sharply suggests that over the country as a whole, for at least 50 of the next 80 years down to 1742 – the year of Walpole's fall – Englishmen at best little more than reproduced themselves. Only in the last decade of the seventeenth century and during the first two decades of the new century did a slow recovery set in. There is evidence of a rising birth-rate in certain regions;[9] of some relief by the 1690s from the very high basic levels of mortality experienced since the late 1650s; and of a remarkable intermission in those waves of epidemics which had regularly broken over England from 1658 to 1686, and which returned to fill the churchyards up and down the land between 1719 and 1742, with an especially massive slaughter in 1728–29. But for the loss of young men in the wars of 1689–1713 and for the persistence of endemic diseases such as smallpox, the recovery of 1690–1720 would have added more than a modest 300,000–400,000 to England's inhabitants. As it was, the population of England and Wale together, at around 5.8 million in 1736, had crept up by no more than four, and probably as little as three, per cent over the previous 80 years.[10]

Even in isolation so significant a check to the population growth of Tudor and early Stuart England must have been a powerful stabilizing factor. What was politically crucial was that in the context of a population which remained so stable, and actually declined slightly between 1660 and 1688, the other two elements that concern us, economic resources and employment opportunities, both increased. Moreover this increase was maintained, variably in the case of the economy, otherwise substantially, during the next 50 years, thereby guaranteeing that the moderate population growth which did take place between 1690 and 1720 could be accommodated with minimal social dislocation. The force of this argument can be appreciated by glancing next at the economic resources of England in our period and their political implications. And keeping in mind, to begin with, the popular threat to the achievement of stability, it is primarily to the changing face of agrarian England and to a standard of living which, with a few setbacks, rose steadily in the late seventeenth and early eighteenth centuries that we must look.

Although not every economic historian would agree with it, a very convincing case has been made of late for advancing the effective beginning of England's 'agricultural revolution' by something like a hundred years before its traditional starting-point in the middle of the eighteenth century. It is a simple enough matter, of course, to demonstrate that agrarian improvement after 1660 was uneven and often slow, and that innovations often had to struggle painfully up a mountain of caution and ignorance. Yet so many unassailable facts have now been established that historians interested in the ordinary Englishman's standard of living can no longer ignore them. It is plain, for instance, that agricultural prices remained remarkably low for the greater part of the years 1660–1750; and quite apart from the benefit to consumers, it is hard to credit that this price depression did not provide farmers and go-ahead landowners with a strong and sustained incentive to 'improve'. Certainly improved pasturage and winter feeding had enabled England by 1700 to become a country of meat-eaters to a degree that had not been possible a hundred years earlier. In 1722 the author of a best-selling contemporary description of England was to write:

> What Don Pedro de Ronquillo, the Spanish Ambassador, said of Leadenhall Market in London, that there was more meat sold in it in one week than in all Spain in a year, I believe to be perfectly true; for there are few tradesmen in London, *but have a hot joint every day.*[11]

Another firmly established fact is that England became a grain-exporting country from the 1670s and a heavy exporter after 1715.[12] Of course, all was not plain sailing with the harvest. There was a worrying run of meagre wheat yields in the period 1693–1700 and a 'pinching time' for the poor after the dismally wet summers of 1708 and 1709.[13] And yet it is now clear that at no time between 1679 and 1742 was

England in any danger of a genuine famine of the kind that struck Scotland with terrible force in the 1690s, or France in 1693 and 1709. A true 'famine', by definition, must cause heavy mortality, either directly or indirectly; and the parish registers tell us that the application of this emotive word even to 1709, when bread was dearer in southern England than in any year except one in the whole century from 1660 to 1760, is totally unjustifiable.

Although parish relief must have played its part in averting disasters, the main explanation must lie in the growth of agricultural productivity in most regions of England since 1650, to the point at which a population of little more than five million was not only guaranteed a comfortable surplus in an average year but at least a bare sufficiency in a bad one. English farmers were especially successful during the seventeenth century in extending the acreage given over to the lesser grains. Obsessed with the well known indices of wheat prices, historians have too often overlooked the fact that a failure of the winter-sown wheat crop did not mean the automatic failure of spring-sown barley and oats, and that rye, though winter-sown, was hardier than wheat.[14] It is surely no coincidence that only three times between 1670 and 1741 did English governments, sensitive though they were to any possible threat to public order, feel it necessary to exert their discretionary power under statute to place a temporary embargo on the export of grain. It is equally instructive that food riots in the reigns of William III and Anne appear to have been remarkably infrequent. They were predominantly Midlands or East Anglian phenomena, and even there concentrated mainly in the years 1693−95 and 1709.[15]

Agricultural progress was not alone in affecting the standard of living of ordinary Englishmen during the half-century after 1680. The rapidly cheapening prices of some colonial and East Indian goods, imported in great quantities during and after the trade boom of Charles II's later years, also contributed; refined sugar and tobacco had ceased to be luxuries by 1700, and tea by 1730.[16] Thirdly, there was an ample supply by the early eighteenth century of inexpensive clothing, especially the new calicoes and 'prints' of the Orient and Lancashire,[17] and also of household furniture and hardware produced for a large consumer market. Most important of all was the fact that before the end of the seventeenth century wages were at last winning the battle with food prices and the prices of consumer goods, for in an era of largely static population and exceptional wartime demands for manpower, labour had become a scarce commodity. In fact, some leading authorities are now convinced that in decades of especially good harvests and cheap food, most notably the 1680s and the 1730s, circumstances yielded the steady wage-earner an exceptional surplus spending capacity. The shrewd contemporary judgement of Defoe in the

1720s would seem to bear them out:

> As the people get greater wages [he wrote], so they, I mean the same poorer part of the people, clothe better and furnish better; and this increases the consumption of the very manufactures they make.

And it was 'the working *manufacturing* people of England' whom he considered to be the most favoured of all the wage-earners, spending more of their growing earnings 'upon their backs and bellies than in any other country'.[18]

Of course, there was much seasonal and some permanent unemployment in the England of 1680–1730, and for the late seventeenth century, at least, Hearth Tax returns and Poor Rate contributions have revealed considerable poverty. But for the political historian this should not obscure the other side of the coin. Population growth that was never more, and frequently far less, than steady; rising wages in many industries, involving in some cases increases of up to 25 per cent between 1680 and 1720; food that was in general cheaper, more plentiful and more varied than earlier in the seventeenth century, and at no time dangerously scarce: these elements together constituted an integral part of the fabric of political stability. More than anything else, they account for the almost total quiescence of genuinely radical politics between 1689 and the age of Walpole and Newcastle.

Although popular passions could often be inflamed by political or politico-religious issues, it is remarkable to what extent their expression was confined within conventional bounds. When popular feeling spilled over on any major scale it did so almost always into moulds already shaped by the feuds of the governing classes and of the electorate – an electorate overwhelmingly composed of men with some stake, however small, in property. It is surely valid to ask why it was that the Protestant mobs, the Whig and Tory mobs, the Church and Jacobite mobs, and the 'No Excise' mobs of 1688–1734 continually voiced the slogans of their masters, rather than articulating any distinctive grievances of their own? Or why it was that even when most powerfully stirred, and even in overcrowded, combustible London, the English lower orders showed no apparent interest in popular liberties, in rectifying some of the grosser inequalities in their society, or even in securing electoral recognition? There were, after all, radical, extra-parliamentary forces clearly identifiable in English politics as late as 1685. They were conjured into life in 1680–81 by the first Earl of Shaftesbury, desperate to keep up the momentum of his Exclusion campaign, and in 1683 government intelligence uncovered disturbing links between well-organized London republicans and radical groups in Dorset and the West Country. A recent scholarly study of the Monmouth rebels of 1685 suggests that some of them, at least, had imbibed the heady democratic wine of the Interregnum.[19]

Yet in general it would be true to say that for over a century between Venner's 1661 Rising and the late 1760s such popular forces, where (or if) they existed, were astonishingly inert. The brave words uttered on the scaffold in 1686 by Richard Rumbold, former proprietor of the Rye House, that 'there was no man born marked of God above another; for none comes into the world with a saddle on his back, neither any booted or spurred to ride him'[20] was a voice from the past, not a clarion call to the present or to the foreseeable future. Although Tory propaganda in Anne's reign did its best to wring what capital it could out of the supposed existence of 'Calve's-Head clubs' – cells of republican dissenters – in London, it is clear that from the 1690s onwards 'Commonwealth' ideas became, for the most part, the preserve of a handful of intellectuals or idiosyncratic political independents. Nothing illustrates more strikingly this change of custody than John Toland's legerdemain in 1698, when he re-wrote the *Memoirs* of Edmund Ludlow in such a way as to portray that old Cromwellian warhorse as a respectable Country Whig gentlemen.[21] Meanwhile *popular* radicalism came increasingly to resemble not so much an inactive volcano as a burnt-out crater. The fact was of crucial importance to the chances of building a politically stable state. With a constitution under considerable stress, from the 1680s at least to King William's death, with an uncertain succession thereafter, and with a political world violently embroiled until well into the 1720s in party and faction strife, even a mild eruption could have proved highly dangerous. Yet in 1688–89 there was scarcely so much as a warning puff of smoke, and in 1710, in 1715–16 and in 1733 it was impossible to detect even that.

It is an extraordinary fact that while a *jure divino* king was being turned off the throne in 1688, with no parliament sitting and for seven weeks no legally constituted government in England, the popular rôle in the revolution was limited to a short burst of ritual anti-Catholic rioting and game-poaching from 'Popish' landlords.[22] Scarcely less revealing is the political crisis of 1710, coming as it did at the fag end of a war of which the bulk of the nation had more than had its fill, after 18 months of exceptionally scarce and dear wheat, and when indirect taxation had begun to bite hard on 'necessaries' such as salt and meat. It was accompanied from March to October by a 'mobbish time' which most discomfited the Whigs. Yet no one in authority, either before or after the change of ministry, appears to have genuinely feared sedition, still less revolution; no one even called for the suspension of Habeas Corpus. The attempt of the London mob in March 1710 to pull down the Bank of England was not an act of egalitarian subversion: it had exactly the same basic motive as the more successful attempts at the same time to sack dissenting meeting-houses.[23] 'High Church and Sacheverell', 'God save the Queeen and the Doctor', the commonest utterances of the crowd all over England in 1710, were also the toasts of every Tory squire and parson. They were slogans that would sweep one party out of power and another in; but they signified no threat to either the social or political order in which these parties flourished.

The absence of a popular and spontaneous dimension to politics has not gone completely unnoticed, of course. Credit has been given to the Junto for swiftly weaning the Whig party after the Revolution from its uneasy association with its former plebeian, crypto-republican allies. It has also been suggested that any radical movements of a socially subversive nature were inhibited by the hierarchical emphases of Anglican teaching under the later Stuarts, combined with the still powerful Puritan legacy of providentialism.[24] It is clear, however, that among a proletariat increasingly untouched by organized religion, ingrained notions of social deference could not be taken for granted: the case of the Waltham Blacks underlined this in the 1720s, as did the growing suspicion that the new SPCK charity schools, by making children 'impatient of the condition they were born to', might undermine the very social assumptions their syllabuses were designed to endorse.[25] On a different tack, it has been argued that frequent General Elections during the lifetime of the Triennial Act from 1694 to 1716 provided a politically overcharged society with a safety valve; and this may well have been of importance in London and some of the most populous provincial towns where electoral disorders, involving both voters and nonvoters, were endemic.[26] The electorate itself is now known to have been both larger and socially humbler in the late seventeenth and early eighteenth centuries than we had imagined, and the fact that it was growing at a faster rate than the population, and was still capable of giving a rough-and-ready representation to the opinions of the man in the street, may have been a far more effective antidote to political radicalism than historians have generally realized.[27]

All these hypotheses, especially the last, have something to offer us. Yet none of them should be strained. Only one of the conditions they emphasize (the element of Anglican social control) applied for most of the 1680s, and only one (Whig dissociation) was operative after 1720. More to the point, they all leave out of the reckoning the most pervading and persistent condition of all. It is difficult to believe that popular radicalism would not have found some outlet in the years between Exclusion and the fall of Walpole, despite all discouragements or distractions, had there been any *sustained* popular grievances that could have been appealed to. Transitory or sectional grievances there were, of course, as there always had been; but none that were sustained. And the reasons must be sought not primarily in politics, or in religion, but in an exceptionally favourable long-term conjunction of economic and social circumstances. Of the variety of explanations posited to account for the 'respectability' of the Glorious Revolution, how many touch on the most vital fact of all, that the 1680s had seen year after year of 'marvellous bounty' from the land and the most important period of commercial expansion and prosperity in living memory?[28] The mid and late 1690s were hard years by comparison; yet by far the most important cause of popular unrest – the Recoinage of 1696 – was non-political. 'Country' campaigns in parliament in those years evoked no popular response, except in the 1698 Election. So too with the 1710 crisis. It is true that it burst upon a country which in many parts of the south had just suffered the two most appalling wheat harvests for half a century. Yet the barley and rye harvests of 1708–9 were more resilient and the food situation never got out of control. What is more, these were freak years: from 1700 to 1707 bread in many parts of England had been slightly cheaper on average even than in the plenteous 1680s.[29]

Only in the years 1715–16, when there were frequent disorderly demonstrations by Londoners in sympathy with the Jacobite cause, did a post-Revolution government half persuade itself that some threat existed to the established political and social order. But in this the Whig ministers of George I were utterly mistaken. True, there was much economic dislocation in the southeast in 1715 to lend a sharper edge to expressions of popular hostility to the new dynasty and to the Whigs. Nevertheless, after a most thorough analysis of this unrest, Nicholas Rogers has concluded that although 'the London plebeians were a more formidable and less malleable force than recent historians have taken them to be', theirs was no radical groundswell. Their main battlecry, of 'High Church and Ormonde', was no more than a variant on the theme of 1710: 'their political notions were basically derivative, . . . defined within terms of the existing political structure which allowed them a vicarious birthright.'[30] In this they were typical of their time. A fundamental conservatism stamps virtually every outbreak of popular disorder in England from 1688 to 1716, from the full-scale London riot to the smallest local protest against enclosure, 'forestalling' or impressment, and it can only be fully understood within the context of economic and demographic trends which placed no intolerable stress on the lower or lower-middling storeys of the social structure. The same goes for the continuing quiescence not merely of popular but also of petty-bourgeois radicalism long after the much-exercised electorate of 1689–1715 had succumbed to atrophy. Can it be coincidence that radical politics, linked to popular unrest, ultimately revived in the years 1768–70, at the end of a decade when a rapidly rising population suffered both hunger and industrial troubles infinitely more serious than anything England's population had experienced from the 1680s to the 1730s?

*   *   *

The basic demographic conditions which are so important in elucidating the first of the questions posed in this paper are equally relevant to the second. In the generation before the Revolution fewer children were produced, and crucially fewer survived to teenage and manhood, than in the generation before the Civil War; in the two generations following 1688 their number only moderately increased. This was not peculiar to the lower social strata. So far as we know it was common to every level of English society. Dr Hollingsworth has demonstrated that aristocratic families followed the same trend;[31] and there are no rational grounds for supposing that the gentry constituted a special case if the peerage did not. The political relevance of this has been completely overlooked. Yet it points directly to a further link of prime importance between political and social stability, annealed once again by economic prosperity.

There were in England in the 1680s hundreds of Whig gentry families, and, after 1714, several thousand families of Tory gentry, who found themselves confronted with the bleak prospect of prolonged official disfavour. To both these groups there seemed little doubt that the doors of government patronage and even of local honour had crashed to in their faces for good. For most Tories under the first two Hanoverians this proved only too true. And for the post-Exclusion Whigs there could have been no reprieve if Charles II had not obligingly died in February 1685. Had such massive proscriptions taken place in the very different social and economic context of the early seventeenth century they would have spelt disaster in terms of political stability. The frustrated cadets of the squirearchy, especially of those lesser gentry whose prospects of providing an 'independence' for their younger sons out of landed patrimony were virtually nil, were for two centuries after 1550 the likeliest material from which reckless men could hope to fashion a dangerous political *coup* in England.

Why was such a *coup* not attempted after the dissolution of the Oxford Parliament in 1681? Why was it ill-planned and bungled in 1683? Why did the rebellion which did materialize in 1685 fail so abysmally to attract 'true gentry' (as opposed to 'pseudo-gentry') support, even in the old Puritan strongholds of the west?[32] Do not these events, or non-events, suggest that a ready supply of martial material, primed by economic stringency or by an acute sense of social grievance, was no longer forthcoming? Admittedly, several years of repression had either removed or frightened off many potential leaders and subalterns of Monmouth's army by 1685. But the same cannot be said of the events of 1715. The unwillingness of the English Tory gentry to commit themselves openly to the Pretender's cause should be pondered, not taken for granted: for after 1688, 1715 was the year of all years that could have changed the political future of Britain, had the political desperation felt by many Tory gentlemen been matched by desperation of a more material kind. But it was precisely this material desperation – the kind of desperation that drives men beyond mere pot-valour – which was lacking; and the fact that it was lacking, despite all the rhetoric the Tories had expended during the recent wars on the wretched plight of the landed interest, gives us more insight into the real foundations of stability in early eighteenth-century England than we can get from the manipulation of places, pensions or boroughs. The same factor may be equally relevant to the surprising frailty of the Jacobite conspiratorial base in England between 1716 and 1727, to the total inertia of the English Jacobites, for example, at moments of opportunity such as the Atterbury Plot or the sudden death abroad of George I. With every year that passed after the Septennial Act of 1716, and especially after the decisive Tory election failure of 1722, the chances that the stability of oligarchic Whiggery would be disturbed at the polling booths steadily diminished. Yet Tory squires overwhelmingly chose to take their cue from their own shrinking body of representatives on the back benches of the Commons, who as Atterbury wrote despairingly in 1722 were 'a rope of sand', men whose 'thoughts both within doors and without are employed about nothing but securing their approaching elections.'[33]

The unwillingness of politically alienated gentry – even when they constituted a clear majority of their class – to attempt the overthrow of an inimical régime by force must not, of course, be simplistically interpreted. It would be absurd to seek the clues to it simply in the demography of the Augustan ruling class or purely in an economic context. We know that the psychological pressure exerted by the memories of 1642–60, shared by virtually all men of property in late Stuart England, had an important restraining effect on the embittered Whigs in 1681 and in 1685. The avoidance of another civil war in 1688, miraculous as it seemed to all concerned at the time, strengthened the determination of the next generation not to tempt Providence again. Such sentiments pervade the arguments on both sides during the Sacheverell debate in 1709–10, but above all on the Tory side where the influence of the passive obedience school of Anglican clergy had recently revived and touched new heights.

Nevertheless, even instincts as deep as these could have been overcome (as they had been in 1688) had things become too much to bear. This is why it was the ambivalent position of so many landed families which held the key and to the prospects of political stability. For however bleak the position must have seemed *politically* for the Tory gentry after 1714 (as with the Whigs in the 1680s), *socially* it was tolerable. Between 1680 and 1740 an exceptionally favourable combination of circumstances conspired to cosset England's governing classes, making not merely political frustrations but the trials of two burdensome wars and the resentments aroused by novel social groups more supportable. It was a combination made up, on the one hand, of a lower birth-rate than that of their Tudor and early Stuart forebears and a high rate of child mortality; and, on the other hand, of the fresh channels of social mobility and the unprecedented range of respectable employment opportunities that were now open to their younger sons. In the very decades that gentry families began to shrink significantly in size and so bring the responsibilities of family heads within more manageable compass, the first phase of the great 'Commercial Revolution' of the seventeenth century was unfolding. Of even greater importance in the long run was the redoubling of demand, at the very same period, for a range of professional services unthought of two generations earlier. Together these developments guaranteed that few younger sons of gentle birth who survived to manhood need be inadequately provided for, and that the aspirations of the majority could be satisfied with little loss of status. This is not to say the landed interest was without its problems, particularly in the war years. But historians have taken too little account of the fact that, though the Lord took away with one hand from many country gentlemen, He often gave with the other.

In 1694 Edward Chamberlayne remarked of the younger brothers of the gentry that, with 'small estates in land', they were commonly 'bred up to divinity, the law, physic, to court and military employment; but of late [he added, with marked distaste] too many of them to shopkeeping.'[34] Because in the long run it was the expansion of the professions which offered the stoutest lifeline to the gentry, it is easy to overlook the significance for them, and ultimately for politics, of the spectacular burgeoning of England's foreign and colonial trade in the 1670s and 1680s. This undoubtely increased the options of the lesser gentry, in particular, as the case of the Heathcote brothers – who came of stock uncharacteristically prolific for its time – perfectly illustrates. 'Gilbert Heathcote, gentleman', who died in 1690, belonged to the younger branch of a minor Derbyshire landed gentry family and owned properties at Monyash and Tapton, and at Barnsley in Yorkshire, as well as houses and tenements in Chesterfield, where he resided. To lay out premiums for the apprenticeship of seven sons, mostly in London, between 1667 and 1683, and then to find £500 to launch each into the world, was not easy for him. But the sons almost all served their apprenticeships in the expanding trade branches of Charles II's later years and the eldest – the great Sir Gilbert, wine merchant and Bank of England tycoon – was later able to thank God, not only for 'one of the best of fathers' but for having 'so particularly blessed his care in our education as to let him live to see his seven sons all merchants in good esteem, a thing scarce to be paralleled.'[35] The Heathcote brothers differed only in number and breadth of achievement from many other young men from comparable backgrounds, or better, who followed similar tracks in the years between the Restoration and the Revolution. The Heysham brothers of north Lancashire and the Scawens of Buckinghamshire provide four examples among many. And like Sir Gilbert Heathcote, the two Scawens were able to graduate after the Revolution from overseas trade to positions of great influence in the Bank and the attainment of enormous wealth.[36]

However, the benefits of the 'Commercial Revolution' were not limited to London. In the thirty years after the Restoration many outports cashed in on the new trading opportunities in northern Europe, Iberia, the Mediterranean lands and the New World, and the long years of war thereafter enabled them to consolidate their gains and continue their slow erosion of London's mercantile dominance. At the same time domestic industries which grew in response to these commercial stimuli brought new vitality and wealth to the manufacturing and commercial classes in those towns which were their chief foci. These changes were important to the rank-and-file gentry of Lancashire and Yorkshire, of the north and west midlands, of East Anglia and the southwest. Nor were some of their better-off county neighbours too proud to benefit from them. Provincial apprenticeships, to merchants, tradesmen or manufacturers, now pointed to viable careers for gentlemen's younger sons;[37] they were cheaper than London apprenticeships[38] and there is evidence to suggest that between 1680 and 1740 they were becoming more popular. They must surely have been balm to the politically frustrated. The wealthy merchant clothiers of Leeds between William III's reign and George I's were taking apprentices even from major families, like the Kayes of Woodsome, Tory knights of the shire, as well as from such lesser gentry as the Micklethwaites of Terrington and the Oateses of Chickenley. Merchant houses were not the sole attraction to gentle families: Manchester and Bolton linen drapers had begun to recruit from the squirearchy, outside as well as inside Lancashire, as early as 1680, and we hear of John Anderson, born into 'as considerable a family as any in Lincolnshire', serving his apprenticeship with a linen draper around the turn of the century. But merchants did enjoy a special cachet, and just as Leeds and Hull became magnets for the Yorkshire gentry so did Liverpool for those of Lancashire. Among the prospering traders who laid the foundations of the town's greatness in the years from 1690 to 1720 were younger sons of the Norrises of Speke and the Claytons of Fulwood, along with William Cleveland who was a transplant from a Leicestershire family.[39]

The case of the Norrises is instructive in more ways than one. Like

Heathcotes they were an unusually fecund stock. Thomas Norris, who inherited the encumbered Speke estates in the 1680s, had five younger brothers in 1685. Two of them went into trade; but of the three others, one went to sea in the merchant service, another trained in Oxford for the Church, and the third qualified as a physician and practised in Cheshire. It would be difficult to exaggerate the importance of the unprecedented expansion of the English professions after 1660 in satis-fying both the economic needs and the social aspirations of the great majority of country gentlemen who had younger sons, or brothers, to establish creditably. The Church of England did not share significantly in the physical expansion; yet it did achieve higher prestige than it had ever done before 1642, and began to attract a greater proportion of recruits from armigerous families. Medicine was able to maintain its status as a suitable profession for gentlemen under the later Stuarts, owing not a little success in attracting their sons into 'physic' to the fact that by 1700 a Continental training could be had more speedily, more efficiently and more cheaply than one at home.[40] Its attractions could never compete, however, with those of the law. With demands for legal services heavier even than in the litigious early seventeenth century, calls to the bar maintained record levels throughout the 1670s and 1680s; and it is striking how often from now on barristers from pro-vincial gentry stock chose to make their base not in London, where the competition was ferocious, but in the towns of their native heaths. At the same time, the rising profits of the 'lesser degrees' of the law began to tempt more of the gentry, especially those in straitened circum-stances, into the more economical course of apprenticing their younger sons to attorneys or solicitors as articled clerks.[41] Despite the presence of too many black sheep in the profession, the properly qualified and regis-tered attorney had already begun even before 1688 to establish his claim to the status of 'gentleman', and by 1730, this transmutation was com-plete for *bona fide* solicitors as well as for attorneys.[42]

For the gentry one of the most promising achievements of the Resto-ration monarchy was the success of Charles II and Pepys in making the new naval profession more attractive to young men of good breeding. Significantly, a narrow majority of the men who earned distinction as admirals during the wars of 1689–1713 were of gentle birth and had taken up 'the sea-service' as a career before the Revolution.[43] Such officers had been far less prominent in the 1650s. Once these wars began it was new professions rather than old ones which surged ahead, making it easier than ever before for the appetites of the gentry to be assuaged. The Royal Navy had become by far the most imposing force of its kind in the world by the beginning of the eighteenth century. Even so, during the 20 years after the Revolution it offered fewer career opportunities than the army; for land warfare on an entirely new scale raised the number of commissioned officers in the army by the later years of Anne to at least 4,000, well over six times their number at the end of Charles II's reign. The purchase system guaranteed that men of some birth and connection would enjoy most of the pickings, but the fact that its demands were not excessive in wartime, so far as the ordinary foot regiments were concerned, proved a boon to many poorer gentry families. In addition to the purchase system there was also by Anne's reign a half-pay system for 'military men', a system institutionalized for the peacetime army in 1713;[44] and this guaranteed that the massive contraction of the army from 1712 onwards was not accompanied by a proportional contraction of the profession.

Between 1680 and 1725 the bureaucracy of the Crown grew out of all recognition, and many of its largest departments achieved a new professionalism. Most of all was this true of the revenue service. The London offices of the Exchequer, the Treasury, the Customs and the Excise, the Post Office, and the large new revenue offices of the war years all teemed with gentlemen's sons. Many of their fathers had been well content to secure them clerkships of as little as £50 to £60 a year initially, in the hope that they would lead to better things in a civil service which now offered far greater career security, as well as hundreds more London jobs, than had been the case before 1680: indeed in many offices clerkships were the only way to promotion. Little is known as yet about recruitment to the local posts in the revenue departments which accounted for almost half the new bureaucracy: there were over 6,000 of them by the 1720s. But there are indications that to landed families still scratching along on rental incomes of £80–£200 a year in the early eighteenth century, the prospects of placing a younger son in, say, one of the 2,900 local gaugerships in the Excise, at £50 a year, was not a horrifying one. The route that could lead to Supervisorships, worth £90 a year by 1715, or to Collectorships of £120 a year, posts of considerable local status, was not to be lightly ignored.

The growth of the professions was one of the essential elements from which the fabric of political stability was created in the years from the 1680s to the 1730s. It was of great moment, both at the time and for the future, that in the course of this half century the English gentry acquired a gilt-edged investment, commonly (though not always) regardless of political affiliation, in this major social change. And to the achievement of stability not least important was the acquisition before 1714 by so many gentry families of a vital stake in those new professions, now firmly wedded to the service of the state through pen or sword.

*   *   *

Trends that with hindsight can be recognized by historians were not all equally plain at the time. To many contemporaries that 'sense of common identity in those who wielded economic, social and political power' which, as J. H. Plumb reminds us,[45] was so essential a prerequisite of stability, still seemed far from realization as late as the second half of Anne's reign. And in the eyes of some thousands of country gentlemen, especially, at least two of the major changes taking place in recent years in the fields of commerce and the professions caused unease: so far from relieving social stresses they appeared to be creating unhealthy new tensions and thereby aggravating party-political animosities. War had led to the diversion of much London capital investment from overseas trade either into the new funded loans, at enticing rates of interest, or into the stocks of the big City corporations, three of them post-1689 creations; and in the process a financial élite of startling wealth and influence had emerged. War had also provided another ladder to unacceptably rapid social advancement by necessitating armed forces of unprecedented size. Looking at these developments with a jaundiced eye, and fearful of their further extension, many country gentlemen in Queen Anne's England – especially Tory squires who were readily convinced that the Whigs were scooping the pool – would have been hard to persuade that the governing class of their day was moving towards fusion rather than towards greater fission. Sir John Pakington voiced their fears when he spoke in 1709 of the danger of 'the moneyed and military men becoming lords of us who have the lands'; and in the winter of 1710–11 the fire of Swift's *Examiner* was turned against this same unholy, socially disruptive alliance.[46]

It is with the reality behind these fears, and the light which recent work on society and the economy can throw upon it, that the third and final question in this essay is concerned. Were the assimilation of novel social groups, the forging of links of mutual interest running through the governing class and across the lines of party loyalty and in the end the removal of social conflict from the causes of political dissension, achieved with great suddenness in the 1720s, and then only because a prolonged period of peace had removed the worst element of friction? Or were these processes far more gradual, and far earlier in their beginnings, than most political historians have assumed – or indeed than the noisy battle-cries of the early eighteenth-century 'conflict of interests' would seem to suggest?

Some points are certainly clearer today than they were a decade ago. They do not alter the fact that after its eruption in the 1690s the 'conflict of interests' did put the achievement of political stability in greater jeopardy. Neither do they relegate to the level of a phoney emotion the alarm expressed about it, at a time when war and party fury were wracking the nation. The rise of a 'new interest' in the City, incorporating 'a sort of property which was not known' in 1688,[47] was no figment of Tory imaginations. It was a blazing comet across the London sky, and in its garish light a few emotive incidents, such as the Bank's ill-considered deputation to the queen in June 1710, not unnaturally took on a sinister significance. But one can also understand how Westminster politicians, dazzled at the time by the comet's light, became blind during Anne's reign to those reassuring signs which can now be distinguished. They were loth to recognize that the 'conflict of interests' was primarily a metropolitan phenomenon: a source of genuine stress in London and the heavily taxed southeast, but of less account to the many counties where the Land Tax was lightly assessed and no 'new interest' had intruded into economic life. They either did not realize, or chose not to see, that the numbers of 'monied men' pure and simple – those 'retailers of money' whom Swift denounced as a threat to the constitution – were very few; that fundholders or company directors were more catholic in function, and often more traditional in background and more assimilable socially than hostile propaganda allowed. While noting with apprehension the cautious attitude of London businessmen towards land purchase, interpreting it as a device for evading a just contribution 'to the public charge', country gentlemen rarely observed that this trend pre-dated the financial revolution and even the war, and did not anticipate that it would be reversed once a saner balance was achieved between land values and rents and profits from trade or paper investment.[48] The years that immediately followed the Peace of Utrecht did much to prove the pessimists wrong, while the South Sea Bubble and its aftermath completed their re-education. Not merely did the 1720 crisis bring land back into a degree of favour with the City investor it had not known since the 1650s; it also killed for good the dangerous myth that all the 'knavery and cousenage' which the country gentlemen had been coached into attributing to the monied men was purely the monopoly of the Whig side in the City.

The 'military men' had always been rather more of a paper tiger than the 'monied men', because even at the height of the wars they were readier to translate their professional profits into landed security and assume the social and fiscal obligations of 'men of estates'. And in any case, the quintessential military men of the quarter of a century after the wars were no longer those ogres of Swift's *Examiner*, that favoured minority of 'generals and colonels' who were accused of jostling honest squires out of their borough seats in 1710 and jamming London's streets with their coaches. Far more typical of the early Georgian social scene were the hundreds of half-pay army officers, who spun out precarious genteel existences round the card tables of Tunbridge Wells or Bath, the coffee houses of Stamford, or the assembly rooms of York or Winchester.[49] They were men whose stereotype social peccadillo –

hanging out for a well endowed wife from the county society from which most of them originally sprang – was a subject rather for mild satire than for deep social or political unease.

The chief beneficiaries of the army's expansion between 1685 and 1712 were the younger sons of the country gentry. But they were not the sole beneficiaries. In the years of ample opportunity and rapid promotion under William and Anne the new officer corps absorbed both scions of the aristocracy and representatives of the urban bourgeoisie.[50] As well as the great economic advantages it conferred on the gentry, the growth of the professions did bring wider benefits to political society in Augustan England. Indeed, in the context of the long haul towards stability it was important that the gentry, while richly participating in the profits, as in the army, did not monopolize them. For the professions were the most active vehicle of social mobility in this period; and as such they had a crucial contribution to make to that burgeoning 'sense of common identity' within the political nation which concerns us. Most professions recruited widely – far more widely, indeed, than did the army. They were consequently able to provide invaluable milieux in which thousands of men of landed and often armigerous families could find common ground with thousands more from very different backgrounds. Here a community of interest could genuinely be experienced, based on mutual concerns and respect. Professional status itself became a bond that served more tightly to integrate many units of local society. Mutual professional interests even helped to heal the breach between Anglicans and Dissenters.

We may take this line of argument, in conclusion, one stage further. Professional men, almost by definition, were a predominantly urban breed. And the towns of Augustan England had an important contribution to make to the achievement of stability. The new social and cultural attraction of the provincial urban community proved a remarkably successful solvent of both social and political distinctions within educated society, in both its upper and middling ranks, as our period unfolded. By 1730 contemporaries were far more alive than their predecessors of early Restoration England to the social advantages of the growing town. They had become aware of it as a place where the gentleman's son (or daughter) living on an annuity or on investment income, the lawyer or doctor, the army officer awaiting re-employment, the retired or even still practising merchant, the smart innkeeper, and not least the squire for whom the country life had lost its charm, could live together in a habitat that was congenial, increasingly well appointed and relatively cultivated. Furthermore, these revivified towns were being recognized as places where the genteel could by and large live more cheaply than elsewhere: no negligible consideration in an age of high taxation. Not even the presence of trade or developing industry was yet seen as a deterrent by neighbouring gentry: Shrewsbury, Chester, Derby and Nottingham seemed scarcely less attractive than Bury St Edmunds, Warwick, York and Beverley. The early eighteenth-century provincial town had, in fact, become a social welder of exceptional importance.[51] In London, with its profusion of coffee houses, taverns, mug-houses and clubs, there persisted a good deal of both social and political segregation. But the social commerce of provincial towns and cities between the 1680s and the age of Walpole, as typified by, say, the race meeting, the public concert, or that supreme symbol of the new provincial 'culture', the assembly room, was not the exclusive preserve of the families of the town gentry, the clergy and other professional men, and the neighbouring squires. The assemblies of Sheffield and Birmingham catered alike for merchants, wealthy 'hardwaremen', ironmongers and goldsmiths, for parsons, medical men and attorneys, and for the squires who came in from their grand houses outside the towns. And in Leeds R. G. Wilson has shown us vividly how, in the first half of the eighteenth century 'not only did the close association between gentry and merchants . . . create a society that was far more open than on the Continent, but also there was a perfect mutual understanding of each other's world.'[52] I know of no parallel in any growing or prospering late seventeenth or early eighteenth-century town to the social segregation which the new manufacturers of the 1770s and 1780s were to experience.

Without social stability, as J. H. Plumb has argued, there could have been no political stability. And it has been the contention of this essay that outside London and the southeast the fabric of social stability in England from the 1680s onwards was basically strong and growing steadily more secure. This fabric was woven not from artificial fibres but from natural ones: from the necessary 'sense of common identity' within the political nation itself, and the necessary measure of acquiescence from those who stood outside and below it. They were fibres that owed their toughness and resilience to organic growths, rooted in the social and economic evolution of England since the Civil Wars. Walpole's consensus policies of the 1720s and 1730s possibly made the growths still healthier; but they did not produce them.

Naturally it is impossible to quantify, and difficult even to pinpoint with concrete examples, the precise contribution of demographic stasis or the growing real wages of labour to the process whereby social stability was finally translated by 1730 into political stability. Still more is this true of such intangibles as the expansion of the professions and 'the urban renaissance'. But that such factors made their contributions we can be sure. Of course, provincial party politics delayed the completion of the work, particularly in towns which experienced frequent and often rancorous elections. But the altogether slower pulse-rate of political life after the passing of the Septennial Act in 1716 ensured that even in such parliamentary boroughs the logic of social change could not be resisted. When John Macky visited York soon after George I's accession, the city's 'polite' society was still embarrassed by the convention, established in the acrimonious atmosphere of the previous reign, of holding two weekly assemblies: Monday being a Tory day, Thursday reserved for the Whigs. Such anti-social doings could not however be tolerated in more tranquil times. Lord Carlisle, staunch Whig though he was, took the initiative by 'carrying mixed company' to both assemblies; and Macky learned that 'the officers of the army' had subsequently played their part in the healing process by themselves 'making no distinction'. Although the rival gatherings had merged harmoniously long before it, the appropriate epilogue was played out in 1730 when work began on the building of Lord Burlington's splendid assembly rooms, one of the urban showpieces of the north.[53] Of a thousand bricks such as these, small though each may have been, was much of the solid edifice of early Georgian political stability constructed.

Colloquy on chapter 1

H.T. Dickinson

Discussion on this paper focused on three issues: the achievement of political stability, the economic and social foundations of Holmes's thesis, and the reasons for the absence of popular radicalism in an age of intense party rivalry.

Cannon wondered whether Holmes was retreating from the position which he had taken up in earlier works when he had been at pains to stress the intensity of party rivalry during Anne's reign.[1] Holmes saw no reason to retract his earlier claim that Whigs and Tories had then been sharply divided on a whole range of issues, but was prepared to tone down his previously unqualified emphasis on how divided English society had been. In looking at the period from a different vantage and with different priorities in mind he had become more aware of the long-term social and economic factors which helped to promote stability. Neither the rage of party nor the 'Divided Society' of which he and Speck had written in 1967 were illusory; but it was possible that in the past he had overstressed Whig—Tory disputes as a *cause* of political instability, whereas he would now concede that they were rather a *symptom*. Some progress towards political stability had clearly been made before 1714. There was much greater ministerial stability during the last decade of Anne's reign than in the 1690s. The queen's ministers only lost one Commons division in the period 1708 to 1714 and the relations between Crown and parliament had been put on a fairly even keel before 1714.

O'Gorman was not convinced that there was a divided society in the reigns of William III and Queen Anne when there were so many signs of social and economic stability. In his view the similarities and continuities between the periods before and after 1714 were more significant than the contrasts. Holmes, supported by Speck, was not prepared to go so far. Both saw a marked change in the political situation between Anne's reign and the 1720s. Party divisions before 1714 ran very deep on a number of issues – on religion, the war, and the succession to the throne in particular. While politicians had made some progress in adapting to post-1688 circumstances, they were not in agreement on these crucial issues. Holmes suggested that the governmental instability of Anne's reign was due in part to the refusal of the queen and her leading political managers, Godolphin and Harley, to submit to one-party rule. St John and the high Tories might well have instituted a one-party oligarchy after 1710 as ruthlessly as the Whigs had done after 1714 had Harley and the queen not frustrated their ambitions.

The discussions on the social and economic evidence presented by Holmes were more central to the thesis of his paper. Speck questioned whether the demographic evidence was as firm as Holmes supposed. (pp. 5–6) Population statistics for this period were not entirely reliable; estimates for the population of England and Wales in 1688 varied between 5,200,000 and 5,800,000; 'this is so large a discrepancy that we cannot say there is a firm base to start from'. Holmes accepted that population figures were only estimates and for this reason he had preferred to base his case on the general trends of demographic change. His figures were largely gathered from Anne Whiteman and the group of Cambridge scholars engaged in research on population.[2] They had proved that the population of England and Wales was larger in 1660 than historians had previously thought, that the population was fairly stable in the period 1660 to 1690, grew moderately in the years from 1690 to 1720, and then levelled off again during the following 20 years. Speck feared that Holmes was asking his readers to accept the Cambridge estimates prematurely as a new orthodoxy.

Speck went on to ask whether it was significant that demographic growth reached a plateau in the period of political stability whereas a faster rate of growth had occurred during the era of political instability. Dickinson added that commercial and financial growth were also slower in the years of political stability than they had been in the previous decades. Holmes admitted the superficial attractions of these arguments but he would not like to draw any sharp distinction between the social and economic developments before and after 1714. Although he accepted that the financial revolution of the 1690s had caused most trouble in the reigns of William III and Queen Anne, he preferred in general to consider the period from 1680 to 1740 as a whole when examining social and economic developments. He also disputed any suggestion that the economy was stagnant between 1720 and 1740; Little's thesis was far too extreme.[3] Growth was slower, but in almost all sectors of the economy it was continuous during these decades: 'The general trend was inexorably upwards'. He accepted Dickinson's point that slower economic growth might have been a factor in promoting political stability in the age of Walpole, but was not convinced that faster economic growth in the earlier decades had been a significant cause of political instability. On the whole, Holmes believed that the results of the commercial revolution had been beneficial for society at large.

McCord thought that Holmes's case could actually be strengthened by showing that there was not necessarily any conflict of interest between those involved in agriculture, manufacturing and mining. Indeed, it was often landed men who developed all three sectors of the economy. Most towns, even those experiencing significant growth, were still quite small and were closely involved with the social and economic life of their rural hinterland. Holmes agreed with these observations. In most areas there were close social and economic links between the urban merchant oligarchy and the local landed gentry. While several towns such as Liverpool and Birmingham did grow significantly, no town, except London, had a population larger than 35,000 to 40,000 in 1730.

Cannon wondered how significant the growth of the professions was by 1720, and how great were the opportunities for profitable employment for the younger sons of the gentry. (pp. 14–17) Some professions —medicine, teaching, even the law for example—were not very palatable for the gentry because of their long training and uncertain financial rewards. Holmes replied that the slowing down of the growth in the professions by the 1720s had to be seen against the background of a relatively static population. Certainly after 1713 there were fewer opportunities in the army and navy while opportunities for a career in the Church did not grow significantly. There were, however, more opportunities in teaching. Tutors employed by rich families could be rewarded quite handsomely.

There was considerable discussion of the absence of popular radicalism in the period 1680 to 1740 (pp. 8–12). It was agreed that there had certainly been many disturbances of a bread-and-butter kind, such as turnpike riots, press gang riots and industrial disorders. While these could be regarded as expressions of dissatisfaction with social and economic developments, they were not overtly political and offered no serious challenge to the governing élite. O'Gorman drew attention to Hayter's work which showed that most riots and demonstrations at that period were short-lived: 'we are talking about popular unrest rather than radicalism, which presupposes some ideological objective.'[4] McCord stressed that the forces of law and order generally handled the disturbances with considerable skill. Speck objected that the Riot Act of 1715 had certainly been a panic measure. Holmes accepted this, but argued that the act put the military firmly under the control of the civil magistrates. The troops were less likely to resort to violent measures to suppress riots after 1715 but, once ordered to use force, were inclined to act more firmly than before.

Dickinson remarked that popular radicalism in the earlier seventeenth century had not been led by men drawn from the lower orders but by men who possessed some property, enjoyed some education and resented being excluded from political, social and economic advancement. After

1688 opportunities for upward mobility did exist and these syphoned off the potential leaders of popular radicalism. O'Gorman, Cannon and Derry agreed with Dickinson that the governing élite was determined that its own internal political disagreements must not be pushed so far as to give the lower orders a chance to make political mischief: it had clearly learned the political lesson of the 1640s.

Holmes accepted this line of reasoning. He conceded that, in retrospect, it was the most serious deficiency in his whole argument and that it was the single most important modification that he would wish to make. The bulk of the gentry, even when shut out of power, were not willing to whip up popular support in order to challenge the political system and to undermine social and economic stability. He had argued that economic prosperity meant that the gentry did not wish to encourage popular unrest, while this same prosperity meant that both the lower and 'middling' orders lacked the serious and sustained grievances which might have provoked them into radical political action. It was significant that there were far fewer riots, especially food riots, in this period than in the later eighteenth century.[5]

Dickinson also pointed out that the political radicalism of the 1640s had been stimulated and influenced by the religious radicalism of the period. In the decades covered by Holmes's paper there was little religious radicalism of this type. The High-Church clergy were certainly prepared to stir up popular hostility to Dissenters and to Methodists, but they did not preach political radicalism or social revolution. Holmes agreed. His own research on the Sacheverell disturbances of 1710 convinced him that the clergy and gentry, who had helped to foment the disorder, were confident that the trouble could be contained: 'they kept popular emotions on a fairly tight chain and it was their chain'.

Note on further reading

The starting-point for any further reading must be J.H. Plumb, *The Growth of Political Stability in England, 1675–1725* (1967). This remains one of the most fertile and truly original historical works written in the past thirty years. The tight lecture-format made it impossible, however, for all its abundant ideas to be developed with equal clarity and emphasis.

Some subsequent qualifications to Plumb's thesis can be found in J.R. Jones, *The Revolution of 1688 in England* and J.R. Western, *Monarchy and Revolution: The English State in the 1680s*, which both emphasize how far the common interests of the governing classes, above all their mutual stake in property and the Protestant religion, were revealed and reinforced by the policies of James II; in G. Holmes, 'Post-Revolution

Britain and the Historian' (in *idem*, editor, *Britain after the Glorious Revolution 1688–1714* [1969]) and 'Sir Robert Walpole' (in H. Van Thal, editor, *The Prime Ministers* [1974], I, pp. 29–46), which point out how favourable, in some respect, for the prospect of greater stability, was the political legacy of the years 1702–21 which Walpole inherited; and in P. Langford, *The Excise Crisis* (1975), especially pp. 4–23, and J.P. Kenyon, *Revolution Principles: The Politics of Party, 1689–1720* (1977), ch. 11, which both question, conversely, how far we are justified in describing Walpole's England as politically 'stable'.

Among excellent recent textbooks, L.A. Clarkson, *The Pre-Industrial Economy in England 1500–1750* (1971), B.A. Holderness, *Pre-Industrial England: Economy and Society from 1500–1750* (1976) and D.C. Coleman, *The Economy of England, 1450–1750* (1977) can all be read with great profit, as, in its more distinctive way, can J.D. Chambers, *Population, Economy and Society in Pre-Industrial England* (1972). Charles Wilson's *England's Apprenticeship, 1603–1763* (1965) is an enduring classic.

Among more detailed work bearing on the socio-economic background, valuable articles are reprinted in E.M. Carus-Wilson, editor, *Essays in Economic History* II (1962), notably those by E.H. Phelps Brown and S.V. Hopkins (two—dealing with wages), R. Davis (foreign trade) and A.H. John (economic growth and the standard of living). Two other articles of importance are reprinted in E.L. Jones, editor, *Agriculture and Economic Growth in England, 1650–1815* (1967), viz. the editor's 'Agriculture and Economic Growth in England 1660–1750: Agricultural Change' and A.H. John, 'Agricultural Productivity and Economic Growth in England 1700–1760', which *inter alia* touches helpfully on wages. See also John's 'English Agricultural Improvements, 1660–1765', in D.C. Coleman and A.H. John, editors, *Trade, Government and Economy in Pre-Industrial Britain* (1976). E.W. Gilboy, *Wages in Eighteenth Century England* (1934) remains a standard work. M. Beloff, *Public Order and Popular Disturbances, 1660–1714* (1938) remains of some value, despite its brevity and dependence on central archives. A more orthodox treatment of the 'conflict of interests' in society and politics than that offered above is provided by W.A. Speck, 'Conflict in Society', in G. Holmes, editor, *Britain after the Glorious Revolution*, and by G. Holmes, *British Politics in the Age of Anne* (1967), ch. 5. Although there yet exists no survey history of the professions in England, there are useful pointers in E. Hughes, 'The Professions in the Eighteenth Century', *Durham University Journal* XIII (1951), and W.A. Speck, *Stability and Strife: England 1714–1760* (1977), p. 290, provides bibliographical guidance. The social implications of provincial urban development are best illuminated in P. Borsay, 'The English Urban Renaissance: the Development of Provincial Urban Culture, *c.* 1680–*c.* 1760', in *Social History* V (1977).

2

Whiggism in the eighteenth century
H. T. Dickinson

I

The term 'Whig' was first applied to a political group in parliament during the Exclusion crisis of 1679–81. Previously a label for Scottish covenanting rebels it was used as a term of abuse to condemn those who wished to prevent James, Duke of York, from succeeding to his brother's throne.[1] Although applied to a political group which was soon defeated and dispersed the term did not disappear with the Exclusionists, but was in constant use as a descriptive label for political groups and political attitudes until well into the nineteenth century. The supporters of Shaftesbury and the Junto peers, of Walpole and Newcastle, of Rockingham and Charles James Fox, and of Charles Grey and Lord John Russell were all labelled Whigs. From at least the 1750s to the 1780s almost all the prominent, front-bench politicians regarded themselves as Whigs whether they were in office or in opposition. The term 'Whig' was evidently broad and flexible, even ambiguous and confusing. Historians prefer to use it with caution. They usually eschew any attempt to define *Whiggism* as such and prefer instead to identify Whig policies and principles during those specific periods when the Whigs were well organized in parliament and were very active in disseminating party propaganda to the wider political nation. This has led them to concentrate on the late Stuart and late Hanoverian periods.[2] Little attempt has been made to define Whiggism during the period from 1714 to the 1760s; ironically the period often described as the age of the Whig supremacy.[3]

This reluctance to define Whiggism over a long period of time and, in particular, this hesitation about defining Whiggism in the middle decades of the eighteenth century is hardly surprising. Whiggism was never a rigid body of principles that dictated precisely how men should respond to every political issue. Whiggism clearly altered over time as personnel changed, as old issues disappeared and new issues arose, and as political opportunities fluctuated. Charles James Fox was not another Lord Wharton nor Charles Grey another Robert Walpole. The problems created by the American and the French revolutions were not identical to those raised by the Glorious Revolution or the Hanoverian succession. Long years in opposition undoubtedly presented very different problems and opportunities when compared with decades in office. The Whigs not only changed over time however. They were rarely united in action or completely agreed on policy. All political groups or parties fall prey to internal disputes about how to respond to major issues and no political platform or political ideology provides an obvious answer to every problem. Whigs and Whiggism are no exception to these general rules. Even when the Whigs were a very coherent and well organized party, as in Anne's reign, they sometimes disagreed sharply about how to respond to specific problems. Any effort to curb the Crown's influence over the House of Commons, by enacting Place and Pension bills for example, split the party.[4] After the 1688 Revolution the Whigs were in fact always liable to divide into those who were prepared to compromise their principles in order to secure power and those who would rather be in opposition than attract the charge of having sacrificed their political integrity.

Nonetheless, while Whiggism never laid down a precise rule of conduct for all politicians at all times, it was a fairly coherent body of attitudes, prejudices and principles and it did offer general political guidance to its adherents. It prescribed certain actions and it proscribed others. Although it was not a coherent political philosophy nor a logically integrated system of beliefs to which all Whigs were obliged to subscribe, Whiggism did give philosophic purpose to the state and provided a set of normative values by which to judge the political and social order.

While asserting that Whiggism was a political ideology of some sophistication I am not claiming that Whig politicians were motivated solely or even chiefly by abstract notions and high moral principles. On the contrary, the strength, durability and popularity of Whig ideology lay not so much in its moral appeal and its rational qualities (though these were stressed by some Whig propagandists) as in its ability to promote and defend the interests of the property-owning classes. Whiggism provided philosophical and ideological justification for those political and social privileges which men of property already enjoyed or wished to enjoy. Whig principles were not therefore opposed to self-interest, but were in fact the means of furthering the political interests of important elements in eighteenth-century society. The Whigs employed philosophical and ideological arguments to promote an ideal political and social order in which they could reap considerable material benefits.[5]

II

Whiggism developed its characteristic commitment to a balance between liberty and order largely, though not entirely, in response to the Tory ideology of the late seventeenth century and the radical ideology of the late eighteenth century. By examining the Whig response to Tory and radical propaganda it is possible to assert with some confidence which political principles the Whigs opposed and which systems of government they proscribed. The Whigs regarded both absolute monarchy and a democratic republic as inimical to that political and social order which they believed was natural and best suited to England. They therefore rejected the full-blown Toryism of the late seventeenth century and the extreme radicalism of the late eighteenth century. Whiggism was opposed to all the fundamental tenets of the Tory theory of order: namely, absolute monarchy, divine right, indefeasible hereditary succession, non-resistance and passive obedience. Whigs recognized the need for an absolute and irresistible authority in the state, but they refused to confer such authority on a single magistrate. In their view no monarch could be trusted with the power to rule by arbitrary will or with the right to set aside statute or customary law. Subjects, particularly those with a substantial stake in the country, could not be expected to put their life, liberty and property at the mercy of an absolute monarch. The power of the Crown had to be limited by a system of laws. Furthermore, since the monarch existed for the benefit of his subjects and not vice-versa, and since all governments were man-made and not specifically ordained by God, no ruler could claim his title by divine right. Rulers could govern only with the consent of the people. Hence their authority was not only limited but might be forfeited altogether if it were systematically abused. In the last resort monarchs who persistently overturned the law and consistently threatened the life, liberty and property of their subjects could be forcibly resisted. The principle of hereditary succession therefore, while generally just and expedient, could be infringed in order to protect subjects from a ruler who would not accept the moral and legal limitations upon his authority.

Although they were chiefly concerned to protect subjects from the arbitrary will of an absolute monarch, the Whigs refused to endorse the doctrine of effective popular sovereignty. While they acknowledged that all men might have the right to resist manifest tyranny they did not accept that all subjects, no matter how poor and dependent, possessed an equal right to participate in the public affairs of the nation. Whiggism never prescribed a political system in which all men were politically equal. On the contrary, the Whigs always believed that democracy was inherently unstable and would inevitably degenerate into anarchy. They therefore rejected the radical claim that all men were invested by God with the natural and inalienable right to a positive voice in how they should be governed. To confer equal political rights on all men would be to undermine limited monarchy and a responsible aristocracy. On the basis of one man one vote all power would reside in the people. This would not only end in a democratic republic, but would provoke an attack on all social and economic distinctions and so end in tyranny by way of lawlessness. A democratic republic could not exist in a country where the structure of society was hierarchical and where the distribution of property was clearly unequal. Despite all their protests to the contrary political radicals would inevitably become social revolutionaries. They would promote policies which would in the end level all social and economic distinctions. The rights and liberties of all men would then be at the mercy of a lawless multitude.

It is possible to define Whiggism in positive as well as negative terms since the Whigs endeavoured to show what benefits their principles and policies would bring. The Whigs rejected the Tory theory of order because they were concerned to protect the liberty of the subject and they resisted the demands of the radicals because they were convinced that these would undermine all order in the State. The Whigs were always preoccupied with the fundamental problem of how to achieve a balance between liberty and order. They fully recognized that these two objectives could and often did conflict. An overemphasis on liberty could lead to anarchy and the breakdown of all order. A preoccupation with order on the other hand could easily lead to the acceptance of a regulated tyranny. The Whigs wished to distinguish liberty from license and the maintenance of order from arbitrary tyranny. They insisted that where there was no freedom there could be no legitimate government and where there was no law there could be no real freedom. A balance between liberty and order could best be achieved by preserving limited monarchy, the Protestant succession and the rule of law: the essential gains achieved by the Glorious Revolution.

Throughout the eighteenth century the Whigs opposed both absolute monarchy and popular sovereignty and supported a constitutional monarchy, the Protestant succession and the rule of law. In order to understand the wider aspects and the deeper implications of Whiggism however we need to look beyond the specific actions of the Whigs in parliament. We need to examine those assumptions, attitudes and beliefs which informed the Whig view of the political and social order. These principles were not simply the practical response to particular circumstances. They emerged from and were strengthened by the Whig interpretation of the nature of man and of the natural social order, of the origins of civil society and civil government, of the ends and objectives of civil government, and of the means by which these ends could be achieved. The Whigs did more than discover moral and intellectual support for the narrow political platform on which they had stood in 1688. They also deepened and extended their political principles so that

Whiggism came to mean far more than just a commitment to limited monarchy, the Protestant succession and the rule of law.

The political and social order which the Whigs believed to be most appropriate was determined by their view of natural man and natural society. The Tories and the arch-conservatives of the eighteenth century were very conscious of the sinfulness of man. They insisted that unless his natural passions and selfishness were restrained then anarchy and bloody strife would ensue. This conviction led them to favour an absolute, divinely ordained monarchy and to reject the claim that all men possessed natural rights which no ruler could infringe. The radicals and ultra-libertarians of the eighteenth century were ready to proclaim the natural goodness of man and were convinced of his ability to obey the dictates of pure reason. This led them not only to claim that all men possessed extensive natural rights but to assert that these rights were inalienable and could easily be translated into civil liberties in a properly constituted society. The Whig view of man was neither excessively pessimistic nor ludicrously optimistic. They believed that man was inherently selfish, but was capable of improvement if his passionate nature were controlled by his reason. This view that man was a mixture of passion *and* reason can be found in the works of John Locke. His observations on the nature of man were not as pessimistic as those of Robert Filmer nor as optimistic as those of Thomas Paine. Locke acknowledged the virtues of natural man and the benefits of natural society while stressing that civil society and civil government were necessary to restrain the selfish qualities of man. All Whigs agreed that the passionate side of man's nature could be most effectively restrained and his rational capacity and benevolent qualities best cultivated by a well ordered civil society and by the institutions of a well constructed civil government.

This view of man led the Whigs to conclude that it was a mistake to regard men as naturally equal in all important respects just as it was wrong to claim that all men were naturally so unequal that most men could be justifiably enslaved by the arbitrary will of one man or a few men. The Whigs insisted that all men shared a common nature and that all men were equal in the sight of God. They went further than these pious platitudes. They agreed with the radicals that *all* men enjoyed certain natural rights – in Locke's phrase, 'the right to life, liberty and property.' These rights were largely negative or defensive. They consisted of the right to enjoy life, liberty and property free from the unjustified interference and arbitrary will of other men. All men had the right to enjoy personal freedom, liberty of conscience, freedom of expression, their personal and private property, and the fruits of their labour. Since *all* men enjoyed these natural rights then no man could interfere with these rights without the consent, either explicit or tacit, of the individuals concerned. Absolute, arbitrary authority was hence unnatural and illegitimate and could be resisted.

Although the Whigs – from Locke through to Burke – recognized the natural right to life, liberty and property, they did not conclude that all men were equal in other respects or that an egalitarian or democratic society was natural to man. Like the Tories they invariably stressed that men differed in their intelligence, strength and talents to such a degree that inequality was ineradicable. Men, even in their most natural state, lived in an ordered hierarchy where differences in rank and status were quite apparent. Locke, and his views on this were widely adopted, stressed that the natural inequalities of men inevitably led to the disproportionate acquisition of property. Locke was eager to point out that this disproportionate acquisition occurred in man's natural state and hence considerable, if not gross, inequality was natural and inevitable. Those who owned substantial property would naturally rank higher and be in a position to exert greater influence than those who were dependent upon selling their labour. In the state of nature there was a property-owning elite and large numbers of men dependent upon and hence subordinate to these men of property. No eighteenth-century Whig challenged this comforting conclusion that a property-based hierarchy was the natural order of society. Their notion of the natural social order was almost as conservative as that of the Tories.[6]

The Whigs endeavoured to convert their concept of natural rights into civil liberties and to transform their notion of the natural social order into the political order of civil society. They tried to preserve a man's life and personal freedom from arbitrary interference by limiting the power of the Crown, by abolishing prerogative courts, by establishing an independent judiciary, by making all subjects equal before the law, and by ending arbitrary imprisonment and torture. In practice of course the rich could generally defend themselves in court more effectively than the poor, but in the eyes of the law all men were equal. Liberty of conscience and freedom of worship were gradually extended to all those who were not a threat to the State even though civil disabilities were placed upon those who did not belong to the established Church, that privileged ally of the State. Since Protestant Dissenters could in general be trusted to support a Whiggish constitution, whereas for a long time Roman Catholics were suspected of favouring a Stuart restoration, it is hardly surprising that more was conceded to the former than to the latter. The commitment to religious toleration for Protestant Dissenters, if not the granting of full civil equality, was in fact one of the truly distinctive features of Whiggism. Once the Roman Catholics proved that they too were not necessarily enemies of the State then the penal laws against them were also gradually relaxed. Throughout the eighteenth century all subjects were allowed to petition Crown or

parliament for the redress of grievances, even after the repressive legislation of the 1790s,[7] while the freedom of the press was widely regarded
as one of the greatest safeguards of English liberties. Indeed, the press
steadily increased its political influence throughout the eighteenth
century.[8]

It was in their defence of property, however, that the Whigs were
most active in converting a natural right into a civil liberty. Certainly
both the legislature and the courts more often used the law to protect the
property than to extend the liberties of the subject. Parliament was used
by the propertied classes to pass numerous private members' bills on
such matters as turnpikes, enclosures and river navigation and to establish regulations about the wages and conditions of work of the labouring
classes. Parliament also greatly increased the number of capital crimes
involving offences against property. During the eighteenth century
there was a mass of legislation about offences involving grain, wood,
hedges, fruit, cattle, horses, dogs and game – all crimes which affected
men of property in particular – that allowed these cases to be tried by
summary conviction. Thus, men of property did not have to worry
about the problems of drawing up formal legal indictments or about
acquittals being granted by tender-minded juries. As JPs they could deal
summarily with those who dared to attack their property.[9] It can therefore be fairly concluded that the Whigs were concerned to preserve the
liberties of the subject in general but that they were chiefly preoccupied
with the defence of private property.

When it came to conferring active or positive political rights upon
subjects, the Whigs adopted a restrictive policy. The one political right
which they were prepared to grant to all men was the right to resist
arbitrary tyranny. Indeed, the right of resistance was one of the most
distinctive features of Whig ideology. It clearly marked them off from
the Tories, but their interpretation of this right also distinguished them
from the extreme radicals. The Whigs were well aware that this right
could be abused and could become a threat to all order. They were therefore careful to point out that subjects had no right to use force in order to
resist minor or isolated examples of injustice. Subjects certainly had no
right to overturn an established government simply because they
wished to set up a better one. The right of resistance was a last resort.

The Whigs disagreed with the radicals even more sharply over the
latter's claim that all men had a natural and inalienable right to influence
and shape the legislative and executive functions of the State. While
they acknowledged that the people had the right to good government
they denied that this meant that they must have self-government. The
Whigs were nearer to the Tories in their desire to exclude all women and
children and most of the adult male population from a direct rôle in the
decision-making processes of the State. They were convinced that civil

society was most in accord with natural society when it was essentially hierarchical and when the aristocratic élite assumed authority over, and responsibility for, the lower orders. The majority of men, so it was claimed, lacked the ability and the opportunities to develop those capacities needed for the proper exercise of political responsibility. Only a minority of men developed their inherent rational capacity; only a minority of men owned sufficient property to be able to afford an education and to enjoy a life of leisure free from the necessity to work for a living; and only a minority of men owned enough property to be independent of the will and commands of other men. There was therefore a natural aristocracy in the State that happily coincided very closely with the actual property-owning élite.

Property therefore became both the qualification for, and the mark of, active citizenship. It became a commonly expressed Whig maxim that power always follows property. The right to protect private property was regarded as the prime motive for the creation of civil society and civil government. The protection of property must therefore be of major concern to society and to the government. In order to ensure this, men of property must be able to exercise power directly for themselves or at least have their property rights protected by representatives chosen by them. Conversely, the propertyless masses must be denied any active voice in the decisions of the civil government. The Whigs condemned the radical demand for full political equality as both dangerous and absurd. They argued that the natural inequality of wealth in society made it impossible to establish a democratic system of government. The lower orders were simply not equipped to exercise power. They would therefore either be compelled to submit to the natural influence of their masters and employers or they would fall under the influence of demagogues and those who offered bribes. Furthermore, if the propertyless were given real power one of their first aims would be to redress the inequitable distribution of property. Political equality would lead inevitably to demands for social levelling and economic egalitarianism. The results of any attempt to establish a democratic system of government would be social revolution, civil war and then either unrelieved anarchy or the forcible imposition of some form of tyranny.

Although the Whigs were convinced that the distribution of power ought to harmonize with the actual distribution of property they were not in entire agreement about what kinds of property and what extent of ownership should confer particular political rights. The Whigs undoubtedly shared with the Tories the conviction that landed property should confer the greatest social prestige and political privileges. Land was still regarded as, and indeed in the eighteenth century was, the most important sector of the nation's economy. Landed proprietors could be expected to enjoy leisure, education and independence. Because of the large number of tenants, servants, labourers and tradesmen who were dependent upon them for their livelihood landed men were used to giving orders and to exercising responsibility for the welfare of others. Moreover, landed men had a genuine stake in the fortunes of their country. They could not escape their responsibility to defend the country without sacrificing all that they possessed, whereas monied men with liquid capital could escape from danger. Nonetheless, while conferring primacy on the possession of land, the Whigs went much further than most Tories in recognizing that property could include more than real estate. In their opinion it should be construed to mean the wealth and possessions of merchants, manufacturers and even financiers. The Whigs could never bring themselves to regard the possessors of this kind of property as being the social equals or even the political equals of large landed proprietors, but they did recognize their claim to some influence. Men with wealth invested in trade, industry or financial institutions were expected to operate at the local level, in town corporations for example, or to ally themselves with landed men if they expected to act on the national political stage. Nonetheless, the Whigs did come to recognize that commercial, industrial and financial prosperity were essential both to social stability and national strength. Since these forms of wealth were in fact a source of power then those who controlled this wealth must be allowed a rôle in the decision-making processes of the State. Parliament therefore must represent these forms of property, although it was expected to be most responsive to the interests and influence of landed men.

The Whigs did not agree with the radicals that parliament should directly represent every subject in the country. Its prime function was to represent all the powerful and influential interests in the nation. The distribution of seats and the franchise must be such that the landed, commercial, industrial and financial wealth of the nation and the interests of all the great professions must be represented. All these various interests could be represented without there being any need to accept the radical demand for equal electoral districts and universal manhood suffrage. If there were a wide variety of constituencies across the length and breadth of the country and if the great majority of those who were of independent means could vote then parliament would be responsible and responsive to the powerful interests in the State. Moreover, these interests could be trusted to protect the welfare of the lower orders since their own prosperity rested on the labour of the poor and they had a sense of duty towards those dependent upon them for employment.

In the late seventeenth and early eighteenth centuries the overwhelming majority of Whigs had no quarrel with the existing distribution of parliamentary seats or with the various types of propertied franchise operating in county and borough constituencies. By the late eighteenth century, partly because of changes in the economic and social structure, partly because of the need to combat the political influence of the Crown, and partly because of pressure from radical opinion out-of-doors, a small body of Whigs was now ready to consider a moderate measure of parliamentary reform. They were prepared to move some parliamentary seats from very small constituencies to the counties and larger boroughs and to extend the franchise perhaps so far as to include all independent male householders. These proposals, which were not enacted in the eighteenth century, were not put forward with the aim of democratizing the constitution. Even the more liberal Whigs still regarded the active citizens in the country as a minority of the population. In their estimation the only public opinion worth deferring to was that expressed not only by the propertied élite but by the propertied middle classes. Even the middling orders of society however could not expect to govern. They might vote, they might sit on juries and on town corporations, they might hold minor posts in the administration, but the helmsmen of the ship of state must be men of substantial landed property. They stood as a bulwark between Crown and people, ready and able when necessary to protect the legitimate rights of either from the unjustified demands of the other. While all men might theoretically retain the right to resist manifest tyranny, this right would never need to be exercised so long as men of substantial property performed their political duties.

The Whigs were convinced that civil society should seek to transform all men's natural rights into civil liberties while restricting active political rights to the property-owning élite. Only then could liberty and order, the two prime objectives of civil society, be secured. The Whigs believed that no civil government could achieve these ends unless it was founded on consent. Indeed, government by consent was one of the fundamental doctrines of Whiggism. The Whigs claimed that the English constitution and the English system of government in the eighteenth century did rest on the principle of consent, yet they could not agree about how this had in fact been achieved. It has been too readily assumed that all Whigs believed that the English constitution was the creation of an original contract. John Locke certainly propagated a contract theory, but a great many Whigs never endorsed this notion.[10] Only the radical minority claimed that the original contract had been made by the explicit and express consent of all men and that such a contract had been the foundation of the English constitution. Locke himself and the other Whig supporters of the contract theory knew that no such contract could be found and they also admitted that consent was likely to have been tacit rather than explicit. Only a minority of the population, the freeholders and independent householders at best, would have participated in drawing up the original contract. Labourers and servants, no less than women and children, would have accepted the decision of their superiors.

Many Whigs did not believe it was possible to trace the English constitution back to an original contract and they came to fear that in any case the contract theory provided too much justification for the doctrine of popular sovereignty. They therefore preferred a more conservative explanation for the origins of government by consent in England. Some conservative Whigs sought the origins of the English constitution no further back than the Glorious Revolution of 1688. This provided them with a firm basis for limiting the power of the Crown without conceding sovereign authority to the people at large. Most Whigs however preferred to argue that the Glorious Revolution did not establish a new constitution but simply restored England's ancient constitution to its true principles. They claimed that England's constitution, like her system of common law, was customary and immemorial. It had not been created by any one man or at any one time. Rather it was the accumulation of the wisdom of ages because it had made thousands of adjustments to the needs created by altered circumstances and the changing habits of the people. It was possible nonetheless to claim that this ancient, prescriptive constitution frequently reinforced its basic principles. This might be seen in the coronation oaths of English monarchs, in Magna Carta, and, most recently and most significantly, in the terms of the Revolution settlement of 1689.

The Whigs believed that the essential political objectives of liberty and order and government by consent were best secured by a constitution which possessed the inestimable virtues of being both mixed and balanced. These particular features could be traced more readily in the ancient constitution or in the constitution established by the Revolution settlement than in the abstract notion of an original contract. Because it established a mixed form of government England's eighteenth-century constitution was praised for securing the greatest number of advantages and suffering the fewest disadvantages of any political system. The Whigs recognized three pure forms of government: namely, monarchy, aristocracy and democracy. Unfortunately, whereas each had its merits it also incorporated a serious threat either to liberty or stability. Monarchy avoided disputes over who could legitimately exercise authority and it allowed the chief magistrate to act promptly in an emergency, but it placed the life, liberty and property of all subjects at the mercy of one man who might act as an arbitrary ruler. Aristocracy provided an élite capable of leading, but often degenerated into a narrow oligarchy of warring, self-interested factions. Democracy offered the greatest sphere of liberty to the ordinary subject, but was too slow to act and so inherently unstable that it invariably collapsed quite quickly into mob rule. Only a mixed form of government, which incorporated elements of monarchy, aristocracy and democracy, could secure the benefits of each while avoiding their disadvantages.

The Whigs (indeed, in the middle decades of the eighteenth century, almost all shades of political opinion) were convinced that England under the Hanoverians was in the fortunate position of being able to enjoy the benefit of mixed government through the political institutions of Crown, Lords and Commons. The mixture of monarchy, aristocracy and democracy was preserved by the balance of power between these three institutions. Each of them possessed its own peculiar privileges and performed its own distinct functions. As chief magistrate the monarch was the fount of honours, the unchallenged head of the executive, and retained various prerogative powers, including the right to summon, prorogue and dissolve parliament. The peers of the realm enjoyed the highest honours in the state, sat in the legislature as of right, and formed the highest court of justice in the land. The House of Commons represented the people and, as such, defended the liberties and put forward the grievances of the subjects. It also enjoyed the privilege of initiating all votes of supply. In addition to these individual and distinct functions the three institutions of Crown, Lords and Commons combined together to form the sovereign legislature. No bill could become law and no tax could be levied unless and until it was approved by all three branches of the legislature during the same session of parliament. There was no strict separation of powers even though the monarch was head of the executive, the House of Lords was the supreme court of law, and the House of Commons raised the revenue needed by the government. Both the executive and the judiciary were expected to interact with the legislature and in fact did so. The leading members of the executive invariably sat in one or other of the houses of parliament and could therefore act as a channel of communication between government and legislature. Judges were appointed by the Crown and could be dismissed after a resolution of both houses of parliament. The most important legal officers of the State were members of the government and sat in parliament. Thus, the constitution was a sophisticated and complicated system of checks and balances. In order to preserve this delicate balance the various estates and interests in society must be allowed to influence the three institutions in the combined legislature and each of these three institutions must be allowed to influence the other two. But in neither case was this influence to extend so far as to culminate in outright control. If one of the three components of the legislature came to dominate the other two or if elements out-of-doors were able to control the legislature then the delicate balance of the constitution would be disturbed and the benefits of mixed government would be lost. The constitution would degenerate into a pure form of monarchy, aristocracy, or democracy with its attendant flaws.

In order to secure the benefits of mixed government and the balanced constitution the Whigs were ready to resist those developments which would give any one of these institutions the upper hand. While the monarch retained some of his prerogative powers and remained at the head of the executive the Whigs insisted that parliament should control the Crown's supply of money if not the actual distribution of its revenue. Although not deliberately planned the consequence of this decision was that the monarch was forced to meet parliament every year after 1688. While the actual terms of the Revolution Settlement did not ensure a constitutional monarchy responsible to parliament this was the eventual outcome of the new system of public credit and the Crown's constant need for the extraordinary revenue voted by parliament. In order to ensure that the monarch would accept the limitations placed on his authority the Whigs always insisted that in the last resort parliament could alter the succession to the throne. Roman Catholics were explicitly debarred from ascending the throne because it was generally believed that they were not prepared to rule as limited and constitutional monarchs. Even though there was some support for the relaxation of the penal laws against Roman Catholics in the later eighteenth century the Whigs always regarded the constitution as essentially Protestant.

The prerogatives of the Crown were rarely a matter of dispute among the Whigs in the eighteenth century, and these disputes were never as intense as in the seventeenth century. Royal patronage however was a different matter. Most Whigs were ready to tolerate a reasonable number of royal ministers, servants and clients in the two houses of parliament. They accepted the monarch's efforts to distribute places, pensions and favours in order to build up a Court interest. It was only when this exercise of Crown patronage became so extensive and so frequent that it threatened to undermine the independence of parliament, particularly the independence of the House of Commons, that the Whigs came to the conclusion that it must be resisted. Economical reform, designed to reduce Crown influence over the composition and the decisions of parliament, became an essential plank in the Whig platform when they grew to distrust the ambitions of the monarch and his advisers. The Whigs also had no objection to members of the House of Lords holding many key positions at Court and in the government or employing their electoral influence to build up a following in the House of Commons. Such power would become excessive only if the monarch became a prisoner of the aristocracy or if the House of Commons came to represent the interests of the peerage to the exclusion of the other important interests in the State. The radicals of the late eighteenth century did claim that the House of Commons had indeed lost its independence because of the electoral stranglehold exerted by the peerage, but only a minority of Whigs was prepared to countenance such a charge. Finally, the Whigs agreed that the House of Commons could initiate votes of supply and could refuse to countenance the policies or appointments of the Crown, but they denied that the lower house could command the monarch or the House of Lords to obey the decisions taken by the representatives of the people.

The Whigs were even more concerned to reject the claim that any other institution or interest in the State or any force out-of-doors could limit or control the actions of the legislature. This would be to destroy its independence. The stability of the balanced constitution required that the authority of the combined legislature of Crown, Lords and Commons should be sovereign, absolute and irresistible. The legislature might protect and represent, but could not be subordinate to, the powerful interests and institutions in the State. The Whigs recognized the power of the Church of England, for example, but they did not accept that the alliance between Church and State was a union between equals, each sovereign within its own spiritual or temporal sphere. The Whigs insisted that in this world, if not in the next, the claims of the State were superior. Although no attempt was ever made to disestablish the Church of England, a strong streak of anti-clericalism did permeate Whiggism throughout the eighteenth century.

The Whigs were convinced that the sovereign legislature was the essential means of achieving the rule of law. They were not therefore willing to allow even the people as a whole to dictate to the legislature. When the Whigs referred to the sovereignty of the people – which was only rarely in any event – they meant to imply that no civil society or civil government could prosper or survive for long without the tacit support of the bulk of the population or at least of the middling and upper ranks of society. They recognized that widespread resistance, whether active or passive, would undermine any civil government and might even destroy civil society. But this conclusion did not lead the Whigs to assert that the people must be a continuous force and an active agent in civil governments. Once given, consent could not be withdrawn whenever subjects wished to do so. The Whigs insisted that the English had long ago tacitly consented to be governed by a combined legislature of Crown, Lords and Commons and this decision was irrevocable unless and until that legislature thoroughly abused the trust placed in it. In order to ensure that the legislature did not become subordinate to the people its members must be free to act to the best of their abilities and in accordance with their independent judgement. While opinion out-of-doors might offer advice to the legislature it could not control it. Even the voters could not bind their own representatives to a particular policy or instruct them how to act in the House of Commons. In order to serve the community at large members of parliament must be independent representatives and not delegates under instruction from their constituents or from any special interest group.[11] By securing the independence and the sovereignty of the legislature the Whigs believed that they could preserve the rule of law and free men from arbitrary will, whether this was exercised by one man or a multitude. Without the rule of law there was no liberty and no order, only arbitrary will (where might was right) or unrestrained licentiousness.

III

Politicians cannot always remain completely loyal to their declared principles nor entirely consistent in their policies. Power has to be secured before any political aim can be achieved and thus alliances and bargains with different groups and interests may have to be made. Once in power politicians are often compelled to choose between conflicting objectives or forced to reconcile competing interests. During their years in politics moreover circumstances may change considerably and force politicians to shift their ground and amend their arguments. It is therefore an easy task to make politicians appear unprincipled and hypocritical. This is particularly the case if we focus too closely on the twists and turns of individual politicians as they engage in their day-to-day manoeuvres. If, on the other hand, we look at the fundamental attitudes and the long-term objectives of political groups and parties we can sometimes discover loyalty to basic principles and consistency of purpose. It is possible in fact to discover an irreducible core of Whiggism. An examination of Whig *actions* in the eighteenth century shows that they were always pursuing certain policies: support for the Revolution Settlement, the Hanoverian succession, the sovereignty of King-in-Parliament, freedom of worship for Protestant Dissenters, and the rule of law. An examination of Whig assumptions, rhetoric and propaganda reveals a consistent adherence to other political principles. The Whigs certainly favoured an aristocratic and hierarchical social order and a limited monarchy but they were also committed to the idea of government by consent and to the right of subjects to resist manifest tyranny. Although the day-to-day political behaviour of the Whigs reveals considerable shifts of emphasis and gives the impression of inconsistency their support for these overriding political objectives remained in fact remarkably constant throughout the eighteenth century. Whig politicians always attempted to keep the prerogatives of the Crown within reasonable bounds, to preserve the sovereign authority of the combined legislature of Crown, Lords and Commons, and to protect the civil liberties of the subject while allowing the propertied classes to guide the ship of state. The Whigs of the late seventeenth and early eighteenth century did this by putting statutory limitations on the royal prerogative, by defending the Revolution settlement and the Protestant succession, and by leaving the parliamentary classes not the people to make the decisions. The Whigs of the later eighteenth century may have criticized the Crown's influence and may have desired a modest reform of parliament, but this did not make them democrats or social levellers. Their support for mixed government, a balanced constitution and a hierarchical society based on rank, status and property remained unchanged.

Throughout the eighteenth century the fundamental objectives of Whiggism remained remarkably constant although there was considerable disagreement among Whig politicians about how best to achieve these basic aims. In nearly all the disputes the conflict was over the relative importance of the two central strands of Whiggism: the need to protect individual liberty and the need to preserve public order. The more liberal Whigs ranked the rights of the subject and the importance of government by consent higher than parliamentary sovereignty and the rule of law. The more conservative Whigs reversed these priorities. Thus, under the early Hanoverians, for example, some Whigs defended Crown patronage because it appeared to be a lubricant essential to the smooth working of a mixed government and a balanced constitution. Other Whigs (as well as opposition Tories) feared that Crown patronage was increasing to such an extent that it was threatening the independence of both houses of parliament by packing them with members devoted to the interests of the government. This dispute should not be allowed to conceal the fact that both sides were trying to defend mixed government and a balanced constitution.[12] By the same token the Whigs in the early years of George III's reign could disagree about how to handle the dispute with the American colonies without reneging on Whig principles. Many Whigs believed that Britain's much-vaunted constitution could be preserved only by defending the sovereignty of parliament and by suppressing disorder in the colonies. A smaller element protested that successive British administrations were destroying the right of the colonists not to be taxed without first giving their consent. Both sides could claim, with some justice, to be upholding Whig principles.[13] By the 1790s Whig opinion was even more sharply and indeed irrevocably divided. While the friends of Fox responded to the unrest at home and abroad by advocating limitations on the power of the executive, a moderate reform of parliament and peace with France, the supporters of Pitt were prepared to adopt repressive measures in order to defeat radicalism at home and revolution abroad. Ironically, despite their very different tactical responses to the crisis, both sides would have wished to secure the kind of political and social order long enshrined in Whiggish principles.[14] The label 'Tory' was eventually applied to the Pittites, but the party was largely composed of former Whigs and its constitutional ideals certainly had more in common with eighteenth-century Whiggism than seventeenth-century Toryism. Its ideology was shaped by that quintessential Whig, Edmund Burke.[15]

Although Whiggism established general objectives it did not lay down clear guidelines on how precisely these ends were to be achieved in changing political, social and economic circumstances. This helps to account for many apparent inconsistencies in Whig behaviour. This does not mean however that Whigs never betrayed their principles. On the contrary, numerous examples could be given of how personal ambition, political expediency and the fear of disorder persuaded individual Whig politicians to compromise their principles. Despite its pragmatic and prudential features Whiggism was in essence an ideal view of the political and social order considered to be best suited to eighteenth-century Britain. Like all ideals it was sometimes betrayed even by those who regarded themselves as among the faithful. When the principles of Whiggism were betrayed blatantly and repeatedly then those responsible lost their right to be regarded as Whigs by their contemporaries. The supporters of Lord North and still more the disciples of the younger Pitt came to be labelled Tories because they appeared to be reneging on too many Whig principles. Whenever political actions could not readily be defended on the principles of Whiggism they became the subject of heated debate. Even such staunch Whigs as the Junto peers, James Stanhope and Robert Walpole were attacked by those who believed that political ambition had tempted these politicians into increasing the power of the Crown. The result was division in the Whig ranks. Even as an ideal therefore Whiggism exerted a profound and pervasive influence on politicians and political events in the eighteenth century.[16]

Colloquy on chapter 2
Frank O'Gorman

At the outset Dickinson stressed that he was dealing with Whiggism not in terms of political ideals or high moral principles but as a practical ideology, rooted in social and economic reality. Men adopted Whiggism for a variety of reasons. Among these, no doubt, could be included self-interest and material gain. This, however, did not render Whig ideology redundant, for even in these cases ideology served to define, to limit and to narrow possible courses of political action. The extent to which men are sincerely attached to the creed or ideology which they profess can never be thoroughly determined, since the historian cannot see into the innermost recesses of the mind. Nevertheless, there is much to suggest that many men professed their Whiggism seriously and that Whiggism was something far more sensitive than an ideological justification for a particular regime.

Cannon took up Dickinson's remark that 'Whiggism was in essence an ideal view of the political and social order . . .' (p. 44). Did this mean that Whiggism had become independent of the men or class who professed it? Dickinson agreed that ideas do acquire a life and integrity of their own: Whiggism was a moral as well as a pragmatic entity and its appeal to men was at different levels of experience. McCord agreed that a simple class theory was nonsense, noting that by no means all members of the landed classes in Hanoverian England were Whigs. Dickinson observed that Whiggism had certain other qualities which help to explain its long life and its wide appeal: it was a good system of incorporating people and was less exclusive than Toryism. Cannon objected that Toryism, in the early eighteenth century, was a more popular political creed than Whiggism. Holmes, on the other hand, stressed the indigenous nature of Whiggism, its popular origins in the xenophobic contempt for foreigners, which was felt by many in Britain. He went on to argue that, though Whiggism might be the creed of the propertied classes, it should be remembered that property was quite widely, if unequally, distributed in Hanoverian England. 'Property' could be an estate of 40,000 acres, but it could also be a 40-shilling free-hold, a clerkship in the Exchequer, a parish constableship, and so on.

Did Whiggism have anything to offer the lower orders? Dickinson denied that Whiggism was no more than the ideology of a repressive upper class: he pointed to the civil and political rights, such as Habeas Corpus, which were enjoyed by all Englishmen and contended that the constitution was regarded with affection, as the loyalist reaction in the 1790s testified. Speck took a rather different view of the early eighteenth century, when Whiggism had not yet established itself. Fearing that their triumph might be short-lived, the Whigs passed a series of repressive measures, the Riot Act, the Septennial Act, Acts against combinations, the Waltham Black Act, and so on. Dickinson accepted some of this, but was not convinced that such Acts were intolerable. The Riot Act was very little used. How many people were killed by the military in riots? Combinations proliferated in the Hanoverian period. The Black Act may have been horrific, but how many people were, in fact, executed? Bearing in mind the threat of Jacobitism, the early Whig régimes do not appear to have been gratuitously repressive – certainly not by comparison with some continental régimes at the same period.

The discussion moved on to consider whether the theory of Whiggism corresponded to constitutional reality. The ideal of a balanced constitution, for example, was belied by the fact that the House of Commons dominated the political system. There was no balance. Similarly, the Whig ideal of representation looked unconvincing because the electoral system was becoming increasingly unrepresentative. Dickinson conceded to O'Gorman that the reality of politics might not accurately reflect the theory, but pointed out that the three elements of the balanced constitution – king, Lords and Commons – were ever-present in Whig theory. The three parts should work in harmony. How this was to be done, and where the emphasis was to be placed, might vary with circumstances, but the Whigs were agreed that good government had to be mixed government.

O'Gorman offered a further objection to Whiggism. Admitting the list of political objectives which the Whigs consistently upheld (p. 42), he yet found Whiggism somewhat static, uninventive and even reactionary when compared with 'enlightened' governments in many other European states. Dickinson replied that an essential aspect of Whiggism was its suspicion of the executive and its distaste for government intervention. Whigs did not believe that civil liberties could coexist with bureaucratic government: 'they simply said "we prefer the liberty of the subject to be the supreme right".'

Among these liberties, religious toleration ranked high. Holmes believed that what really separated the Whigs from the Tories was the Whig commitment to religious toleration. Cannon was less impressed with the Whig record on toleration: they had done little for the Protestant Dissenters and had taken over the old Tory defence of the Anglican Church. Speck had some sympathy for Cannon's view: Walpole's behaviour over Occasional Conformity was indeed cynical.

Nevertheless, the Whigs had to take tactical considerations into account: they had to maintain the Anglican establishment in order to assuage Tory doubts and fears. Dickinson thought that Walpole had probably gone as far as anyone could have done down the road to religious toleration in the 1730s. He did not think it extraordinary that the Whigs should defend the Church's position provided that the Whig State dominated it: 'after all, the Church of England in mid-century was very different from the old Tory Church.' There was nothing in Whiggism which said that the Church ought to be dismantled and disestablished. Derry agreed that one did not need to be a Tory to believe in a religious establishment: it was a perfectly defensible attitude for the Whigs to distinguish between toleration and playing a full part in political life: there was no reason why the Whigs should not believe in a religious establishment, though they would define it in a way different from the Tories.

The discussion then turned to Dickinson's comment that 'the prerogatives of the Crown were rarely a matter of dispute among the Whigs in the eighteenth century.' (p. 40) Dickinson contended that the disputes which did exist were not profound constitutional issues, but mere tactical skirmishes. O'Gorman did not deny that the constitutional struggles of the time lacked the convulsive quality of those of the seventeenth century – probably because the element of religious passion was absent – but thought them issues of great importance. When, between 1782 and 1784, certain Whigs argued that the king should not in practice be allowed to choose his ministers, it was more than a difference of emphasis. Derry suggested that all that was at stake was the use to which the prerogative should be put: the opposition did not say that the king should be deprived of his prerogatives or of his veto over legislation. Even the Foxites were not agreed on how far their restrictions upon the use of the prerogative ought to go: their own practice, as the Regency crisis of 1788/9 made plain, was on occasions inconsistent. Cannon agreed with Dickinson that the legal right to the prerogative was little disputed, but its exercise certainly was: 'when the king, undoubtedly within his rights, appointed Lord Bute to the Treasury, some people said "but the prerogative must not be used for private favour but as an act of public policy"; when, in 1783, he appointed Pitt, some people said "but the first minister of the Crown must command a majority in the House of Commons." In a way, they gave him the prerogative with one hand, and took it away with the other'. Dickinson reasserted Derry's point: 'no Whig who remained a Whig could say that the king had no choice over his ministers'. O'Gorman retorted that in attacking the use to which the prerogative was put, and in adopting the view that it should be exercised by bodies other than the monarch, the opposition Whigs in the later eighteenth century were going far in the direction of changing the balance of the constitution.

Next we discussed the relationship between Whiggism and radicalism. Holmes, 'somewhat perplexed', challenged Dickinson's 'black and white' distinction between the two and suggested that most radicals still regarded themselves as Whigs (pp. 34–5). Dickinson explained that the radicals obtained 'their initial body of ideas' from Whiggism, but insisted that it was possible to draw certain boundaries between the two: a radical ceased to be a Whig if he asserted that all men had a natural right to vote; if he argued that the people, not parliament, were sovereign; if he believed that an MP must do what the electors told him or that parliament must blindly obey public opinion or a convention; if he argued for complete religious liberty as a natural right; or, indeed, if he attacked any of the bulwarks of the Whig constitution, such as the existence of the monarchy or the House of Lords. McCord reminded us that there were radicals and radicals: not all radicals would subscribe to these particular propositions. Dickinson agreed that men like Wilkes and Wyvill could be incorporated into the Whig position: men like Tom Paine could not.

Holmes asked about the relationship between political rights and property: to what extent could the middling orders participate in the political system of Hanoverian England? (pp. 35–6) Dickinson contended that the ownership of property was the most essential way in which a man qualified for influence in that society. To have power in parliament or at court clearly required very substantial amounts of property, to which normally only the landed classes could aspire, but increasingly men from the middling orders were staking their claim. The logic of Whig ideology dictated that they be admitted. A kind of 'sliding scale' of property qualifications for the different types of power and influence which existed – the vote, membership of parliament, office as a sheriff, JP, or militia officer – allowed the middling orders different 'entry points' to the system, particularly at local level. In local office, there might well be quite humble men, tenant farmers, professional men, even skilled craftsmen. Holmes added that, by the end of the century, most of these qualifications could scarcely be considered prohibitive: what may have acted as a more effective barrier to participation was the fact that, for the most part, only the landed classes had sufficient leisure to perform the duties properly. McCord noted, with Dickinson's approval, that it was important to remember that for the Whigs responsibility as well as power went with property.

One of the most contentious – and possibly most confusing – issues to arise was evoked by Dickinson's statement on page 44:

> The label 'Tory' was eventually applied to the Pittites, but the party was largely composed of former Whigs and its constitutional ideals certainly had more in common with eighteenth-century Whiggism than seventeenth-

century Toryism. Its ideology was shaped by that quintessential Whig, Edmund Burke.

O'Gorman commented that Burke endowed the early nineteenth-century governing party with a Conservative rather than a Tory philosophy, characterized by an organic theory of the State. Dickinson conceded that the organic theory, a theory of evolutionary change, was not at all common with Whig theorists, who preferred to speak the static and unhistorical language of the Ancient Constitution and of Prescription. O'Gorman suggested that the governing party had gone beyond the boundaries of Whiggism in embracing an organic theory of the State. Dickinson inclined to agree, but pointed out that the governing party retained its belief in such good Whig traditions as the balanced constitution of Lords, king and Commons. McCord, in protest, could not see what the Pittites had done to be deprived of their Whiggism? Dickinson replied that they were better described as Conservative Whigs than as Tories, but that their panic resistance to even moderate reform and measures like the suspension of Habeas Corpus were not symptomatic of traditional Whiggism. McCord and Derry remained unconvinced.

In conclusion, Cannon asked whether 'Whiggism' was to be understood as a term rather like 'democrat', in that it conveyed a specific meaning, excluded certain alternatives, yet was capable of further development, into 'social democrat', 'christian democrat' and the like. Dickinson agreed. The term 'Whig' served the same sort of function for Hanoverians that 'liberal' or 'conservative' serve for us today. It represented a position which the overwhelming majority of the population would accept, though right and left would choose to emphasize different aspects of the tradition.

Note on further reading

The activities of organized Whig groups and parties, from their first appearance during the Exclusion Crisis of the late 1670s to the First Reform Bill of 1832, can be studied in J.R. Jones, *The First Whigs* (1961) and in the books by Horwitz, Holmes, Speck, Hill, Smith, O'Gorman, Roberts and Mitchell listed in note 2. Because party organization and party discipline were weakest in the middle decades of the eighteenth century little has been written about Whiggism during this period. Historians who have worked on the Whigs of the earlier and later decades of the eighteenth century have written much more about the actions of Whig politicians than about their principles, prejudices and assumptions. An attempt to understand the ideological dimensions of political debate during the whole eighteenth century has been made by H.T. Dickinson, *Liberty and Property: Political Ideology in Eighteenth-Century Britain* (1977; paperback, 1979). There are a number of more detailed studies, but these cover shorter periods or particular aspects of the ideological debate. The most important books are: Caroline Robbins, *The Eighteenth Century Commonwealthman* (1959); J.G.A. Pocock, *The Machiavellian Moment* (1975); Isaac Kramnick, *Bolingbroke and His Circle* (1968); H.T. Dickinson, *Bolingbroke* (1970); John Brewer, *Party Ideology and Popular Politics at the Accession of George III* (1976); and Colin Bonwick, *English Radicals and the American Revolution* (1977). One important book which does deal with Whig (and Tory) ideology is J.P. Kenyon, *Revolution Principles* (1977), though this concentrates on the political debate in the reigns of William III and Queen Anne.

3

Whigs and Tories dim their glories: English political parties under the first two Georges
William Speck

The nature of political parties in England during the period 1714 to 1760 is at the moment a subject of controversy. This in itself is a healthy sign of a renewed vitality in the study of eighteenth-century politics. At the same time it can be a source of confusion to students. This essay, therefore, attempts to clarify the nature of the debate over party politics under the first two Hanoverian kings, and to suggest a resolution of it.

In order to make the controversy clear the first part adopts an historiographical approach. This involves describing the views of other historians, an exercise fraught with shortcomings. For one thing, telescoping anybody's ideas inevitably distorts them; and, while part of the intention of the colloquies on each essay is to try to ensure that no injustice is done, the reader is reminded that only he can determine fair play by reading the works referred to in the annotations. Another drawback is that disagreements in print can appear to be of a personal kind. Lest there is the slightest danger of my own criticisms of others being so viewed, I would like to stress here, at the very outset, that I have the highest respect for the interpretations of other authorities on English politics in this period: and one of the many delights of working in the eighteenth century has been to experience a high degree of cooperation from colleagues in the same field.

The starting point in any discussion of the historiography of the period 1714 to 1760 must be the work of Sir Lewis Namier, and especially his epoch-making studies *The Structure of Politics at the Accession of George III* and *England in the Age of the American Revolution*, first published in 1929 and 1930 respectively. In them he deliberately set out to destroy the prevailing concepts which had explained the period to posterity, and succeeded so well that he prevented any coherent interpretation from taking their place for the best part of two generations.

Where prevailing historians had identified politicians of the century as members of the Tory or Whig parties, Namier asserted that 'in the absence of distinct, definable programmes it was becoming increasingly difficult to say who, from the angle of practical politics, should be considered a Tory and who a Whig'. He conceded that the division between Whigs and Tories existed in 1761, as before 'being latent in temperament and outlook, in social types, in old connexions and traditions' but insisted that 'it was not focused on particular problems, and did not therefore supply clear lines of divisions in politics'.[1] Toryism in particular had become a mere mentality. The party, if such it could be called, had no organization 'on a national scale' and 'no acknowledged leader·in parliament'.[2] 'In short', agreed John Brooke, Namier's collaborator in the official *History of Parliament* for the years 1754–1790, 'the Tories were pre-eminently the landed gentry, unconnected with the Court—a social group rather than a political party.'[3]

To Sir Lewis 'the names of Whig and Tory . . . explain little, but require a good deal of explaining'.[4] Instead of classifying MPs as Tories or as Whigs he preferred to distinguish three types.[5]

> In reality three broad divisions, based on type and not on party, can be distinguished in the eighteenth-century House of Commons: on one side were the followers of Court and Administration, the 'placemen', *par excellence* a group of permanent 'ins'; on the opposite side, the independent country gentlemen, of their own choice permanent 'outs'; and in between, occupying as it were the centre of the arena, and focusing upon themselves the attention of the public and of history, stood the political factions contending for power . . .

Although the first type consisted almost entirely of Whigs, while the bulk of the second were Tories, and even the third could be distinguished with 'party' labels, these appellations, whatever their origins, ceased to explain political behaviour under the first two Georges. As far as Namier was concerned 'the political life of the period could be fully described without ever using a party denomination.'[6]

This interpretation of politics in early Hanoverian England became the conventional wisdom, though not without reservations being expressed. By the 1950s it was being extended back in time to the first decade of the eighteenth century, which had previously been regarded as the classic years of party. After investigating English politics during those years, however, Robert Walcott concluded that 'the more one studies the party structure under William and Anne, the less it resembles the two-party system described by Trevelyan . . . and the more it seems to have in common with the structure of politics in the Age of Newcastle as explained to us by Namier.'[7] Thus he claimed that the significant division of the House of Commons was threefold: first there was a 'government interest', composed of members who either held places or pensions from the Court, or were returned to parliament with the help of government influence; then there were seven 'party groups', held together by electoral interests and family and personal relationships; and finally there was a large body of independent members, about half of whom consistently supported the Court while the others were veteran opponents of the administration.

It is astonishing in retrospect that Professor Walcott's version held the field for over a decade, and that though it was regarded as heretical by most students of Anne's reign, his doctrine should have been received as the new orthodoxy by other historians. For his definition of a political party as 'one of the parts into which a legislative body may be divided by questions of public policy or election of public officers'[8] is manifestly inadequate. Questions of public policy frequently create alignments within both Houses of Congress in his native United States of America, which cut right across the lines of Democrat and Republican; but these temporary combinations of Senators and Congressmen cannot seriously be regarded as political parties. Nor could similar *ad hoc* groupings in the House of Commons during the years 1701 to 1708.

More seriously still, parties were not confined to St Stephen's chapel then, any more than they are restricted to the Palace of Westminster today. On the contrary the party battle was waged in the Lords as well as in the Commons; and it reached out from the centre of politics in Court and Cabinet to the remotest constituencies. Yet Walcott dealt with those arenas only as side-shows to the clan warfare he detected in the Commons.

Although others working in the same field expressed scepticism about his conclusions, the most substantial refutation of *English Politics in the Early Eighteenth Century* was provided by Geoffrey Holmes in *British Politics in the Age of Anne*. Professor Holmes reaffirmed that the terms Whig and Tory could be used not only to describe almost every member who sat in the Commons between 1702 and 1714, but also all the Lords who attended the Upper House, and even the bulk of the electors in the constituencies.

It has been suggested that, in refuting Walcott, Holmes and others were repudiating Namier too; but this is not necessarily so. They merely challenged the wholesale translation back into Anne's reign of the conclusions which Sir Lewis had reached for the beginning of George III's. The methods which he had used to arrive at those conclusions were never impugned; quite the reverse, for as far as methodology is concerned we are all Namierites nowadays. The main technique which he bequeathed to historians is the biographical method, which investigates how each MP actually behaved in parliament, instead of relying upon generalizations about political behaviour. The most significant sources for the actual affiliations of MPs are parliamentary lists, which either purport to show how individuals voted in a particular division, or else attribute to them a specific party label. Professor Walcott was the first to use systematically those which have survived for the early eighteenth century. When compiling an index for all MPs returned between 1701 and 1714 he entered information from the lists on each member's card.[9]

This analysis led him to conclude that 'there was theoretically a "Whig" and a "Tory" position, and members should have voted consistently on one side or the other time after time. Unfortunately the lists do not square with this theory. The "Tory" side in any one division inevitably includes many who at other times voted "Whig", and vice-versa'.[10]

This untenable claim made his whole theory a house of filing cards. In fact the parliamentary lists confirm rather than confute the idea that a party label can be given to almost all politicians in the period. The number of men returned to the House of Commons in Anne's reign totalled nearly 1,250. A few of these, some 156, do not feature on any known list. There remain over a thousand whose voting habits can be ascertained. If Walcott's claim held good, then most of these should be found to have voted inconsistently; but on the contrary, the vast majority were remarkably consistent. When the lists are carefully examined, and palpable inaccuracies in them are discounted, 495 are found to have habitually voted Tory, while 439 consistently divided on the Whig side; only 130 wavered in their party allegiances. The Whigs were the better disciplined party, for most of the 130 waverers were Tories whose partisanship weakened in the last years of Anne's reign, no fewer than 59 of them being 'whimsicals' who voted against the treaty of commerce with France in 1713.[11]

The House of Lords was similarly polarized. Of 182 lay peers who feature on parliamentary lists in Anne's reign, only 41 crossed the party lines. As in the Commons the Whigs were the more united, for two-thirds of the inconsistent voters were Tories. Party discipline in the Lords extended beyond voting in person to the organization of proxy votes, few peers leaving their proxies at the disposal of the rival party.[12]

Polling at parliamentary elections was also partisan. Most constituencies in England returned two members, and a typical contest fielded four candidates, two Tories and two Whigs. Although the voters each possessed two votes, and could distribute them as they wished between candidates, the vast majority gave both to the same party. Thus in Bedfordshire in 1705 only 313 out of 2,560 freeholders split their votes, while in 1715 a mere 142 out of 2,529 did not vote along straight party lines; in Buckinghamshire in 1710 there were 164 split votes cast out of 4,301 freeholders, and in 1713 only 197 out of 3,957. London was an even more polarized constituency, for the City returned four members, giving each voter four votes to distribute among candidates. Yet in 1710, when four Tories stood against four Whigs, out of 6,638 electors, 5,939 gave all four votes to one party or the other. When three candidates stood in a two-member constituency the pattern was more complicated, as some voters were reluctant to waste a vote, so that a proportion of them would cast one for the candidate standing on his own and the other for one of the partners. Even in this situation, however, party affiliations could actually be highlighted by the number who did use only one vote and 'plumped', in the contemporary phrase, for the single candidate. In Hampshire 201 split their votes in 1705 when only three candidates stood, while as many as 724 plumped for the sole Tory candidate; another Tory who stood on his own in Buckinghamshire in 1701, 1702 and 1705, received 1,327 single votes at the first election, 1,574 at the second and 1,852 at the third.

With the exception of the Anglican clergy, who by and large voted solidly Tory, and of the Dissenters, who were even more firm in their allegiance to the Whigs, the voters were not as consistent in their support of one party as those they returned to parliament. Between elections there was, in many constituencies, a sizeable floating vote. In Buckinghamshire 13 per cent of those who polled in 1705 and again in 1710 changed sides, while in Westmorland the proportion was as high as 25 per cent between 1701 and 1702. The extent to which voters switched sides seems to have depended on national trends. For example, in Hampshire 20 per cent of the freeholders polling in both 1705 and 1710 changed their votes, four-fifths of them changing from voting Whig to voting Tory. This shift paralleled a swing from the Whigs to the Tories nationally between the two elections.[13]

A reasonable inference from this is that issues of national importance overrode local considerations, at least in the larger constituencies where 'public opinion' counted. It is therefore plausible to argue that the behaviour of peers, MPs and electors was to a large extent conditioned by their attitudes to the great political debates of the day.

Under Anne the main issue which divided Tory from Whig had been raised by the Revolution of 1688 and its implications. By transferring the crown to William and Mary, and ultimately to Anne, the Bill of Rights had broken the strict indefeasible, hereditary right of rulers. A few Tories logically refused to accept this, and became Jacobites, recognizing James II as king until his death in 1701, and thereafter accepting his son as James III; after Anne's death, the accession of a king who decisively broke the hereditary descent added to their ranks. Others refused to take the oaths to the new monarchs and became nonjurors. Most, albeit illogically, acquiesced in the Revolution but still hankered after some kind of divine sanction for government. The Whigs, on the other hand, argued that monarchy in England was limited, some by appealing to the notion of an original contract, others by insisting that historically the fundamental constitution was a balance of king, Lords and Commons; either theory ultimately justified resistance to a ruler who acted arbitrarily. The Toleration Act of 1689 also gave rise to tensions between Tory and Whig, since Tories regretted the concession to Protestant Dissenters, especially when, far from containing dissent as they had hoped, it seemed to encourage its growth. Faced with what they saw as a threat to Anglicanism from nonconformists, particularly after they proceeded to take office in local and national government despite the Corporation and Test Acts which were designed to keep both in the hands of Anglicans, the Tories strove to reverse these tendencies. The Whigs, on the other hand, who welcomed the Dissenters as allies, sought to protect them against Tory reaction. Finally, by involving England in major wars with France, the Revolution also generated party strife. The Whigs emerged as the champions of complete commitment to land wars on the continent while the Tories preferred a so-called 'blue-water' policy of directing England's main war effort to the sea. Towards the end of the War of the Spanish Succession these disagreements over strategy were transcended by the determination of the Whigs to bring France to her knees, contrasted with a growing Tory desire for peace at almost any price.

Most historians now accept that in Anne's reign the terms Tory and Whig were meaningful, and that two parties, if not a two-party system, existed. But if this was the case, and yet Sir Lewis Namier got the structure of politics at the accession of George III right, what happened to the labels and to the parties between the deaths of Anne and George II?

The best answer to this problem by a 'self-confessed member of the so-called "Namier school" ' is to be found in the contributions of John Owen, and particularly in his textbook *The Eighteenth Century 1714–1815*, published in 1974. When describing the pattern of politics he argued that the great issues which had previously divided the parties were all 'overtaken by events', largely because Tory attitudes to them became irrelevant. Thus Tories accepted the Hanoverians, even though the Act of Settlement by which they came to the throne made a much greater breach with the hereditary principle than the Bill of Rights, while 'after 1714 religion ceased to be a central issue of political debate'. Insofar as issues mattered at all under the first two Georges they were such as divided Court from Country rather than Whig from Tory. For example, 'differences of opinion over the conduct of war still continued, but the "blue-water school" had long since become "Country" rather than "Tory" '. More specifically Court–Country were the issues raised by the number of placemen in the Commons, the size of the standing army, and the duration of parliaments after the Septennial Act of 1716, all of which the Country members, the independents, or as Owen prefers to call them the 'non-dependents', wished to reduce. But the crucial political activities were generated by groups of politicians who owed allegiance to major political figures, who struggled to control government. So Owen finally endorsed the pattern established by Namier, which he even reduced to a diagram:[14]

This 'Namierite' model was under attack even before Owen published his able summary of it. A major revision of it came from a somewhat

COURT   COUNTRY

POLITICIANS

COURT + TREASURY PARTY

INDEPENDENTS

unexpected source, the official *History of Parliament* which Sir Lewis had done much to set up. The volumes for 1715–1754, which appeared in 1970, emphasized the survival of party identities throughout the period, thereby contrasting sharply with the volumes for 1754–1790 edited by John Brooke and Namier himself. The contrast was made explicit in the Preface, wherein it is explained that 'a method suitable for 1754–1790, when "the old party denominations of Whig and Tory no longer corresponded to political realities" is not appropriate for 1715–1754, when there was a real difference between the parties.' To many onlookers it must have seemed as though Namier had created a monster which had turned on its master, especially since the volumes appeared under the name of Romney Sedgwick, a close collaborator of Sir Lewis. However, though the voice was Jacob's, the hands were the hands of Esau: Sedgwick was general editor of the volumes, but the introductory survey was written by Dr Eveline Cruickshanks. In it she concluded that the 'available evidence leaves no doubt that up to 1745 the Tories were a predominantly Jacobite party, engaged in attempts to restore the Stuarts by a rising with foreign assistance.'[15]

The chief evidence for this assertion is in the Stuart papers and the French archives. These contain correspondence between Jacobite agents and prominent Tories on the one hand, and the Pretender and the French government on the other, concerning plots to restore James III. Few historians have worked on these and the English papers at the Quai d'Orsay as assiduously as Dr Cruickshanks, though mention must be made of Professor Paul S. Fritz, who used them for his study of *The English Ministers and Jacobitism between the Rebellions of 1715 and 1745* published in 1975. While one can only admire their thorough exploitation of these sources, the conclusion which they base upon it, that the bulk of the Tories were active Jacobites, has left considerable doubt.

There were, of course, many Jacobites, and more fellow travellers, both in the Tory party in parliament and in the country at large. Nor one can refute the charge that the bulk of the Tories were Jacobites merely by pointing out that they did not rise in rebellion when they had the opportunity in 1715 and again in 1745. Thomas Forster, one of the few who had the courage to take up arms on behalf of the Pretender, was right to feel badly let down by many who shared his principles but were afraid to join him in the Fifteen; as he himself complained 'he was blustered into this business by such people as these, but that for the time to come he would never again believe a drunken Tory'.[16] At the same time he went too far when 'he looked on the whole body of the Tories to be in it'.[17] The narrow test of being an active rebel would exclude William Shippen, which is absurd since it was notorious to contemporaries that he was 'the head of the veteran staunch Jacobites'.[18] Shippen did not get himself implicated in the Fifteen, perhaps because he was too prudent to commit himself to such a hopeless cause. We shall never know how many Tories would have shown their true Jacobite colours if the Young Pretender had stood a chance of winning in the Forty-five. Yet if the insistence on active participation in rebellion is too exclusive a test of Jacobitism in the Tory party, willingness to accept that any Tory named on a list of potential rebels sent to the Pretender was in fact an active supporter is far too inclusive. Both Dr Cruickshanks and Professor Fritz publish a list compiled for the Pretender in 1721 by prominent Jacobites, purporting to name his supporters in England and Wales.[19] Something of the unreal optimism which inspired them can be discerned from their comment that Birmingham and Manchester could furnish 27,000 fighting men for the cause – no mean feat when their combined population totalled only 40,000.[20]

They also included men whose Jacobite zeal was, to say the least, suspect.[21] If George Baker of Durham was an active Jacobite, then why was William Cotesworth, a zealous local Whig, undertaking to answer for his parliamentary behaviour in 1718? Acton Baldwin and Sir Edward Stradling were such lukewarm Tories in 1715 that they could be described as often voting with the Whigs in the year of the Jacobite rebellion. Lord Downe was so indifferent to the Tory cause that he sold his burgages in Pontefract to a Court Whig in 1727. Lord Fermanagh was also so moderate a Tory in that year that he was held to be 'unconcerned for any party'. John Hardres actually supported the septennial bill, scarcely a distinguishing mark of Toryism, let alone of Jacobitism, and along with Stephen Parry was in receipt of a bounty from the government at the very time that the list was drawn up. Sir Justinian Isham was so anxious not to be mistaken for a Jacobite that he actually instructed his son to avoid the Pretender when he visited Rome in 1719. Thomas Lewis went over to the Court in 1726, and warned the Commons in 1733 not to reduce the army since 'it was our weakness that encouraged the rebellious plots in the late reign'. William Levinz, so far from joining in the Fifteen on behalf of the Pretender, subscribed £100 towards the cost of raising a regiment in Nottinghamshire to supress it, and was 'as zealous to put the laws in operation against the Roman Catholics as anybody'. Sir Nicholas Morrice referred to George I in his private correspondence as 'this king', something no self-respecting

Jacobite would ever have done. Edward Nicholas, whom the third Earl of Shaftesbury once rightly described as 'so supple a Tory' and a 'sure tool' of the Court, wrote to his Whig nephew Spencer Compton promising his vote and interest for the Speakership of the Commons in 1722. Thomas Palmer upheld the Chancellor of the Exchequer in 1721 when the Jacobites were baying for his blood because of his involvement in the South Sea Bubble.

In the absence of corroboration from other sources, the wishful thinking of the Pretender's adherents cannot be used to substantiate the claim that the Tories were committed to his restoration. Yet the equation of the Tories with Jacobitism is taken to considerable lengths by Dr Cruickshanks. For instance, she attributes their cooperation with opposition Whigs after 1730 to the receipt of instructions from the Pretender, as though they were like a Western European communist party in the 1930s under orders from Moscow. In fact most of them were taking their lead from Sir William Wyndham, who had long since repudiated the Pretender and had reached a working agreement with William Pulteney. Another example of the casual way in which almost all Tories are identified as Jacobites is her description of the Cocoa Tree, a coffee house in Pall Mall, as 'the Jacobite Club', when, as Dr Linda Colley has demonstrated, it was the London base of staunchly Hanoverian Tories.[22]

Although Dr Colley is convinced that the Tories were not Jacobites, she is nevertheless persuaded that they existed as a coherent political party, with effective leadership and organization, throughout the period 1714 to at least 1754. Certainly she has demonstrated that they retained their separate identity in the House of Commons, led by Wyndham until his death in 1740, and thereafter by Sir John Hinde Cotton, Sir Watkin Williams Wynn and Sir John Philipps.[23] When it is claimed that they were ideologically distinct from opposition Whigs, however, difficulties arise. Yet both Dr Colley and Dr B. W. Hill in his recent book *The Growth of Parliamentary Parties 1689–1742* assert this.

Both insist that the great issues which had divided Tory from Whig before 1714 continued to polarize them well into the reign of George II. Thus Dr Hill claims that 'the succession question . . . remained a matter of serious concern to ministries until at least the failure of the Young Pretender's descent in 1745.'[24] This would be a more telling point if he agreed with Dr Cruickshanks that the bulk of the Tories were Jacobites, but he is no more prepared to accept her thesis than is Dr Colley. Of course Walpole and the Pelhams after him used the Jacobite smear to try to prevent opposition Whigs from working with Tories, but between the crises of 1722–23 and 1744–45 it does not appear to have been a very successful gambit. Again, Dr Hill maintains that 'the religious element remained active', but does not even mention it, much less prove it, until his discussion of the session of 1736 when he rather inconsistently talks about 'the revival of religious issues'.[25] In fact, after the repeal of the Occasional Conformity and Schism Acts in 1719, religious controversy diminished in importance rather rapidly. The cry 'the Church in danger', so potent under Anne, was scarcely whispered between 1720 and 1754. Only in two isolated incidents did the old slogan surface, in 1736 and 1753. On the first occasion, a Dissenting bid to repeal the Test and Corporation Acts was firmly stifled by Walpole, though a measure to make it easier for Quakers to protect themselves against prosecutions for non-payment of tithes did temporarily heat up the political atmosphere. The opposition offered to the Tithes Bill by the bishops, however, who were by 1736 Whigs almost to a man, scarcely squares with the notion that it divided politicians along Whig and Tory lines.

Printed division lists provide an excellent test of Dr Hill's claim that 'down to the fall of Walpole, at least, party differentiation remained intact because the issues which had given birth to it were still very much alive.'[26] Divisions which merited the publication of lists were surely those which contemporaries held to be the most important. Those which resulted in such publication under Anne were almost all occasioned by debates involving the succession or religion: in 1703 a division over extending the time for taking the abjuration oath; in 1704 the tacking of the Occasional Conformity Bill to the Land Tax Bill; in 1709 the naturalization of foreign Protestants; in 1710 the trial of Dr Sacheverell; in 1714 the expulsion of Richard Steele for maintaining in print that the succession was in danger. These were all issues which underlined the party struggle.

Apart from the publication of lists of those who voted for and against the repeal of the Occasional Conformity and Schism Acts in 1719, none of those published in the period 1714 to 1742 concerned divisions on issues which fundamentally divided Tory from Whig: the Septennial Bill of 1716; the Peerage Bill in 1719; the civil list in 1729; the payment of Hessian troops in 1730; the army in 1732; the Excise Bill in 1733; the repeal of the Septennial Act in 1734; the Convention of Pardo in 1739; the Place Bill in 1740; the chairmanship of the committee of privileges in 1741; the payment of Hanoverian troops in 1742. These lists do not reflect the survival of issues which polarized the political world into Whig and Tory parties in Anne's reign. On the contrary, they record the eclipse of those issues and their replacement by questions which created tensions between Court and Country.

It is true that the Tories are to be found voting against the Court in all these divisions.[27] Only 14 who sided with them in Anne's reign voted for the Septennial Bill, while 142 opposed it. A mere three supported the repeal of the Occasional Conformity and Schism Acts, and again only three were for the Peerage Bill, with 128 against. Only a few former Tories voted on the Court side in the division lists extant for the period 1729 to 1742. This is an extremely impressive record, especially considering that the Tory party had been much less disciplined than the Whigs under Anne. Yet after 1714 it was essentially an opposition party, with none of its leaders in office. Indeed, to some extent the discipline of the party is an optical illusion, since former Tories who voted with the Court after 1714, and who numbered at least fifty, tended to be classified as Whigs. The acid test of the meaningful survival of party labels is therefore not how the Tories voted but how the Whigs divided. And divided is the word, for on every list Whigs are to be found voting against the Court: 43 against the Septennial Bill; 69 against the repeal of the Occasional Conformity and Schism Acts; 144 against the Peerage Bill, compared with 188 for it. In the division lists for the years 1729 to 1742 the number of Whigs opposing the Court fluctuated between 69 and 115. In the light of these figures it is hard to see how Dr Hill can assert that during Walpole's administration 'a united and continuous opposition was made impossible by the repeated refusal of both Tories and 'patriot' Whigs to act together on important issues.'[28] If the division lists do not document the important issues, it is difficult to see what does.

This crucial qualitative change in the nature of division lists vitiates the quantitative argument which J. C. D. Clark seeks to base upon them.[29] A central feature of his thesis that party distinctions survived Anne's death until the 1750s is that the deviation from normal voting behaviour was not significantly higher under Walpole and the Pelhams than it had been under William and Anne. This is a dubious proposition when by his own account only 10 to 15 per cent of MPs voted inconsistently in the earlier period, while there were two or three times as many inconsistent voters in the House of Commons between 1730 and 1747. It is remarkable evidence of the overriding supremacy of the strife between Tories and Whigs in Anne's reign that the most exhaustive analysis of parliamentary lists from the years 1702 to 1714 failed to establish the existence of a single member who voted consistently against whichever government held office during those years. Under Anne's immediate successors, however, most Tories and a sizeable phalanx of Whigs regularly opposed the government. This can only be explained as a deviation from a Tory/Whig norm if the Court is regarded as Whig, the Tories as Country and the opposition Whigs as deviants. Any historian who accuses opposition Whigs of deviating from a Whig norm when they opposed placemen and soldiers has not appreciated the pedigree of Whig political theory. So far from being inconsistent in their Whiggery, his Whig opponents accused Walpole and the Pelhams of being apostates from Whig principles, and significantly called themselves 'Old' or 'Country' Whigs.

John Owen used the lists in a very revealing way to see how the independent knights of the shire voted between 1714 and 1790.[30] He showed that between 1714 and 1760, whatever their party affiliation – and though most were Tories a significant number were Country Whigs – they voted overwhelmingly against the Court. In the parliaments of 1715–22 and 1723–34, 70 per cent of them divided consistently with the opposition, while in that of 1734–41 'no less than 58 (or 82 per cent) were declared opponents'. This confirms an anonymous riposte to Lord Perceval's notorious tract *Faction detected by the evidence of facts*. First published in the aftermath of Walpole's fall in 1742 to justify the very slight ministerial changes which ensued, Perceval's argument was that Tory and Whig divisions were still the underlying realities in English politics. *A Defence of the People: or full confutation of the pretended facts advanc'd in a late huge angry pamphlet call'd Faction Detected* took issue with him; 'for God's sake how come you to ground a defence of the new part of the administration on this ridiculous exploded jargon about Whig and Tory?' demanded its author:

> How could you possibly forget the joint labours of so many men of genius, to prove, that a solid, well understood, and well cemented coalition had actually taken place; that Whig and Tory were no more, and that Court and Country were, for the future to distinguish the friends and enemies of the people?

Although 'Court' and 'Country' had become more meaningful terms to describe the realities of English politics by 1742, it does not necessarily follow that they described parties which had replaced the former alignments. It is true that the expressions 'Court party' and 'Country party' were used in the mid eighteenth century; more commonly indeed than the term 'Tory party', or even 'Whig party'. Yet the word 'party' is not a precise noun, like say 'army' but a general concept, like 'class', which can mean different things at different times and even convey varied meanings to historians of the same era. The major political parties in modern Britain, for example, have highly developed organizations, with detailed programmes approved at annual conferences, nation-wide electoral machinery and discipline in parliament imposed by whips. When men in the eighteenth century used the word party to describe political associations they did not refer to anything so complex. Burke, for instance, was content with the simple definition 'a body of men united, for promoting by their joint endeavours the national interest, upon some particular principle in which they are all agreed'. Yet this does not invalidate his use of the word. To some modern historians the primacy of political principles is still the vital ingredient of a party, and they would assert the paramount importance of a coherent political philosophy held by the members of a party. Others would argue that·it is not what men think but what they do that counts. This is the view of most Namierite historians. To Sir Lewis Namier ideas were mere 'names and cant'.[31] John Brooke endorsed this when he wrote: 'Political parties do not exist in a void nor are political principles academic intellectual exercises in logical thought. A history of parties is meaningless which does not relate them to the specific political questions which they were called upon to solve.'[32]

Both points of view are valid and can be applied to the problem of what contemporaries meant when they referred to Court and Country parties. Were there 'Court' and 'Country' attitudes of mind, ideologies even? Did those politicians who adopted those attitudes organize joint activities in parliament with the object of securing specific ends?

Court and Country were much older divisions than Whig and Tory, dating back at least to the 1620s, when they had been used to describe the supporters and opponents of James I and Charles I. At one level they merely differentiated between the 'ins' and the 'outs', but to accept this as a complete explanation of the division is to take a worm's eye view of politics, for on the Country side were many critics of government who had no intention whatsoever of taking power themselves. The abiding feature of the Country mentality from the days of the Duke of Buckingham to those of the Duke of Newcastle was a suspicion of government itself, whatever the political complexion of the Court; a distrust of the executive for its own sake, based on a conviction that power corrupts, and that governments govern best which govern least.

During the seventeenth century this attitude was partly inspired by, and partly inspired, Puritanism. This inspiration survived, and found expression in the political attitudes of men like Robert Harley and Sir Richard Cocks. As a Whig member of parliament for Gloucestershire in William's reign, Cocks spoke out strongly against placemen and standing armies. As chairman of the county quarter sessions in George I's reign he charged grand juries to 'punish vice and discountenance immoralities. Punishments and fear of penalties make men considerative, and consideration makes men wise, and wisdom makes men religious.'[33] Attacks on courtiers from Buckingham to Walpole were charged with the puritan conviction that such men were wicked.

Under the first two Georges, however, the Country outlook was reinforced by a more secular tradition. Country writers like Thomas Gordon and John Trenchard drew on the political philosophies of Machiavelli, Hobbes, Harrington and Algernon Sydney to substantiate their view that people were inherently corruptible, that politicians were perpetually bent on depriving people of liberty, and that corruption was the principal means whereby they achieved their object. They documented this view from ancient and modern history. The history of ancient Rome was used to illustrate the erosion of liberty and the advancement of autocratic power through the agency of corruption. Contemporary developments on the continent were cited to demonstrate the collapse of representative government and the rise of absolutism. England had so far averted this fate thanks to its ancient constitution and constant vigilance. To Country writers England had possessed a more durable polity than other nations because its balanced constitution contained elements of monarchy, aristocracy and democracy, which together resisted the inevitable decay of constitutions containing only one of these. The last blatant attempt to destroy the equilibrium had been in James II's reign, when the king himself had tried to expand the monarchical element to the detriment of the aristocratic and democratic. Though the Revolution of 1688 had restored the ancient equilibrium, the expansion of the executive since then threatened once again to undermine it. Four developments in particular were suspect: the growth of governmental expenditure; the increase in the size of the standing army; the rise in the numbers of placemen in parliament; and the extension of the maximum interval between general elections from three to seven years by the Septennial Act of 1716.[34]

Gordon and Trenchard were Whigs, but their arguments were picked up and extended by Tories such as Bolingbroke, Pope and Swift. In their writings the plot thickened, and the arch conspirator was revealed to be Sir Robert Walpole. Pope's final version of the *Dunciad* described him as a 'wizard old' who 'made one mighty Dunciad of the realm'. In the first voyage of Gulliver, Swift showed how Lilliput had degenerated from a perfect polity to a petty and corrupt régime, a process aided by self-seeking politicians who were flimsily disguised Walpoles. *The Craftsman* ransacked history from Sejanus to Wolsey to find precedents for the tyranny of 'The Great Man'. By the time of Walpole's fall in 1742, according to a recent study of *The Tories and the 45*, 'the public demands of the Tory party were: a reduction of the standing army, the organization of an effective militia (in which they would be allowed to serve), a foreign policy based on the national interest, a repeal of the Septennial Act, the Waltham Black Act and the Smuggling Act.'[35] This shows the extent to which Country issues had replaced former party principles, for opposition Whigs could wholeheartedly endorse the entire list.

In Country writings philosophy and history were blended into an ideology which has been described as 'the politics of nostalgia'.[36] Country ideology venerated the rôle of England's traditional ruling class, its great landowners, and deplored the rise of new interests, especially the military-financial complex of the City of London. There was something of the ancient tension between the Country and the City in this propaganda, which depicted a golden age, almost a Garden of Eden, when England had been ruled by country gentlemen and aristocrats in the classical sense of being 'the best'. This idyllic scene was contrasted with the present, in which the City in the modern sense meaning the Bank, the Stock Exchange and other financial institutions had been established within recent memory, and seemed to command government itself. The assets of the City were seen as an inexhaustible fountain of corruption, for which the South Sea Bubble served as a spectacular symbol.

Although much Country thought was based on myth, there was some foundation for it in reality. To some extent the transition from the rage of party to the struggle between Court and Country was due, not merely to the passing of the old issues which had divided Tory from Whig, but also to changes in society which created a conflict of interests cutting across the old party lines. What has been described as the Financial Revolution occurred in England after 1688, largely in response to the government's need for war finance. This created what contemporaries called the monied interest, based mainly in London and the Home Counties, consisting of rentiers who lived off their investments in 'the Funds'. Some of them were real plutocrats, including a number of foreigners and Jews who were prime targets for xenophobic country gentlemen. The growth of the executive in these years was also unprecedented. The taxation needed to service the huge debts which profited the monied interest was administered by a whole new bureaucracy of customs and excise men. The expansion of other agencies of government, such as the Post Office, created a civil service which survived the demobilization of much of the army after the Treaty of Utrecht in 1713 and continued to grow under Walpole. There is even evidence that Walpole systematically deployed the influence of the Crown to build up a Court party in the Commons much more formidable than any body of royal servants at the disposal of his predecessors. All these developments brought Court and Country issues to the fore.

If Country Tories and Whigs thought alike along these lines, then how prepared were they to work together to preserve the ancient constitution? The Country mentality informed backbenchers throughout the later Stuart period, but apart from a few interludes in William's reign, when they had united into a Country party, the magnetic pull of Whig and Tory proved too powerful for them to fuse into one on a permanent basis. After William's death the rivalry of the Whigs and Tories had transcended all other divisions, so much so that, although there were still Country members in their ranks, the expression 'Country party' is very rarely met in Anne's reign. Yet though the rage of party prevented cooperation between them, in 1714 a leading Country Whig could write 'the Country Whigs and Country Tories were not very different in their notions, and nothing has hindered them from joining but the fear that each have of the others bringing in their whole party.'[37]

These fears survived for ten years, kept alive mainly by Tory association with the Jacobite scares of 1715, 1717, 1719 and 1722. But with the
exile of Francis Atterbury, the Jacobite bishop of Rochester in 1723,
and the return of Henry St John, Viscount Bolingbroke, from the
service of the Pretender in the same year, a new situation arose. Bolingbroke, by then completely disillusioned with James Edward Stuart, was
determined to dissociate the Tories from Jacobitism and to persuade
them to cooperate with dissident Whigs. The departure of William
Pulteney from the ministry in 1725 provided him with a Whig ally who
was prepared to urge his followers to combine with the Tories in opposition to Walpole. In 1726 they launched *The Craftsman* to preach the
Country gospel. Thus on 24 April 1727 they called for a coalition of
parties on the grounds that

> those disputes which have divided the nation into two great factions and
> brought about several wonderful revolutions in our government seem, at
> present, to be in a great measure terminated by the firm establishment of the
> Protestant succession against all attempts to defeat it; and by the general
> affection of the people to his Majesty's person, family and government . . .
> let the very names of Whig and Tory be forever buried in oblivion.

Five years later they summed up their editorial policy thus:

> We have . . . us'd our utmost endeavours, through the whole course of these
> papers, to banish these senseless and fatal animosities; to reconcile all parties
> to one another; to unite them in their common interest; the interest and
> cause of their country; and to persuade men, who are equally zealous in the
> pursuit of the same end, though perhaps by different means, not to defeat it
> by unreasonable jealousies and reproachful imputations.

These exhortations were not entirely successful, for Tories and
Country Whigs did not merge into one body but kept their separate
identities. Disagreements over tactics frequently created friction
between the leaders of both groups. For instance, in the aftermath of the
withdrawal of the Excise scheme in 1733, when their euphoria at defeat-
ing the Court might have been expected to keep them together, they disagreed in drawing up a list of members to investigate frauds in the
Customs. Pulteney wanted the list to be composed entirely of opposition Whigs, while Wyndham insisted on the inclusion of some Tories.
This disarray enabled Walpole to carry the Court list for the committee.
Nevertheless the aims of Country strategy were never lost sight of.
The size of the standing army was attacked in virtually every session of
the parliament of 1727–34, as was the award of places and pensions to
MPs. 'The climax of this attack on Walpole's devices for managing
Parliament came in the final session, with the motion . . . for the repeal
of the Septennial Act, which . . . the opposition saw (correctly) as the
lynch-pin of Walpole's managerial success.'[38] Meanwhile the previous

session had witnessed the furore over the Excise scheme, of which Paul Langford noted: 'At a time when the ministry's opponents were anxious to bury party feuds and unite the mixed forces in opposition to the Court, nothing was better calculated than a straightforward Court and Country issue like the Excise to reinforce its strategy.'[39]

The following general election was the first at which it is possible to gauge how far the electorate reacted to the new alignment of Court and Country, for in 1734 the opposition projected itself to the voters as a united party. As *Fog's Weekly Journal* put it,

> If any one had told me in Queen Anne's reign that some time about the year 1732 the invidious names of Whig and Tory, of High Church and Low Church, should be utterly abolish'd and forgot, I should have consider'd him as a false prophet, or a dreamer of dreams, and yet this thing is actually come to pass . . . .

According to the most detailed analysis of the results, however, 'the only areas where the new doctrines made some progress were the economically more advanced, and therefore politically more sophisticated, parts of the country, around London and in the southeast generally and to some extent in Yorkshire.'[41] Certainly in London itself the opposition had overcome former party differences to present a united front to Walpole some time before 1734. Nicholas Rogers has shown how 'City politics in the late 20s and 30s were . . . conspicuously different to those of Queen Anne's reign. One notes an attenuation of old party distinctions and a substantial sector of moderate voters uncommitted to either of the old parties.' The decade 1725 to 1735 saw 'the emergence of a broadly based anti-ministerial coalition, a 'Patriot' party as it was called'.[42]

Elsewhere it seems as though the pattern described by Sir Lewis Namier held good: 'in a good many constituencies the names of Whig and Tory still corresponded to real divisions: partly perhaps because local factions could hardly have been denoted as 'Government' and 'Opposition', and partly because the most enduring distinction between Tory and Whig – High Church *versus* Low Church and Dissent – retained more vitality and significance in local struggles than at Westminster.'[43] This was certainly true in constituencies where the Court was opposed by Tories only, since although they described themselves in 1734 as being 'in the Country interest' this did not appeal to many Whigs to vote for them, even if they were discontented with Walpole. Dissenters especially could not be brought to change their traditional allegiance and support Tories.[44]

However, in the few constituencies where a Tory and a Country Whig stood against Court candidates the electorate appears to have been more discriminating. There were seven in England and Wales where the voters were definitely presented with such a choice, and a further five where they probably were.[45] In the seven contests where candidates can be definitely distinguished as 'Government' and 'Opposition' the numbers which they polled suggest strongly that the voters recognized them as such.

Where four candidates stood, the distribution of votes can be deduced without recourse to poll books. Thus in Kent the Tory Sir Edward Dering and his Country Whig partner scored 4,441 and 4,252 votes against 3,569 and 3,450 cast for the Court Whigs, while in Sussex the Court Whigs Henry Pelham and James Butler were returned with 2,271 and 2,053 against 1,704 cast for the Country Whig Sir Cecil Bishopp and 1581 for the Tory John Fuller. These figures demonstrated that the electorate for the most part voted for a pair of candidates even if this entailed supporting a Tory and a Country Whig. In Yorkshire the situation was slightly more complicated, since the Country Whig Edward Wortley Montagu did not join with the Tory Sir Miles Stapylton but intervened to split the Whig vote so that he would be returned. The stratagem was successful, for Stapylton topped the poll with 7,896 votes, the Court candidates obtained 7,879 and 7,699, while Montagu trailed with 5,898. In the two boroughs where four candidates stood the polarization between Court and Country is even more clear-cut. In Liverpool the Court candidates Thomas Brereton and Richard Gildart polled 1076 and 1030 respectively, while the Country Whig Thomas Bootle and the Tory Foster Cunliffe obtained 990 and 940 votes; in Wareham, where the Country Whig Henry Drax and the Tory John Pitt obtained exactly 208 votes apiece, 75 voted for Sir Nathaniel Gould and 68 for Sir William Wolseley the Court Whig candidates.

Contests, of course, are not the only measure of the degree of electoral support which parties could command. The most striking instance of this in 1734 was Middlesex, where the leading opposition Whig William Pulteney stood with the Tory Sir Francis Child unopposed. The Court prudently decided not to fight an election it knew it could not win. The fact that many Country members were returned from large constituencies even without a contest is a significant sign of the popularity of the opposition to Walpole. Dr Langford has shown how opponents of the Excise scheme were far more prominent in constituencies with over 500 voters than were its defenders, and stood a better chance of being re-elected to parliament.[46] To some extent this justifies the opposition's use of the label 'Country' in the sense that it represented a wider gamut of interests throughout the nation than the more narrowly based Court.

The predominance of the Court interest in small boroughs was due to the growth of the Whig oligarchy since the death of Queen Anne. This in itself was both a cause and a consequence of the demise of the party rage of her reign and its replacement by a conflict between Court and Country. Tories proscribed from office found themselves unable to compete with Whigs backed by the Court in general elections, especially when the cost of contests rose after the passing of the Septennial Act in 1716. As a result the number of contests fell significantly, from a peak of 129 contested English constituencies at the polls in 1722, to a trough of 46 by 1761. Although counties were affected by the decline in contests, the real fall occurred in small boroughs where Tory candidates were squeezed out. This process confirmed the fears that the Commons was ceasing to represent the Country and was beginning to represent the Court, apprehensions which were stock charges in Country propaganda, but which seem to be first justified in the aftermath of the 1734 election, where the ministry was routed in the popular constituencies but still kept a majority in the Lower House.

By the 1730s the language of politics was very different from the vocabulary which had been employed in the reign of Queen Anne. It is true that under George II men still referred to Tories and to Whigs. But where between 1702 and 1714 these had been distinguished as parties, with the Tory party significantly being often dubbed the Church party, after 1730 this distinction is rarely met. Instead one increasingly encounters such expressions as the Court, the Courtiers, the ministry, and opposed to them, Tories, Old Whigs, patriots, the Country party, and above all, the opposition. It was in these years that the expression 'the opposition' first came into general use to describe those who regularly voted in parliament against the government.[47] The reason was that none of the terms used in Anne's day were still felt to be appropriate. The Tories were no longer a party, least of all 'the Church party', in the sense that they had been then. Furthermore, although they were in opposition they were not the only politicians to oppose Walpole, being joined in 1725 by Pulteney and the patriots, and after 1737 by the followers of Frederick, Prince of Wales. In the 1741 election the prince allied with the Cornish Tories to such an extent that his agent there foretold the results in these terms: 'there will be I think 27 members returned in Cornwall on the Country interest and 17 Courtiers.'[48]

The 1740s saw some disruption of this pattern. First, the reconstructed ministry following Walpole's fall appeared to benefit Pulteneyites only, no Tories being taken into office. This led the Tories to accuse Pulteney and his followers of using them to serve their own ends, and some of them were prepared to listen receptively to Pelham's overtures in his struggle for power against former patriot leaders. Thus for the first time since Anne's death Tories entered the ministry and found themselves back on the commissions of the peace in the counties. These trends were set back, however, by the desertion of Lord Gower, who went over to the Government in 1744 after playing a prominent part in Tory counsels for years, and especially by the Jacobite rebellion of 1745, which seemed even to the Country Whigs to vindicate Walpole's charges that the Tories were really Jacobites at heart. By the late 1740s the only Whigs playing a leading role in the opposition were those associated with the prince, whose death in 1751 created a situation momentarily like that which prevailed after Anne died, in which most Whigs supported the ministry while the bulk of the opposition consisted of Tories.

But, as in 1714, this situation did not last long. Whigs like the Duke of Bedford and the Earl of Sandwich went into opposition almost immediately, so that the apparent polarity of Court – Whig and Country – Tory was disturbed. Far more important was the rise of William Pitt, which cannot be explained in terms of a struggle between Tories and Whigs. By the 1750s the last vestiges of ideological distinction between the two former parties had almost completely disappeared. Jacobitism, never more than a minority attitude among Tories even in their hey-day in 1710, became confined to a negligible few after the failure of the Forty-five. Many Tories ostentatiously showed their loyalty to the Hanoverian succession while maintaining an opposition stance by attaching themselves to Prince Frederick. After his death they switched their allegiance to the reversionary interest of the young Prince George, whose cause was also being championed by Pitt. The Great Commoner rallied the Tories, opposition Whigs, patriots and all the Country elements against the Court with attacks upon the Duke of Newcastle's foreign policy and by sponsoring bills to strengthen the militia and the navy which had been the constant platform of the opposition since the accession of George II. For the first time under the Hanoverians these tactics succeeded in removing a prime minister from office and in bringing Pitt to power.

Thus, on the eve of the accession of George III, the political alignments were totally different from those which had obtained on the death of Queen Anne. In 1714 George I had to choose between the Tory and Whig parties. In 1760 the choice was of men who would strengthen the ministerial or Court vote in the Commons, and measures which would appeal to enough backbenchers to prevent the formation of a Country coalition against the Court.

Colloquy on chapter 3
Geoffrey Holmes

The discussion focused on three main issues. First was the validity of
the central thesis: that soon after 1714, and certainly no later than 1725
(p. 66) the Court – Country division became the dominant one in both
political action and debate, and remained so until 1760 – except in the
years 1745 – 51 when there was a final brief reversion to something like
the Whig – Tory dichotomy of Anne's reign. Second was the character
of the Whig and Tory parties under the first two Georges and the question of whether or not a 'Country party' existed at any time in this
period. Third concerned the Commons' division lists of the years
1716 – 42 on which Speck appeared to have rested a substantial part of
his case – how representative were they of prevailing voting patterns
and how should they be interpreted?

O'Gorman felt that the central thesis was overplayed and suggested
that two aspects should be kept in mind, opinion in the country, and
opinion in parliament.

His view was that, in general, party lingered longer in the constituencies than at Westminster – it was still in evidence in the late 1750s
and early 1760s; and that such intensity of political feeling as early
Hanoverian England could muster in General Elections was generated
principally by residual Whig and Tory differences, though he did not
dispute that in some constituencies they could be submerged by
Court – Country loyalties. Speck accepted that the basic division among
voters from 1715 to 1761 remained strongly traditional, but stressed the
qualifications. London quickly departed from the old norms; the
number of contests throughout England declined so much after 1722
that examples of a genuine Whig – Tory schism in the electorate became
increasingly scattered; in a significant number of constituencies
Country Whig and Tory candidates did occupy the same platform in
opposition to ministerialists. Dickinson, however, was not prepared to
concede as much to O'Gorman, arguing that he had begged the question
of what was a Whig and what a Tory. In Anne's reign the same issues
came up in popular constituencies as in Parliament; candidates claimed
to be standing for definite causes, clearly identifiable as Whig or Tory.
But was there any real parallel to this under Walpole? With the Tories,
for example, the same men and families reappeared who had fought the

elections of 1702–15 and there was a residual loyalty to them among the voters, but apart from an element of Church allegiance, and gut hostility to corruption, to the Hanoverians, to 'Whiggism' in general, where was the *positive* Toryism that had been seen in Anne's reign? What gave them their identity as 'Tories' was opposition to the government. O'Gorman agreed there was a change in post-1714 Toryism – a natural reaction to the change in the political world around it – but insisted that it retained its intrinsic electoral importance.

At Westminster the situation was different. There Tories and Country Whigs did coalesce now and again, but never, in O'Gorman's view, to the point of submerging their identities in a common 'party'. Surviving division lists suggested that virtually all Tories consistently opposed the government after 1714 and perhaps 70 to 75 per cent of Whigs consistently supported it. He thought this latter figure 'enormously instructive'; but Dickinson enquired, in what way *were* these post-1714 governments 'Whig' in the old sense, or their opponents 'Tory'? Walpole's and Pelham's administrations had stolen quite a few Tory clothes by then, and the Tories had shed many of their old garments, notably Succession, Church and Non-resistance. Country, not Whig and Tory issues, dominated the parliamentary debates of that period. Cannon recognized that opposition politicians had some success in encouraging Whig and Tory members to work together and even to dine together, but thought that Speck's argument failed one of the acid tests of parliamentary allegiance, the famous vote of No Confidence in Walpole in February 1741. Here, at last, was a real chance of bringing down the government, yet the Tories refused to go into the lobby with the Whigs, because they regarded the vote as impingeing on the prerogative of the Crown. Did this not suggest that they looked upon themselves primarily as opposition Tories, not as opposition Country? Dickinson thought the wording influenced the Tories, but for Holmes this was the very point: an address to the king asking him to dismiss Sir Robert *for ever* from his counsels struck at the heart of *Tory* principles.

Speck, while reminding us that other votes in 1741 revealed that Whigs and Tories could cooperate, was less concerned with specific divisions than with the long-term pattern of politics. He was even inclined to suggest that the Court–Country antithesis was the natural one in late Stuart as well as Hanoverian politics (e.g. 1697–1701) and wondered whether Anne's reign should not be seen in retrospect as the anomaly?

Towards the end of the discussion on the main thesis Derry raised another point: could one use the term 'party' of men remote from power, even though they might act together? Did a Country 'party' ever exist after 1714 and what did Whigs and Tories stand for? Speck called for more analysis of the terms people actually used in talking about their politics. In Anne's reign he knew of only one (dubious) instance of 'the Country party' being mentioned. Yet in the 1720s and 1730s this term was used repeatedly, and 'Tory party', as opposed to 'Tories', relatively rarely. Holmes asked whether, nevertheless, historians could accept the existence of a party without strong evidence of continuity, at least from one parliament through a general election into the heart of the next parliament. He saw no such evidence in this period which justified labelling *ad hoc* combinations of Tories and Country Whigs as 'a party'. Speck replied that he had been careful not to do so!

Holmes suggested the danger of equating 'Country' politicians and stances with *opposition*. In using division lists we had to be particularly careful not to lump together, under one ideological umbrella, Whig power politicians (or even Tories hopeful of power) with the true Country independents, Whig or Tory. All might achieve a Country attitude or consensus at times, but there was no real unity behind it. The union of Country independents with the Pulteneyites and the Excise rebels was, for the latter, a marriage of convenience; and this was even more true of Pulteney's wooing of the Country Tories.

No one dissented from the argument in Speck's paper (pp. 57–9) that the Tories were not a Jacobite party; but O'Gorman thought that Speck had not done full justice to Linda Colley's full and sophisticated case for the persistence of a unitary party after 1727, and Cannon suggested an inconsistency between Speck's denial of 'party' status to the Tories (p. 69) and his concession (p. 61) that no Tories voted with the Court on any extant division list in the years 1729–42. Holmes asked for second thoughts on Speck's dismissal of any 'Church party' basis for Toryism. The anticlerical traditions of the Whigs lingered on through the late 1720s and erupted quite alarmingly in the 1730s. The bitter fight over the attempt to repeal the Test and Corporation Acts and to carry the Quaker Relief Bill (1735–36) should be seen not as isolated sallies but as the culmination of a string of measures, beginning in 1730, viewed by the Tories as hostile to the Church. Certainly Walpole tried to convince them and the clergy that the Church was safe in Whig hands, associating his ministry only with the Quaker Bill; but he failed. McCord agreed: surely, Speck's statement that the 'Church in danger' was 'scarcely whispered' in this period was much too sweeping? (pp. 60).

Speck readily conceded that he had not done full justice to Colley's doctoral thesis. He very much looked forward to its publication since she *had* demonstrated that the Tories retained their separate identity in the Commons into the 1750s. Yet he believed that Tory voting figures were less impressive than they seemed: the fact that the Tories lost their Court wing rapidly after 1714 and were left mainly with a Country rump, gave an 'optical illusion' of solidarity. He had searched in vain for the expression 'the Church party' in the period 1720–60, a phrase synonymous with the Tory party under Anne. He found it odd that if the anti-clerical measures of 1730–36 were so vital to the Tories, the *Craftsman* had not led a propaganda campaign on the Church in danger issue. Holmes did not share his surprise: the measures of the early 1730s were overtaken by the Excise Crisis and, in any case, why should the *Craftsman* be considered representative of Tory opinion, when Bolingbroke was damned in many Tory eyes as a Deist?

Dickinson conceded that there was an identifiable Tory group which voted together fairly consistently, and that there were some issues, especially Church issues, on which Whig–Tory feelings survived. But these were not the key issues in the parliamentary politics of the period. The main political debate was consistently about Court–Country issues: these were the 'platform' issues and provided the real stuff of politics.

All appeared to accept that there was a big difference between the content of the political propaganda of 1689–1714 and that of 1714–60. But Holmes turned the discussion finally to the question of the value of contemporary division lists, since Speck had made so much of these to buttress his Court–Country thesis. (pp. 60–62) Holmes and Cannon expressed qualms. How capricious was the survival and publication of division lists? If they were geared to election propaganda were they not *ipso facto* selective? Did they provide a reliable guide to the voting of such as the Country Whig knights of the shire (p. 62), not merely on these few particular issues but on the whole range of other issues? Do not some of the lists deployed in the paper to support the Court–Country thesis (Hessian troops, Hanover troops) touch matters on which old Tory prejudices were very sensitive?

Speck accepted that the survival of lists does appear capricious, but stressed that they reflected the issues on which the political propagandists of the day wanted to reveal voting records to the electors. It was noted that the last list used was for 1742, and Cannon asked about the reappearance, four or five years after this, of all the old party animosities, with Tories complaining bitterly about being excluded when the opposition Whigs got office. Dickinson traced this back to the period 1742–44 and the horror of many Country members, who had read and believed their *Craftsman*, at the way Pulteney and Carteret had 'sold out' over Country principles: their idols stood revealed as 'wheelers and dealers'. Holmes and Cannon thought most Tories had seen through Pulteney well before this. Speck himself believed the real turning-point came with the Forty five, when some Country Whigs awoke with horror to the possibility that some of the people they had been sitting down and dining with had been Jacobites. In any event, he reminded us, the words of his title had been carefully chosen to cover just such departures from the norm: 'Whigs and Tories *dim* their Glories'. He had never claimed that their lights had been totally extinguished.[1]

Replying to the discussion, Speck admitted that he would modify some of the sharp contrasts made in the initial argument, while leaving the broad lines intact. He would no longer suggest that the division between Court and Country became dominant 'soon after 1714', since it seems clear that the debate between Tories and Whigs remained central to politics at least until the furore raised by the Atterbury trial died down; although by the general election of 1727 other issues dictated the political dialogue. This is reflected in the way that the press discussed election results. In 1722 newspapers still described all those returned as Tories or Whigs, but thereafter other terminology became increasingly necessary, so that in 1734 and 1741 Tories and opposition Whigs were generally said to have been 'in the Country interest.'

As for parliament, he was more convinced than before that, although Court and Country became dominant during Walpole's ministry, one could not go on to say that this dichotomy created Court and Country *parties*. The opposition was too disorganized to support such a contention. Nevertheless he was not persuaded that ideological differences prevented the formation of a Country party. A very wide spread of politicians, from the Tory Sir William Wyndham to the maverick Court Whig Sir Joseph Jekyll, subscribed to the *Craftsman*: it by no means reiterated the views of Bolingbroke. Moreover the famous motion of 1741 did not fail just because of Tory disapproval of its wording, for several opposition Whigs registered their dislike of it. Mistrust of the leaders of the Country opposition, amply justified in the cases of Bolingbroke and Pulteney, made it hard to concert attacks upon the government.

Bolingbroke above all, who had been Secretary of State from 1710 to 1714, was identified with the Tory reaction of those years, not only with the proscription of dissent and the alleged encouragement of the Pretender, but with the betrayal of the allies in the making of the Treaty of Utrecht, the disgrace of Marlborough, the restraining orders sent to the Duke of Ormonde, and a hundred incidents which made that ministry stink in Whig nostrils. As long as he and other Tories associated with those events, such as Shippen and Wyndham, survived, although the Tory party of Anne's reign committed suicide shortly after the queen's death,[2] its ghost continued to haunt politics right into the Hanoverian era. Only the arrival of a new generation of opposition leaders held out the prospect of a genuine realignment of parties.

Note on further reading

As the opening section of the essay is essentially historiographical, detailed discussion of the relevant literature seems superfluous here. I would therefore simply like to point out that there is no sign of the renewed interest in party politics in the eighteenth century flagging. On the contrary, several works are in preparation, if not in the pipeline, which should ensure that the debate continues to be lively. Linda Colley's thesis on the Tory party from 1727 to 1760 is being expanded into a study of the Tories from 1714 to 1760, and is eagerly awaited. It will be a most substantial contribution to the discussion, and I only wish that it had been published earlier so that I could have done justice to it. Yet although Dr Colley kindly allowed me to read her chapters, both revised and new, it seemed to me inappropriate to discuss in detail a major monograph in advance of its publication. J.C.D. Clark's article on the decline of party is but the opening shot from his armoury: further salvos, including a positive bombardment, have been promised. Meanwhile the History of Parliament is actively working on the period 1689 to 1714 under Dr Eveline Cruickshanks, and sparks from its anvil will doubtless illuminate the period after 1714 too, until the official volumes emerge freshly forged. The best way of keeping abreast of these and other developments in the field is to read the reviews in the house magazine for the period, *The Scriblerian*.

Since the above was written, J.C.D. Clark has published 'A General Theory of Party, Opposition and Government, 1688–1832', *Historical Journal* (1980) xxiii, 295–325. In it he asserts that a two-party system under Anne was replaced during the reigns of George I and George II by a three-party system consisting of Court Whigs, Tories and dissident Whigs. We acknowledged in the discussion that the Tories and Whigs in opposition did not succeed in coalescing permanently into a Country party. At the same time, the notion that they retained their separate identities as *parties* raises problems of definition which, in the case of the dissident Whigs above all, appear to be insuperable. Yet they are not adequately discussed, much less resolved, in this article.

4

Party in the later eighteenth century
Frank O'Gorman

British political life after 1760 was distinguished by the gradual rehab-
ilitation of party politics. Although a two-party *system* did not appear for
another fifty years, the Whig party of Lord Rockingham mounted a
challenge to the monarchy of George III in the first decade of the new
reign which culminated in the constitutional crisis 1782–84. The
origins of this conflict between the advocates of party and the defenders
of the traditional role of the monarchy in the constitution are clear
enough. From the earliest days of the new reign, George III showed
himself to be unwilling to maintain the harmonious equilibrium which
had normally obtained between George II and the Pelhams. The new
king hated the old Whigs and was determined to play the political game
according to his, and not their, rules. Thus, while he did not engineer,
he rejoiced in the resignations of Pitt and Newcastle. And while he had
not plotted to oust Newcastle's men as part of a 'Great Outline' he certainly revelled in the 'Massacre of the Pelhamite Innocents'. Early in
1763 he exulted in his victory over the men who had, in his view, mani-
pulated royal powers for their own ends, practised corrupt government
and driven the country into wasteful and immoral wars. But it was
among the old Whigs, thus excluded from favour and office, that the
seeds of the Rockingham Whig party were sown.

Although major political issues were at stake in the struggle between
the Rockingham Whigs and George III, at one level, it concerned the
very legitimacy of party itself. Earlier in the century, parties had been
discredited through their association in the public mind with political
instability, foreign invasion, religious divisions and tumultuous,
popular politics. In spite of attempts made by the opposition to Walpole
to identify party with the alleged corruption and tyranny of the
Walpolean regime, pamphlets justifying party began to appear in the
1730s. In the following decade it was being argued that parties were an
inevitable element of mixed governments.[1] Indeed, their apparent disappearance in the 1750s evoked some unease and alarm; it only needed
George III's attack on party to rally its defenders. Edmund Burke's doctrine of party should be seen, therefore, as a development of an existing
tradition of ideas rather than an innovation. There is, however, little
evidence either that he foresaw the development of a two-party system

or that he believed that party should occupy a permanent role in politics.[2] What is significant about Burke's legitimation of party is that he fused into a coherent, influential and enduring political philosophy the old corps Whigs' collective claim to political power, the Country party's horror of corruption and, to some extent, 'Broad-bottom' permissiveness towards coalitions. In vindicating party, both in opposition and in government, Burke played an important role in persuading his countrymen to accept its value. Indeed, by the 1780s, party had come to be recognized as an essential component of political life. Party expedited business in parliament, exercised vigilance over the executive and protected popular liberties. When Charles James Fox seceded from parliament in 1797 he was widely condemned for deserting his party duties on the grounds that the performance of those duties was vital for the safeguarding of the nation's liberties.

Burke and the Rockingham Whigs believed that party was the remedy for the ills of the state because of their fear and hatred of Lord Bute. The Court's hostility to the old Whigs, the attack on Wilkes and, most sinister of all, Bute's influence with the king after his retirement from politics in April 1763—all pointed in the direction of a Court plot to restore power to the monarchy. While suspicion of Bute was widely shared, it was only in the group around Newcastle and Rockingham that it became an obsession and, indeed, an explanation not only for their own political misfortunes but, more generally, the political and ministerial instability of the 1760s, the supineness of parliament and the apparent revival of authoritarianism at home and in the empire. This obsession set the Rockinghams apart from other groups. It explains their refusal to strengthen their administration of 1765–66 by treating with the friends of Bute and their neurotic desire to seek Pitt's help. Thereafter, the willingness of so many members of Rockingham's group to hitch their wagons to the stars of Chatham and George III in late 1766 was so galling that this too was attributed to the machinations of secret influence.

Their fear of the court and their suspicion of other political groups persuaded the Rockinghams that if they were ever again to come to power then they must do so on their own terms, a demand which, of course, challenged the royal prerogative of appointing ministers. Such an attitude was already apparent in the negotiations of the summer of 1767. Although Rockingham did not yet have in mind an exlusive party administration, he was already envisaging a union of parties, led by his own, which would form a coalition so broad and so all-embracing that the king would not be able to resist it. And in the union of the opposition in 1769 he demanded the support of Chatham and of Grenville, and their followers, in an extended administration on his own terms, with himself at the Treasury. These were high terms, indeed, and in negotiations with the declining North ministry during the years of the American War, Rockingham was to extend them. A complete change of men and measures, a total change in the system and principle of government, peace with America, war on the Bourbons, economical reform and justice for Ireland—this was the lengthy list of conditions which he attempted to impose with creditable consistency upon the Court between 1778 and 1782. It was Rockingham's achievement in 1782, when North fell, to force the king to agree to his measures, although the king refused to surrender to government by party, preferring to ally first with Shelburne and then with the younger Pitt in a desperate attempt to retain his political independence. The price the country paid for the king's refusal to surrender was the constitutional crisis of 1782–84 as well as the loss of the American colonies, but the king's interpretation of the constitution was triumphantly vindicated at the general election of 1784 which condemned the Whig party once again to an indefinite period of opposition.

So thoroughgoing were the consequences of the Rockingham party's suspicion of the Court that some historians have attributed to them 'a "Country" complexion not wholly dissimilar to that of the old Tory party.'[3] The analogy is, to a point, useful, and it is salutary to be reminded of the Country aspects of Rockinghamite Whiggery. For one thing, Rockingham himself was a Yorkshire magnate and knew little of kings and cabinets. In his own county he attracted some Independents and some Tories. His ear was always close to the ground of public opinion. His much vaunted antagonism to Bute, albeit sincere, must have been confirmed by the unpopularity of the favourite in Yorkshire. Further, there is a 'Country' ring about some of the political attitudes which the Rockinghams struck, especially their constant criticism of the executive and their conviction that their cause was hopeless unless supported by the public. A 'Country' tinge may also be observed in their defence of individual and popular liberties against government persecution (Wilkes, the Printers), their defence of chartered rights against government regulation (the East India Company in 1767), and their defence of local privileges against ministerial encroachment (America, Ireland). Nevertheless, to regard the Rockinghams purely as a Country, still more as a 'Tory', party is absurd. The Rockinghams prided themselves upon their Whiggery and, like the old corps, they detested the Tories. It was not long, for example, before they began to attribute Tory characteristics to the régime of Lord Bute. Before the end of 1762, a new criterion for distinguishing Whig from Tory had emerged. Rockingham believed that Bute was implicated in the 'Massacre of the Pelhamite Innocents' 'to make room for his *Tory* friends'.[4] Indeed, the opposition was roundly condemned for reviving the outdated party distinctions of Whig and Tory. But revive them they did and extend them to cast the politics of the reign into a party mould. Thus Almon depicted Bute as the representative of the Tories and Jacobites, bent upon establishing a Tory régime. Within this framework, the function of the American issue was to heighten the party conflict yet further. Although North and his ministers patiently argued that the war they were conducting was parliament's war as much as the king's, the opposition denounced them as Tories. The purpose of the war, they argued, was to attack liberties in Britain and America. As Rockingham remarked:

> The Quintessence of Toryism (wch may synominously [sic] be called the King's Friends system) is both ready and willing if any opportunity offers to reak their vengeance upon us with the assistance of a King of the Brunswick Line, just as they would have been if any of their attempts to reinstate a Stuart had succeeded.[5]

The Rockinghams consciously repudiated what they took to be the revival of a new Toryism. It is hard to take seriously, therefore, the view that they were a 'Country' party tinged with Toryism. Indeed, the essence of Country party ideology had been its rejection of party, whether Whig or Tory. In one sense, the country aspects of Rocking-hamite thought and action, far from denying the Rockinghamite claim to a Whig ancestry, indisputably vindicate that claim for the Whig party of the later seventeenth and early eighteenth century had been charac-terized by the force of its Country traditions. There are, moreover, many differences between the Rockingham Whigs and the Country tradition, their commitment to one of the two great parties and its tradi-tions, their ambition to form a party government, their rejection of 'Measures not Men', their suspicion not merely of the Court but of the Throne, their involvement in imperial politics, their contacts in America, and Ireland, their antagonism towards the Bourbons' power (rather than that of Hanover). The Country element in Rockinghamite Whiggery broadened the (Court) base of Pelhamite Whiggery and, in so doing, liberalized it and rendered it more popular.

The Rockinghams loved to draw attention to their place in the unbroken line of Whiggism stretching back to the Glorious Revolution. But this claim has been much disputed and it has been suggested that they owed little even to their immediate Whig predecessors.[6] But there can be no doubt that Rockingham inherited Newcastle's party. The Rockingham party was not a child of the ministry of 1765–66.[7] Never-theless, some disruption occurred late in 1766 when Rockingham sounded the clarion call to opposition. Of the 111 Rockingham Whigs who can be identified at the fall of the Rockingham Ministry, only 54 remained loyal to Rockingham. Of the remainder, over 30 stayed with Chatham and the rest displayed little political certainty in their alle-giance thereafter. Of Rockingham's 54, 34 had been among Newcastle's

109 'Sure Friends' in 1764. But of those 109 'Sure Friends', 34 had left parliament or politics, and 41 followed Chatham and George III.[8] These desertions were undeniably serious and included what Dr Langford has called 'the great majority of the more ambitious and more useful commoners'.[9] They included about 30 from the old corps Whig professional politicians whose spell in opposition from 1762–65 had been unfamiliar and uncongenial. They also included that group of 'Young Friends' who have been regarded by some historians as the ancestors of the Rockingham party.[10] But they had always hero-worshipped Chatham and were now acting true to their Chathamite impulses. What, in fact, happened in 1766 was not the severing of continuity in Whig history but the divergence or separation of Whiggism into two distinct channels both of which have their source earlier than 1760.

The growing influence of Country ideas upon the Rockingham party was a function of their years in opposition rather than a reflection of the wilful inconsistency of new men in their number. The new men who entered the Newcastle–Rockingham connection did not abruptly modify it. The handful of Tories among them did not, apparently, bring their Toryism with them. In any case, they were swamped by the much larger number of Whig lords, knights and gentlemen whose politics, estates or marriage brought them into contact with Rockingham or one of the other Whig lords. After all, Rockingham did carry with him into opposition in 1766 'the authentic representatives of the earlier old corps', the Whig lords and their dependants who formed the indispensable backbone of the Rockingham party, as they had that of the old corps.[11] Old corps traditions for long inhibited the Rockinghams from adopting aggressively party positions. Newcastle was the epitome of those who disliked 'forcing the Crown – coming in without the king's support, etc.'[12] Yet the same traditions promoted habits of group solidarity and mutual loyalty together with fidelity to the principles of the Glorious Revolution and the Hanoverian Succession. Such men wished to preserve the system of government, not radically to change it, and there may be a connection, however indirect, between the old corps attitudes and their half-hearted attitude towards Economical Reform.[13]

After the political upheavals of 1766 the Rockingham party had few hopes of office. The fortunes of the party waned and then waxed. Its numbers sank to 42 in 1774, partly because of its unpopularity and partly because its electoral strength could not withstand the loss of the Newcastle connection—the Duke died in 1768—and the distractions of Portland with Lowther. But by 1780 the party had over 80 followers in the Commons. Fox proved to be something of a magnet for new MPs and the failure of British arms in America vindicated the party's criticisms of the conduct of the war. Furthermore, the family connections of the party—especially those of the Cavendishes—seemed constantly to be extending themselves. The party had survived the dark years of 1768–74 and had almost doubled its strength. This was a remarkable achievement. Furthermore, the Rockinghams were essentially provincial politicians. Before Fox, at least, the party's home areas were Yorkshire, Derbyshire, Lancashire, Cumberland, Nottinghamshire, the Welsh border counties and, to a much lesser degree, Buckinghamshire and Wiltshire. How could such a party not merely survive in opposition, but maintain the attendance and cohesion which it was able to do without establishing elaborate bureaucratic machinery?

In ensuring the cohesion and durability of his party, the leadership of the Marquis of Rockingham was a vital element. Of his rise to the leadership of the old Newcastle connection little needs to be said. It was less the talents of the Marquis than his position, his wealth, his Northern reputation and, essentially, the elimination through death or alternative political allegiance of any rivals, which brought him the Treasury and, as it happened, the leadership of a party for the rest of his life. But he did much to stamp his own personality upon his group. His distaste for Bute, his suspicion of the king and his pride in party together with a strong desire for public vindication never left him after the ministry of 1765. From a remarkably early date thereafter his leadership was unquestioned. His ability to conciliate, his readiness to consult and to persuade, his ability to represent the opinions of his political friends in parliament and in the provinces and his integrity kept serious political dispute within the party to an astonishingly low level. And Rockingham remained his own man. There were those, like Richmond, Fox, and Keppel who, in the dark years of the American Revolution, believed that Rockingham should weaken his attachment to his party's principles and to seek alliances on almost any terms with others and, even, to enter the ministry. Rockingham never wavered in his steely attachment to his own views. He was, simply, indispensable to his party.

One of Rockingham's greatest strengths was his willingness to consult others and in his leadership of the party he did this through the semi-formal institution of the 'Conciliabulum'. Such a body was reminiscent of the old corps practice of seeking and maintaining harmony through meetings of the great Whig leaders and lords. This had no formal membership but Rockingham maintained its aristocratic complexion. Subject to availability, the leading personalities in both Houses would be invited to these frequent meetings at the London homes of one or other of the great Whig lords. The control of the party was entirely in Rockingham's hands and the direction of its affairs suffered from his indolence, his caution and his timidity. Nevertheless, although too much should not be made of this semi-formal, customary institution, no other group of the time had a comparable institution.[14] If the 'Conciliabula' took the strategic decisions affecting the party, their implementation was left to a smaller group which supervised the day-to-day activities of the party. Until 1774 this group included Rockingham, Dowdeswell and Burke, perhaps supplemented by Richmond and Portland. After 1774 Rockingham and Burke were helped by George Byng and Lord John Cavendish and, after 1777, Charles Fox. House of Lords business would be directed by Rockingham, Richmond, Portland and, during the American War, Manchester and Effingham. Finally, Rockingham used general meetings of the party on the eve of the parliamentary session to disseminate information and instructions. These were organized by Dowdeswell as leader of the party in the Commons and, after his death, by Burke.

Proceedings in parliament were organized by the characteristically Rockinghamite qualities of personal informality and intermittent enthusiasm. Rockingham personally supervised the Lords although he rarely spoke there. He made it a party responsibility to collect proxies, sending out the instrument of proxy for signature himself. He also extended the hitherto apparently infrequent practice of drawing up Lords' Protests, using the pen of Edmund Burke for the purpose, and occasionally publishing them. Although the party's following in the Lords declined between 1763 and 1776, thereafter the decline was arrested. Some degree of stability and cohesion now informed the party's proceedings in the Upper House.[15]

The struggle between the Rockingham party and the ministries of George III was, however, fought in the House of Commons. In general, it may be said that the Rockinghams, secure in the safety of their status as a systematic opposition, developed contemporary practices of party and opposition. The procedures of the day, however, recognized the legitimate status of a systematic opposition, government and opposition cooperating, for example, over the arrangement of parliamentary business. The Rockinghams exploited the traditional opportunities open to opposition parties. Their use of petitions was impressive. They went to the country both in 1769 and in 1780; on the former occasion they frightened a ministry out of existence, on the latter they brought one to its knees and forced it to negotiate. Their use of divisions was selective rather than exhaustive. It was, for example, only after 1774 that they regularly divided on the Address. Their exploitation of such divisions was intended to impress the public; of their numerical inability to bring down ministers they were only too well aware. In the same way, demands for papers, accounts and information were frequently made together with the use of other traditional opposition procedures such as Addresses to the Crown, Motions of No Confidence and Committees on the State of the Nation. The Rockinghams, however, broke new ground when in 1770 and again in 1780 they contested

Division	Maximum Rockingham Vote	Actual Rockingham Vote	% Attendance
Wilkes 22/2/75	60	44	73
America 26/10/75	59	33	59
Civil list 16/4/77	59	32	55
America 2/2/78	61	45	73
America 4/12/78	62	40	64
Contractors bill 12/2/79	62	59	95
Keppel 3/3/79	62	54	87
Pensions division 21/2/80	59	48	81
Economical reform 8/3/80	59	54	90
Abolition of board of trade 13/3/80	59	56	94
Dunning's motion 6/4/80	60	57	95
Motion against prorogation 24/4/80	61	59	97
		AV.	80.2

Division lists, 1774–80

the Speakership. They were also somewhat more conscientious than earlier oppositions had been at proposing legislation of their own.[16] Finally, their ability to whip in their followers should not be underestimated. Professor Ginter has claimed that 'There is as yet no evidence that an opposition group employed a formal whip on the floor of the House of Commons before the 1780s' and that such letters of attendance as were sent out 'were sent by individuals to their friends without system'.[17] Whipping was no longer a personal affair, however. Dowdeswell in the late 1760s and George Byng in the 1770s strove to obtain a decent attendance during sessions. These party organizers would contact patrons or others who, for geographical, personal or other reasons, might be able to contact an MP. An intermediate stage had been reached in which whipping was no longer personal but, with the Rockinghams, a party responsibility. A standardized party whip, however, had not yet appeared. But how effective was this whipping?

The table on p. 84 shows how on the twelve issues on which division lists survive during the parliament of 1774–80 the attendance of Rockingham Whigs ranged from 55 per cent to 97 per cent, averaging 80.2 per cent. This compares favourably, for example, not only with the attendance of the Tories in the middle of the century but also with that of both ministerial and opposition Tories of the same period.[18] Taken together, the evidence suggests that in spite of their indolence, the Rockingham Party, once decided upon a course of action was, as Professor Foord has concluded 'steadier and more resolute than any of its predecessors.'[19]

The Rockinghams maintained a reasonable attendance in parliament not only through the formal process of whipping but also through the establishment of opposition clubs. Wildman's Club in January 1764 provided a convivial wining-and-dining club for those MPs opposed to the ministry of Grenville. What the history of Wildman's demonstrates, however, is the ability of Newcastle and Rockingham to maintain patrician control of the party.[20] Discredited by the disasters of 1762–63, the 'Young Friends' were unable to mount any sort of challenge to the leadership of the Whig lords, although they desired greater vigour in the practice of opposition. Rockingham was able to reconcile the 'Young Friends' to the party leadership until they left it in 1766. After the decline of Wildman's in 1765–66, Almack's became the principal opposition club. Established in 1764, Almack's became Brooks's Club when it moved to St James Street in 1778. It was not as exclusively a Rockingham Club as it was later to become a Foxite retreat. And one further opposition institution was the Thatched House Tavern, a regular venue for opposition and radical dinners.

The Rockinghams were keen to carry their cause to an extra-parliamentary opinion. That most famous of all Whig newspapers, *The Morning Chronicle*, was founded in 1769 and by 1780 *The London Evening Post* had also become a vehicle for Rockinghamite opinion. The party's views of the political world were also conveyed in *The Annual Register*. The dramatic increase in the numbers of newspapers and in their circulation thus gave widespread publicity to the opinions and activities of the party. The party's propagandist activities did not end there. On occasion they employed hack writers such as James Burke, James Bromley, Richard Gardiner, Dr Ferdinand Warren, Richard Wolfall and Sir John Dalrymple. But, in general, Professor Foord's judgment remains sound, that the Rockinghams 'never became assiduous pamphleteers'.[21] Nevertheless, there was more to the party's propagandist activities than Burke's theorizing alone. Several pamphlets were issued in 1769, for example. Sir William Meredith's *The Question Stated* attacked the ministry over the Middlesex election as did William Dowdeswell's *The Sentiments of an English Freeholder*.

It is, however, difficult to determine the impact made by Rockinghamite propaganda on public opinion. The opposition's voice was
heard and its message spread but it is impossible to speak of a major shift
of opinion towards the party. The Rockinghams failed to identify their
potential support. For example, they had enjoyed the support of mercantile opinion during the 1765–66 ministry but that connection was
not maintained. Similarly, the support which the old corps had tradi-
tionally enjoyed among the Dissenters seems to have been somewhat
weakened by the Rockinghams. At the same time there were signs of
party division in certain professions, notably the services.[22]

It was the great achievement of Rockingham and his followers to have
planted the tree of party in the least congenial of soils and to have tended
it to survival. Their dogged adherence to their principles, their frank
expressions of hostility towards the Court and the king, and even their
rejoicing in the defeat of British arms help to explain their neglect and,
at times, their unpopularity. Their anti-Chathamite and anti-monarch-
ical associations left them high and dry until 1782. Yet some historians
complain about the ineffectiveness of the Rockinghams without
recalling that in most of the great wars of modern British history party
gave way to coalition. The Rockinghams, to some extent unconsciously,
succeeded in laying the foundations for a new party tradition while
relating it strongly to the party traditions of the past.

So thoroughly had they done their work that it could not be shaken
significantly by the political upheavals of the crisis of 1782–84.[4] The
ruthless consistency with which Charles James Fox – a new and disturbing influence within the party – tried to give effect to the Rockinghamite tradition transfixed and horrified contemporaries. The coalition
with North, for all its unpopularity, as Mr Brooke remarked over
twenty years ago, 'gave expression to the deepest tradition in the
Rockingham party', its hatred and fear of Chatham and his successors,
those who with the king in 1766 and 1782–84, wished to break party.[24]
In any case, should Fox have waited for Shelburne to have allied with
North? The coalition was neither unnatural nor surprising. The old
issues which had separated Fox and North had passed or were passing
by 1783 and Fox's agreement to 'drop' parliamentary reform, while it
may have damaged his own consistency, did not damage that of his party
since reform of parliament had always been an open question. The real
damage done to party continuity by the Fox—North coalition was in its
impact upon the political allegiance of the Dissenters. By 1784 their
loyalties were divided and thereafter Fox was unable to make religious
toleration a party issue.

Nevertheless, the party of Fox and Portland was punished for the
coalition at the general election of 1784. They went into it with about
210 MPs and emerged with 132. Thereafter, their numbers stabilized

until they reached 144 on the eve of the election of 1790.[25] This cohesion and stability may be explained at various levels. At the personal level, the magnetism, charm and friendship of Fox were as essential to the party as had been Rockingham's very different personal qualities. But it is possible that the idolization of Fox was double-edged. If his mercurial talents were indispensable to the party, then the cocoon of hero-worship all too frequently sheltered him from reality. At the level of the legitimacy of party, earlier inhibitions operated much less strongly than they once had done. Indeed, the Fox—North coalition was so vehemently criticized because it seemed to be such a dramatic departure from party politics. Party now needed no defence, no justification. Cooperation between government and opposition became much more systematic than it had been earlier. The routine of parliamentary practice was coming to accommodate formed opposition and party in parliament. At a third level, the party of Fox owed its cohesion to the polarization of politics after 1784, the proscription of the opposition and its condemnations of the illegitimate, unconstitutional nature of Pitt's ministry.

This underlying cohesion in the Whig party was reflected in its organizational development. Professor Ginter has performed a valuable service in unearthing the centralized institutions which the Whig party developed after the death of Rockingham.[26] There can be no gainsaying the significance of the emergence of a bureaucratic party machine, the growth of a party manager, the existence of party offices, party officials, party agents, party writers, party whips, party funds, party campaigns and party propaganda. But two comments must be made. In his eagerness to interpret these developments as the origins of modern party politics, Professor Ginter minimizes the significance of the activities of the Rockingham Whigs, although no one would wish to contend that their achievements equalled those of Adam and Portland. Secondly, he tends to exaggerate the significance of the developments of the 1780s.

In the first place, he notes the reluctance of the Rockinghams 'to support candidates outside the circle of their own intimate or family connections' and their failure to regard a general election as 'an opportunity to expand the bases of their political power beyond the bounds of their connection'.[27] To generalize outwards a party's appeal is, for Ginter, an essential characteristic of a modern political party. But there are some instances of the Rockinghams doing just this.[28] They were prepared on occasion to take the initiative in expanding the geographical scope of their party's influence. Further, the voluntary attachment of hitherto Independent MPs was an important element in Rockinghamite politics, as indeed it continued to be in the Portland party. It is to the *developing* cohesion of the Whig party that we should draw attention, not the presence or absence of a definitional criterion.

The Rockinghams have been further criticized because they were not inclined to improve their strength out-of-doors 'by a sustained, extensive and systematic effort'. Perhaps not, but it does not follow that their efforts 'were almost wholly oriented toward parliament itself'.[29] On the one hand, we have already noticed the strength of Rockingham's own 'Country' inheritance in his native Yorkshire. On the other hand, it had been a cardinal element in old corps politics to seek extra-parliamentary support and Rockingham himself was studiously aware of the importance of commerce. Hence his careful cultivation of commercial contacts during the ministry of 1765–66, the raising of petitions from mercantile centres and the reception of deputations and addresses which greeted him on the downfall of that administration. Rockinghamite involvement in the Petitioning Movement of 1769, moreover, was extensive, in eleven of the fifteen counties and six of the twelve boroughs which petitioned. All the party leaders were willing to harness their local influence to their national campaign to protect the rights of electors and to overthrow the Grafton ministry. In 1780 the Rockinghams did much to provoke and to organize the Petitioning Movement; they were active in inspiring 12 of 27 county meetings and supported 11 others. Early in 1782 when North's ministry was reeling to disaster, Rockingham was still keen to raise more county meetings and petitions to deliver the ministry one fatal blow. The Rockingham party may have been essentially a gathering of amiable aristocrats but it could make vigorous and, at times, impressive, coordinated appeals to the nation.

It is, of course, the scale of the developments of the 1780s and their bureaucratic character which are so impressive together with the fact that party and party institutions were coming to embrace all sections of the opposition after 1784. Reservations must however be entered. First, the reality of the party's organizing activities is indisputable but in the constituencies it certainly remained much less important than the autonomous activities of magnates and their agents.[30] Second, how extensive was it? Although the party intervened in 83 constituencies, in over half of these there already existed an MP sympathetic to opposition. And in only about one quarter of all the cases cited did the 'activity' extend to much more than the writing or receiving of a letter and in only eight to the payment of even part of the election expenses. In more than half the cases cited, party activity consisted of bringing together candidates and constituencies. Third, how effective was it? Professor Ginter's own figures show that the party's support in the Commons declined from 229 to 193 at the general election of 1790, a startling fall of almost 16 per cent. Fourth, it is not clear why the whole party simultaneously became 'outwardly oriented' nor why the older quality (presumably 'inward orientation') could not coexist with the newer in accounting for this dramatic transition. Ginter emphasizes the 'shift in political attitudes' which took place towards the end of the American War of Independence, the importance of extra-parliamentary opinion and the organizational requirements of an opposition group which had suffered defeat in 1782–84, thereafter to be proscribed by the king.[31] There is no doubt much to be urged in favour of these explanations. What needs to be emphasized, however, is the critical and decisive character of political conflict between 1782 and 1784. Fox and his party were fighting to effect a permanent change in the balance of the constitution and George III fought back ruthlessly. The Rockingham party, on the other hand, had failed to establish sophisticated party institutions at the general elections of 1768, 1774 or 1780, for example, because on none of these occasions was the government mounting a campaign to oust and destroy the party. The election of 1784 threatened to be a Massacre of the Foxite as well as Northite Innocents. Consequently, the opposition had to make unusually sophisticated attempts to defend itself. Thereafter, the utility of these institutions was recognized and they continued to operate. Finally, party institutions of a bureaucratic character may have been necessary to weld together the Fox – North coalition and the other groups in opposition ranged under Fox's leadership. Such practical considerations translated the informal organization of the Rockingham party into the experimental, tentative attempts at bureaucratic party organization of the party of Portland and Adam, but it was a development of degree rather than of kind, inspired by political realities rather than by a conscious attempt to transcend one ideal of party by another.

The organizational cohesion of the Whig party after 1784 is sometimes contrasted with its ideological heterogeneity. No one would claim that it had the same ideological motivation as the Rockinghams had but it does not follow that its political divisions were ominous causal precursors of the party divisions of the 1790s.[32] The essential division in politics remained that between those who upheld and those who opposed the influence of the Crown in the routine of government, in the appointment and dismissal of ministers, and in the elevation of party as the cure for the ills of the state. The king's notorious intervention in the House of Lords in December 1783 renewed Rockinghamite accusations of the Court's unconstitutional behaviour. There were, of course, political divisions in the opposition, especially over the issue of the reform of parliament, but that division does not square with the ultimate lines of fission in the party.[33] There is no reason why historians should not take seriously Fox's professions of his constitutional principle. Contemporaries did so. And he adhered faithfully to those principles for the rest of his life. The opposition was less fond of wearing its principles on its sleeve than the Rockinghams but that is perhaps explained by the hopelessness of its position, by the rejection of its party ideas at the election of 1784 and by the retreat of Burke from the centre of Whig politics. Not only this, until the Regency Crisis, at least, the party was repairing its shattered morale and strengthening its position in the country.[34]

What really threatened the party were less its ideological differences than the bitter personal enmities which were worsened by the failures, duplicities and humiliations of the Regency Crisis of 1788–89. These did not cause or anticipate the breach in the party of 1792–94 but they made it very much harder to deal satisfactorily with the momentous issues thrown up by the French Revolution, and seriously damaged the standing of the party in the country.[35] Yet too much should not be made of these divisions in explaining the split in the party of the early 1790s. After all, the source of the most serious divisions within the opposition had been the activities of the Prince of Wales, yet his affairs were an insignificant issue after 1789. Similarly, no more critical agency of party disruption could have been found than the formation of the Association of the Friends of the People in 1792, yet it cannot be traced back to the 1780s. It was a creature of the rising political expectancy of the times. In truth, there was to hand no answer to the basic question raised by the French Revolution: at this unique hour of crisis, was the greater danger to be expected, as Burke and then Portland and Fitzwilliam argued, to come from fomenting popular unrest or, as Fox and his friends maintained, from renewed instances of ministerial despotism and royal corruption? Both sides argued that their respective positions were vindicated by the party's past history. Although the crisis deepened and political divisions within the opposition intensified – especially on the issues of civil liberties and reform – the final break-up of the party did not come until July 1794. The entire process is a reflection of the relevance and importance of party since it amounted to a struggle for present control – and thus future direction – of the party's activities, as well as of its history. The schism in the Whig party was not a repudiation of party but a bitter struggle for consistency, popularity and power through conflicting interpretations of the agency of party.

After the political realignment of 1794 the Foxite Whigs inherited the mantle of party. Together with his 70 or so followers, Fox found in the 1790s an important role for party to play in defending the constitutional liberties of Englishmen. At this crisis in the history of Europe the public-spirited endeavours of men of independent fortune were more needed than ever. Like the Rockinghams earlier, the Foxites prided themselves on their consistency. During the ministerial uncertainty of 1801, Fox laid down a policy of

> simplicity and consistency, Removal and censure of Pitt and his associates, Religious liberty to its utmost extent, Reform in Parliament, liberty of the press and indemnity to others, not only peace but a good understanding with Boneparte. [sic].[36]

These principles condemned Fox and his party to years of opposition. Yet these principles existed within the framework of Whig historical mythology pioneered by the Rockingham Whigs and, especially, by Burke. Into this framework they placed every condemnation of Pitt and every issue old and new. These party convictions did much to sustain the Foxite Whigs. Even Fox's death and the fall of the Talents ministry in 1807 did not seriously endanger the party's existence or growth. Their ideological and psychological exclusiveness enabled the Foxites to remain a party without Fox, and, after his death, even without active leaders. His successors lacked not only his charm, charisma and notoriety but also his qualities of leadership and of ambition, but the Whig party had come to stay.

Clearly, then, the Foxite Whig party sprang from its earlier, Whig, origins. The continuity of personnel, of language, of attitude and of principle is unmistakable. The twin great questions of the last decade of the eighteenth century – the war and reform – remained to dominate political life up to and beyond 1815. Even thereafter a sympathetic line to European liberal movements was merely an extension of Foxite liberalism. Gradually, Foxites extended the range of their concerns and became friendly to reformist and humanitarian causes of many types. The ideological centre of Rockinghamite politics, its suspicion of the Court, was being expanded into a substantive and reformist liberalism which was to be of immense relevance from the 1830s to the 1860s. The Rockinghamite ancestry of Foxite Whiggism should not be overlooked. As Dr Mitchell has remarked, 'the resilience of the experiences of 1782–84 is astonishing' and these, of course, were themselves the culmination of two decades of party warfare.[37] At the same time, there had been a strong element of liberal feeling among the Rockingham Whigs – on America, on religious toleration, late in the 1770s on Ireland. We should not exaggerate the obvious differences between the Foxites and the Rockinghams.[38] There are, indeed, interesting similarities between the two parties and not merely those of ideology and principle. They were both small parties of similar size, similarly unpopular in their opposition to a popular war, both of them capable of appealing to the public in petitioning movements but also of seceding from parliament when the political prospects were absolutely hopeless, as the Rockinghams did in 1776–77 and the Foxites from 1797–1801. Yet the differences should also be noted, especially the Foxites' greater commitment to reform, their readiness to trust the people, and their acceptance of party as a permanent element in political life. The Whig organization of the 1780s continued into the nineteenth century, although it gradually became less bureaucratic. Fundamentally, the Whigs were averse to over-vigorous leadership and this, together with the still powerful position of local patrons within the party, continued to inhibit the emergence of strongly centralized party institutions. When keen efforts were made, the Whigs were capable of fairly efficient organization of meetings, whips and attendance notes. It is not clear, however, that the party organization of the 1780s survived in its entirety: there certainly existed a Chief Party Whip. Membership of the Whig party thus had an institutionalized criterion. Grenville's MPs, for example, were regarded as separate and were only sent to with his permission.[39] The great London Clubs, Brooks's and the Whig Club, together with a smattering of local imitations of the latter, existed and Fox's death gave rise to the inevitable Fox Clubs; these flowered for about 20 years and then began to disappear. Such clubs were the only nationwide party organizations in existence. The party funds of the 1780s revived in the excitement of 1806–07 but have not been traced thereafter. Party organization undeniably existed but it was much less streamlined and coordinated than it had been in the 1780s.

As for the Tories, as the period covered by this essay comes to an end, signs of their re-emergence as a party are discernible. Although the story is as yet untold, the coalition of Portland with Pitt in 1794 did much to translate party attitudes to the government side of the House. But it was the years before Pitt's death which appear to have been vital in beginning to transform Pitt's anti-party faction into something resembling a party. About 60 Pittites, led by Lowther, Castlereagh, Hawkesbury, Fitzharris, Perceval, Canning and Ryder, but not by Pitt himself, sought to give practical effect to Pitt's principles, to support the ministry of Addington, and prosecute the war, to defend the king and the constitution. To these ends they wished to keep Pitt's followers together as a body of organizing them. It is, however, impossible to speak of a 'Tory party' so long as Pitt, the anti-party Whig, was alive. Nevertheless, in the years after Pitt's death, Portland did much to hold his followers together out of office, and his successors, Perceval and Liverpool, kept in being the old Pittite following which had saved the country. By 1812 or a little later there can be no mistaking the revival of party terminology, the revival of party passions – already manifested at the general elections of 1806 and 1807 – and contemporary awareness of parties and their affiliations, principles and members.[40] Furthermore, as royal and ministerial patronage continued to decline it became harder for government to sustain itself, unless it appealed to specific sectors of opinion in the country. Liverpool's ministry was acknowledged as a Tory ministry pursuing Tory policies and resting upon Tory sentiment in the country.

Nevertheless, the historian should resist the temptation to exaggerate the nature of the 'two-party system' which had emerged by 1815. Older anti-party traditions died hard. Although there were now fewer Independents in the House, Independency remained a widespread rhetorical refuge. At the same time, loyalty to the monarch continued to be a powerful political force. There could be no effective two-party system until the monarch retreated from the centre of the stage. That cannot be said to have happened before the early years of the nineteenth century and the prince regent retained considerable constitutional authority. Nevertheless, he was not, as his father had been, the first of party leaders, a fact which permitted a Tory, as distinct from a Court and Administration party, to develop.[41] Furthermore, minor factions continued to exist and to exert great influence: those of Canning, Wellesley and, of course, Grenville played a rôle in politics out of all proportion to their numbers. Party did not yet entirely dominate parliament. Politicians were divided not predominantly between reformers and reactionaries – a cleavage which might have permeated most political issues – but between those who adopted one view of royal prerogative and another. This explains why many issues were not party issues: they were not prejudiced or influenced in advance by their attitude to the prerogative. Finally, the Napoleonic Wars aroused patriotism, temporarily retarded political partisanship and renewed traditional cries against the legitimacy of party and opposition.

However, by the end of the war parliament had succumbed to the parties of government and opposition. The oposition was no longer a rump. By the time of the Talents ministry the Foxites numbered around 150 and for the next quarter of a century wavered between 150 and 180. Dr Mitchell has calculated that only 114 MPs out of 683 in the 1820 Parliament wavered in their allegiance, while in the sessions of 1821 and 1822, however, only 23 MPs out of 546 voting MPs wavered and switched their allegiance.[42] In 1766, 'hardly a quarter of the House of Commons could be described as party men'.[43] Fifty years later well over three-quarters could be. Stability of party cohesion is thus one of the most characteristic features of the period. By 1830 even the House of Lords was rent by party.[44] All this was accompanied by the revival of party terminology and the growth of party sentiment in the country. Coexisting with certain older, traditional practices and traditions, party was well on the way to becoming the lynch-pin of the British political system.

Colloquy on chapter 4
John Derry

The main themes of the discussion on this paper were whether undue emphasis had been placed on the Rockingham Whigs in the writing of the history of party; how coherent had been their attitude towards party; to what extent it changed under the leadership of Charles Fox, and in what respect the attitude of the Rockinghams and the Foxites towards the Crown was different from that of other contemporary politicians.

O'Gorman maintained that the Rockinghams were unique, particularly in the importance they themselves attached to party; the Bedfords and Grenvilles, by contrast, were not much interested in the idea, while the Chathamites were positively anti-party. Dickinson challenged the uniqueness of the Rockinghams, seeing considerable continuity between them and the old corps Whigs, such as Walpole and the Pelhams. This O'Gorman did not deny; there was a 'continuity of habit' between the two groups, a passing of the baton. Dickinson suggested that it was possible to put too much emphasis on the structural or mechanical aspect of party and would have liked more discussion of the political attitude of the Rockinghams, particularly as enunciated by Burke, towards George III and the prerogative, or towards America. O'Gorman was not sure that Burke had all that much impact on the party: the ideological bond of the Rockinghams was their fear of the Court, 'their incredible neurosis about Bute,' and so on. It had been quite deliberate to pay less attention to ideology, which he thought had been overplayed: he had tried to demonstrate that the organization of the Rockinghams was more impresive than Ginter, for example, had maintained.[1]

McCord sounded a note of caution in attributing to the Rockinghams a belief in the permanent role of party in the constitution. (pp. 83–6). O'Gorman thought that the views of the Rockinghams had developed over a period of time: in 1770 they were not yet claiming a permanent place for party, but 12 years later, their claims for party were much greater. Even in the 1760s they were advancing rather strong demands against the king – 'Rockingham is already talking in high dictatorial terms in 1767' – before Burke had written his *Thoughts* and before they had begun to see themselves as a permanent party.

Holmes accepted that there was a strong element of liberalism among the Rockingham Whigs (p. 91), but was not clear how this could be a natural development from their suspicion of the Court. How, for example, did it link up with the suggestion that the Rockinghams retained many Country attitudes? O'Gorman thought that the critical development took place in the 1790s and that by the 1800s the polarity in political life was between reactionary Tories and liberal Whigs. The Whigs developed from an essentially anti-Court party, which the Rockinghams had been, into something much more reformist. Cannon objected that this was no new development of the 1790s: in the 1760s the Rockinghams had tried hard to depict themselves as a liberal-minded party, struggling against reactionary adversaries, at home and abroad. Dickinson agreed with the suggestion that Fox led the Rockinghams in the 1790s into a more liberal political position, even committing them to a moderate form of parliamentary reform.

McCord raised a new point about the coherence of the political attitude of the Foxites. How could they advocate reform of parliament while maintaining their hold on their own pocket boroughs? Was it not absurd that a party which prided itself upon its close links with the people should remain so very unpopular, both over America in the 1770s and over France in the 1790s? O'Gorman conceded that neither the Rockinghams nor the Foxites were good at rousing public opinion: they tended to make their case and then sit back. Derry was uneasy about the emphasis placed upon the Foxites' liberalism: particularly after they had allied with the Grenvilles they became, in some respects, a rather conservative party. O'Gorman agreed that the Grenville connection acted as a drag on Foxite liberalism: nevertheless, the Grenvilles were but a small party and by 1815 he thought that the Foxites could put forward a reasonably coherent liberal programme – Catholic Emancipation, repeal of the Test and Corporation Acts, a measure of parliamentary reform, and a liberal foreign policy.

If the Rockinghams did not have a fully fledged theory of party, Holmes asked if it was possible to identify a moment of transition, when the Foxites adopted a more advanced doctrine. O'Gorman thought that this was essentially Fox's contribution, a view of party which he had held and put forward for most of his life – 'Fox did more for the notion of party than Burke ever did.' Cannon agreed that Fox had certainly justified the propriety of opposition, arguing that it performed a constructive function: 'but then again, one is stuck to know whether Fox's view is a modern and forward-looking glimpse of the Victorian party system, or merely a reversion to the old Country attitude that one must always be on guard against a dictatorial and tyrannical executive.'

Speck brought the discussion back to Ginter, who had argued that a real party should have, or attempt to have, an organization extending outside its immediate and personal area of influence (p. 87). Was that

a helpful view? Ginter had argued that, by this standard, the Rockinghams were not a party but merely a faction. O'Gorman thought that the
Rockinghams were much more than a faction and that they had tried to
extend their electoral base. Speck objected that their methods were the
traditional ones of beer and bribery rather than handing out pamphlets
to educate the electorate, as a 'forward-looking' party might have been
expected to do. McCord wondered whether the 'liberalism' with which
the Rockinghams were credited had revealed itself in any interest in the
social and economic problems of the day. O'Gorman replied that there
were signs in the later 1770s of a development in their political thinking,
with reformist policies on Ireland and India, some interest in poor-law
reform, economical reform, and so on.

Cannon posed the old question 'when is a party not a party?' Why
should one distinguish so sharply between the Bedfords and the Rockinghams? The Bedfords had a reasonably coherent, if authoritarian,
attitude towards Wilkes and towards America; they had some organization at Westminster for whipping-in; they understood the value of newspapers and published pamphlets; they tried to coordinate their electoral
activities. Did this not entitle them to be considered a party? O'Gorman
replied that the Bedfords were totally uninterested in party ideology, in
the rôle of party in the constitution. Party was, to them, merely 'a closet-
storming mechanism'. Although they had a remarkable capacity for
survival and were around in politics for 40 or 50 years, neither their
ideas nor their organization ever developed.

The discussion then moved on to the Rockinghams' attitude towards
the Crown, and particularly its prerogatives (p. 78). Cannon asked
whether the Rockinghams really challenged the king's *right* to choose
his ministers, or merely the way in which he exercised that right.
O'Gorman agreed that there was no formal challenge to the royal prerogative, but in practice the Rockinghams had shown themselves determined to diminish the king's rôle. Cannon thought that this was really
forced upon them: 'they, and particularly Charles Fox, had made themselves so disagreeable to George III, that if they went on maintaining
the king's unfettered right to choose his ministers, they would stay
in opposition for ever.' Dickinson thought that the Rockinghams'
challenge was implicit rather than explicit. Cannon doubted whether
this attitude of the Rockinghams was particularly novel: after all,
the Pelhams in 1746 had ganged up against the king; did not all politicians push their luck sometimes? Derry agreed: Wellington and Liverpool in the 1820s had been very sharp with George IV, yet they were
not politicians who, at least in theory, wished to deprive the Crown
of its prerogatives. McCord thought that it did not much matter why
the Rockinghams adopted their stance: personal interest coincided
with a constitutional appraisal to produce a new doctrine. O'Gorman

maintained that the Rockinghams pursued their demands against the king with such determination and such consistency that it did differentiate them from other politicians, who occasionally, and on specific issues, clashed with the king.

Holmes asked who were the natural forerunners of the Rockinghams? Did they regard themselves as successors to the Whigs of Anne's reign (p. 80) The Whigs of that period had believed in getting into and working within the system, rather than imposing terms and conditions on the monarch. Theirs was a kind of Court Whiggery, whereas the Rockinghams always seemed to harbour a deep suspicion of the Crown. O'Gorman thought that the Rockinghams were not all that much interested in tracing political pedigrees, judging by their speeches and correspondence. This was disputed. Speck pointed to Burke's *Appeal from the New to the Old Whigs* – was not that directly concerned with pedigree? Derry remarked that Fox himself was sufficiently interested to begin work on a history of the reign of James II, believing that it would justify Whig principles to the nation.

In conclusion, O'Gorman reiterated three major themes. First, that his concentration on the Rockinghams was justified. It was true that their political conduct left much to be desired and that, in many ways, their party characteristic did not conform to the expectations of a modern party man. Nevertheless, their *raison d'être* was their view of their duty to establish party in the British political system, as a guarantee of liberty and accountability. Other groups certainly existed, some of them organized and some of them with consistent policies. But the Chathamites prided themselves on not being a party and were prepared to ally with the Court to destroy party. The Bedfords contributed little to party, either in its organizational or ideological aspects. The Grenvilles did not survive the death of their leader in 1770. But the Rockinghams did survive the death of Rockingham in 1782 and handed over the mantle of party to Portland and Fox.

Secondly, his treatment of the Rockinghams had been consciously structural. They had been treated so often as essentially an ideologically motivated group that it was helpful to look at them as a body, and to examine the more tangible elements of cohesion. They were by no means as incompetent at party organization as many historians had argued.

Thirdly, he believed – perhaps somewhat Whiggishly – that over the time-span 1760–1832 party did show unmistakeable signs of development. The touchstone of political allegiance had for long been the extent to which a man trusted that the powers of the Crown were being applied to the national interest: in the early nineteenth century, a different touchstone emerged, the extent to which a man was prepared to further liberal or reformist causes.

Party development has always been intermittent rather than steady. Attitudes and practices of earlier days tend to persist. Two good examples of this are of the persistence of country notions into the nineteenth century and the practice of secession as late as the end of the eighteenth century. The historian should, nevertheless, be prepared to commit himself and to detect in the paradoxes of historical survivals the grey line of development.

Note on further reading

The general scepticism concerning the relevance of party to Hanoverian politics expressed by Sir Lewis Namier, *England in the Age of the American Revolution* (2nd ed. 1961, pp. 179–203) has not been shared by most recent historians. Although John Brooke has suggested that 'Namier always maintained that the conclusions he had reached about the middle years of the century might not necessarily be true for an earlier or later period' (*The House of Commons*, 1754–90 (1964), i.p.ix), the 'Namierite' view of party often seems to have been given such general application, e.g. J. Brooke, *The Chatham Administration* (1956), pp. 218–47 or L. B. Namier, 'Monarchy and the party system', in *Personalities and Powers* (1955).

But the conclusions Namier reached for the 1760s have now been challenged from two standpoints in F. O'Gorman, *The Rise of Party in England, 1760–82* (1975) and J. Brewer, *Political Ideology and Popular Politics at the Accession of George III* (1976). A more traditional interpretation of the Rockingham Whigs may be found in Paul Langford, *The First Rockingham Administration, 1765–66* (1973), pp. 264–89. Nevertheless, the general direction of recent writing has been to substantiate the sympathetic attitude adopted towards the Rockinghams by Herbert Butterfield, *George III and the Historians* (1957) and G. H. Guttridge, *English Whiggism and the American Revolution* (1966).

The relevance of party to the post-Rockinghamite period has been strongly asserted in a number of works. John Cannon argued that the constitutional crisis of 1782–84 could not be understood without reference to party: *The Fox–North Coalition* (1969). The institutionalization of party has been thoroughly discussed by Donald E. Ginter in *Whig Organization in the General Election of 1790* (1967) and in 'The financing of the Whig party organization, 1783–93', *American Historical Review* (1966). These organizational aspects of party are discussed and placed within a broad political framework by F. O'Gorman, *The Whig party and the French Revolution* (1967). However, two recent articles raise questions about these attempts to rehabiliate party: Paul Kelly, 'British Political Parties, 1784–88', *Historical Journal* (1974) and B. Hill, 'The Whig Party and the Question of Principles, 1784–89', *English Historical Review* (1974).

5

New lamps for old: the end of Hanoverian England

John Cannon

The political stability for which Hanoverian England is celebrated was a plant of slow growth and blossomed, in the end, for a comparatively short time. Based upon the Glorious Revolution of 1688, and strengthened by the successful transfer of the throne to the House of Hanover in 1714, it was not firmly established until the middle years of Walpole's ministry. Even as late as 1745, Highlanders marched to the very centre of the kingdom at Derby: not until the total rout of the Jacobites at Culloden was the settlement secure against all comers. Yet, by the 1760s we see the first signs, however slight, of those stresses which were to undermine and, at length, destroy the old political order.

It is important not to overstate the problem. In the first place, we must not exaggerate the stability of the 1750s. That decade began with an acrimonious dispute over the Jew Bill, followed by fierce party conflict at the general election of 1754. The Seven Years War, which broke out two years later, was a bloody and exhausting struggle, and the first event of the war – the capture of Minorca by the French – sent a tremor through the nation. The year 1757 produced a political crisis and arrest of government of unprecedented length, followed by widespread and serious militia riots. We may be sure that people at the time did not feel that they were living in an age of peculiar stability. In October 1757 John Wilkes, then a government supporter and not the most timid of men, wrote that there was 'the most general discontent I ever knew, and every person I converse with, of all parties, seems to be under the dread of something very terrible approaching.'[1] Perhaps stability, like prosperity, is most easily recognized when it has gone.

Nor should we exaggerate the collapse of the system. England did not lurch into chaos and revolution: the monarchy, the House of Lords and the established Church all survived, and the landed classes continued to wield powerful influence throughout the nineteenth century. Nevertheless, the period 1798 to 1830 witnessed, in succession, the Irish rebellion, the Despard and Emmet plots, Luddism, the Burdett riots, the Spa Fields affair, the East Anglian 'bread or blood' riots, the Derbyshire rising, Peterloo, the Cato Street conspiracy, the Caroline riots and the 'Swing' riots of 1830. We do not have to presume that any one of the episodes constituted a serious threat to the established order, but, at the least, they suggest that all was not well.

The years 1828 to 1835 saw the transformation of the old system. Five pieces of legislation – the repeal of the Test and Corporation Acts, Catholic Emancipation, the Reform Act of 1832, the Poor Law Amendment Act of 1834 and the Municipal Corporations Act of 1835 – meant a grand reconstruction of the political order.[2] With pardonable exaggeration, a contributor to the *Quarterly Review* in 1835 drew the conclusion that the country was in a new political era, operating under a new constitution.[3]

The five Acts were connected not merely chronologically but by internal political logic. Repeal of the Test and Corporation Acts pointed directly to Catholic Emancipation. Emancipation led on to reform of parliament, not merely because change in one area encouraged those who wanted change in another, but because in the process the Tory party, defenders of the Hanoverian constitution, had been dealt a mortal blow. Municipal reform was linked both to civil and ecclesiastical reform. Lord John Russell insisted that it was 'in strict accordance with the spirit and intention of the Reform Act', and Joseph Parkes improved upon the description by writing that municipal reform was 'the steam engine for the mill built by parliamentary reform.'[4] To open up the snug corporations to popular influence was essential if the concessions to religious dissenters were not to remain token ones.[5] J. W. Croker, out of parliament by his own desire after the passing of the Reform Act, agreed with Russell that municipal reform was the natural corollary, though he drew a different moral, deploring the annihilation of those corporations 'which had repelled and destroyed the despotism of James II and were the bulwarks and the safeguards of the Protestant interests in the State.'[6] Lastly, the provisions of the Poor Law Amendment Act went some way to depriving the landed classes of one of their main functions in the counties. Though, as with parliamentary reform, the outcome was a compromise and the gentry retained great influence, much of the business of petty and quarter sessions was removed and an important step taken towards extending the power of central government into areas it had scarcely reached in the past.

It would help to focus the discussion if we could establish at what period the signs of a collapse of confidence in the traditional institutions became apparent. Much recent work has drawn attention to the spread of radical attitudes in the decades before the French Revolution. Dr John Brewer has argued that the 1760s was the 'crucial decade' in the formation of a critical public opinion and Dr Colin Bonwick has suggested that radicalism made 'giant strides' in the 1760s and 1770s.[7] Dr Jarrett has written that the 1760s was 'a time of ferment' and that the established order of things was severely shaken by the Seven Years War. Dr Shelton claims that the hunger riots of the 1760s sent 'shock waves' through English society and constituted a greater threat to the social order than either Luddism or Chartism.[8] Sir Herbert Butterfield thought that the popular movements of the early 1780s were 'quasi-revolutionary' in character.[9]

No doubt each of these decades contributed something to the development of a watchful public opinion. In particular, discussion of proposals for religious concessions or for reform of parliament familiarized people with the idea of innovation. But my own feeling is that the traditional institutions were not substantially weakened by the end of the century. There is not space here to do justice to the subtleties of argumentation. It is a matter, in Burke's famous phrase, of reckoning the great silent cattle against the importunate grasshoppers: though the volume of criticism was growing, most Englishmen still admired their ancient constitution. Whatever their other differences, George III and *Junius* were united in praise of 'the venerable fabric'.[10] During the 1790s and 1800s traditional respect for the constitution was powerfully reinforced by patriotic feelings aroused by the wars with France. A writer in *Blackwood's Magazine* in 1821 rejoiced that at least the agricultural population remained uncontaminated by French principles, were proud of their country's renown, and 'never called to question the virtues of that system of government that had won so much honour'.[11]

*　　*　　*

One of the most essential features of the old constitution was the identification of Church and State, dovetailed together under aristocratic supervision. Though the term 'Protestant Ascendancy' is usually applied to Ireland, it serves to describe England as well. The basic assumption was that only persons of property – preferably landed property – were fit to be trusted with political power and that they should be in communion with the Church of England. This assumption also prevailed at local level where in the counties power was exercised by the Lords Lieutenant and the JPs, and in most of the boroughs by self-electing Anglican oligarchies.[12] The theoretical defence of this settlement was, basically, threefold. First, that only persons of property could be trusted to act responsibly since they alone had something to lose in the wreck of the community; secondly, that Catholic and Protestant dissenters had, by their conduct in the seventeenth century, shown themselves to be subversive and unreliable; thirdly, that the three sources of power in parliament – king, Lords and Commons – balanced each other, the resulting equilibrium preventing the constitution from sliding into royal despotism, aristocratic oligarchy or popular licence.

In practice these neat categories and functions were difficult to maintain and the assumptions behind them seemed increasingly dubious.

Looking back to the convulsions of the seventeenth century, eighteenth-century Englishmen were ever on guard against a reassertion of royal authority and were still gloomily anticipating despotism long after it had ceased to be a practicable possibility: Dunning's famous motion of 1780, that the influence of the Crown had increased, was increasing and ought to be diminished, was an inaccurate as it was elegant. The gradual decline of the power of the Crown put the constitutional balance in jeopardy and prepared the way for a struggle between the aristocratic and popular elements.

These constitutional arrangements depended also upon another unspoken assumption – that those excluded from power were unlikely to join forces to obtain concessions. This assumption is, perhaps, most apparent in the religious sphere, where for many years the hostility between Catholic and Protestant Dissenters was such that common action against the Anglicans was out of the question. Nor, for most of the eighteenth century, did it seem possible that members of the middling class, whose wealth and ambitions were not adequately recognized, would ever collaborate with the propertyless. William Beckford, a man of vast imperial wealth, inveighed bitterly in the 1760s against the aristocracy – 'those two hundred great lords who received more from government than they paid to it' – but he had little sympathy for the lower orders: 'those who raise mobs raise the devil.'[13]

One way, therefore, of explaining why the old system came to be dismantled is that the excluded grew stronger, better organized and less divided, while the conviction of the governing classes that those exclusions were justifiable grew correspondingly weaker. Timid Anglicans still shuddered at the time when Catholics had tried to blow up king and parliament or when fierce Puritans had stabled their horses in the great cathedrals, and Sir Robert Inglis, resisting the repeal of the Test and Corporation Acts, tried to pluck the old chord:[14]

> They (the penal laws) are the power which the constitution of England keeps in her own hand to protect the Church and herself, whenever such a combination of circumstances shall again arise as that which, two centuries ago, overthrew the altar and the throne, the Church and the State, in one common destruction.

But it was growing difficult to believe that such circumstances would recur and that Catholics and Dissenters were merely biding their time for a repeat performance.[15]

The great strength of the old system – that it was an interlocking relationship – turned out to be, in the hour of crisis, a weakness also. William Huskisson, attacking Russell's motion for repeal of the Test and Corporation Acts, insisted that it could not be viewed in isolation: the Acts were, he insisted, part of 'the system as a whole, one portion of which could not be properly dealt with. . . . The strength, and security, and prosperity, of the empire mainly depended on the present system.'[16] The strength of the system was therefore the strength of its weakest link. By 1828, the weakest link appeared to be the continued exclusion of thousands of loyal Protestants from full participation in the public life of their country. In 1689, England had been in the vanguard of religious toleration: by 1828, after a century of Enlightenment, it lagged behind the rest of Europe, as Lord John Russell pointed out:[17]

> Is it now the case, that persons who do not profess the religion of the State are excluded from civil and military employment in all countries? The fact is notoriously otherwise. In France, the Netherlands, Germany, Austria, and Austria in Italy, no such law exists; but persons of all religious persuasions are eligible to office. The English Protestant Dissenter, if he were to leave his country, might be admitted to all the employments of Catholic Austria, might go from exclusion at Bath or Huntingdon, to sit in the municipality of Prague or of Milan.

*   *   *   *

Most discussion of the demise of the old political order has been in rather general terms: one of the objects of this paper is to attempt to sharpen up the explanation by identifying which groups had begun to lose confidence in the traditional institutions. When trying to gauge great shifts in public opinion, the historian is obliged to be content with approximate explanations. There is no way of examining the views of the twenty-one million people who made up the population of the United Kingdom in 1821. I intend therefore to look at four main groups, each to some extent outside the old unreformed system— religious dissent, the Irish, the lower orders and the middling classes. I am acutely aware of the objections to these categories and am far from believing that opinion in each group was homogeneous or static. Nor are the groups mutually exclusive. But provided that we bear in mind these reservations, the scheme may assist analysis.[18]

There are, of course, peculiar difficulties in making any numerical assessment of religious affiliation. But the overall position seems reasonably clear. By the middle of the eighteenth century, membership of old belief may have fallen as low as 50,000:[19] coupled with the stagnant position of Catholicism,[20] this suggested that by a process of erosion religious nonconformity might, in the course of time, be worn away. This prospect was destroyed by two developments—the spread of Methodism and its gradual alienation from the Church of England, and the beginning of large-scale Irish immigration into England, which restored Catholicism as a popular religion. By the end of Wesley's life in 1791, the membership of his sect was 72,000; by 1827 it had risen to

237,000, and the dissenting bodies could claim to represent two million people. The success of the Methodist campaigns was followed by a recovery among the Baptists and Congregationalists: the three communities had some 2,391 places of worship between them in 1801; 50 years later, they could claim 17,040.[21] The Catholic community which, on the basis of the 1767 returns, has been estimated at 80,000, was powerfully reinforced at the turn of the century from Ireland. The four Lancashire towns of Preston, Wigan, Liverpool and Manchester which in 1767 had some 4,000 catholics, had 22,000 by 1810, 37,000 by 1819, and 120,000 by 1851.[22] The 1851 religious census revealed that, in church attendance, the dissenting sects could claim parity with the Church of England.

Nor had the Dissenters, particularly the Protestants, grown only in numbers. They had grown greatly in wealth and in standing in the community, and John Smith, seconding Russell's motion for repeal, was at pains to shrug off the 'king-killing' image:[23]

> The Dissenters of the present day were as intelligent, as loyal, as prosperous, and as industrious, a class of people as any within his majesty's dominions. . . . They could boast of eminent men in all professions – of useful men in all the avocations of life. It was ridiculous, absurd and mischievous, at that time of day, to slander such a class of persons by keeping on the statute book Acts which, though they were not enforced, amounted to a gross insult.

The implications of this massive shift in religious loyalty for the old partnership of Church and State were serious, and at times the question was less whether concessions would have to be made to non-Anglicans than whether the established Church could survive at all. The growing unpopularity of the Church of England had become a liability to the revolution settlement and the first breach was in the ecclesiastical provisions.

The debate on repeal of the Test and Corporation Acts took place in the shadow of Catholic emancipation. Opponents of emancipation suspected that repeal was no more than a stalking-horse, and the historian of emancipation agrees that many pro-Catholics supported repeal 'to establish the principle of breaking in upon the constitution.'[24] Huskisson, an uncomfortable member of Wellington's newly formed government, made a different diagnosis, arguing that repeal would work against the chances of Catholic emancipation: the Protestant Dissenters, their main grievances met, would leave the Catholics in the lurch. He therefore, somewhat to the surprise of the House, spoke and voted against repeal. Others in the government were opposed both to repeal and to Catholic emancipation. These differences of opinion, and others about corn and the Penryn Bill, meant that resistance to Russell's motion was badly coordinated. Not until a very late stage was it decided that the motion should be resisted by the government and, according to Ellenborough, the whip was half-hearted. The outer ramparts of the old system were therefore carried while the defence was still organizing itself, leaving, as Sir Robert Inglis put it, the citadel itself to be attacked in due course.[25]

In the House of Lords, where the defenders of the old order might have been more confident, resistance was slight. Not a single bishop protested against repeal, and though a number of lay peers fought back, they were in the awkward position of being more zealous for the Church than the bench of bishops itself.[26] Lord Kenyon protested:[27]

> All he looked for was the security of the Established Church, which he venerated not only for its spiritual character, but for the political influence exercised for the support of the constitution. The great majority of the bench of bishops, he observed, had shown little or no concern for either.

The bishops, it transpired, thought the safeguards useless. The Archbishop of York argued that the tests only encouraged insincerity, and the Bishop of Lincoln thought that they should be retained only as long as the Church was in evident peril, which was no longer the case. The attitude of the bishops to this issue was in marked contrast to the hostility they showed towards reform of parliament, when 21 bishops were in the majority in September 1831 which threw out the first Reform Bill. By a curious irony, the laymen were keener to defend the Church and the clerics the State.[28]

*   *   *   *

Most of the Irish had also been excluded from power since the seventeenth century and, indeed, the success of the Hanoverian settlement had depended to a considerable extent upon the subjugation or pacification of Ireland. But the situation changed towards the end of the eighteenth century. First, demographic developments altered the balance between the two countries. It seems probable that the population of England and Wales at the time of the Glorious Revolution was about five and a half million: there is less certainty about the Irish population, but it can hardly have been as high as two millions, and some estimates are considerably lower. According to the census of 1821, there were some 6,800,000 Irish to 12,000,000 in England and Wales – i.e. the Irish had increased to well over half the relative population. Secondly, the success of the Volunteer movement in the 1780s in prising concessions from the English government was a sign that Ireland was once more stirring and this was confirmed in dramatic form by the rebellion of 1798. Thirdly, the Act of Union of 1801 not only brought Irish problems to Westminster but, contrary to Pitt's original intentions, brought in the Irish without Catholic emancipation, which had been intended as the basis for a more sympathetic and stable relationship between the two countries.

Nor was the arrival of one hundred Irish MPs in the House of Commons the only invasion. In the course of the 1800s, and more particularly after the sharp famine of 1821, thousands of Irish immigrants began to enter England. The consequences were considerable. Increasing strain was placed on an already overburdened poor-law system. The Act of Settlement of 1662, which laid down that paupers should be returned to their parishes of origin, had not been devised for difficulties on this scale. Lancashire in particular was hard hit, the Bristol overseers of the poor petitioned for assistance, and select parliamentary committees looked into the matter in 1823 and again in 1828.[29] The presence in English cities of thousands of Catholic Irish also carried a political threat which was widely appreciated – indeed, as it transpired, exaggerated. W.H. Trant, member for Dover, opposing Catholic emancipation, accused O'Connell of saying 'What if the hundred thousand Irish Catholics in London were to set fire to the four corners of the city?'[30] The nightmare vision did not materialize but for decades to come governments were haunted by the spectre of Irish nationalism joining forces with radical agitation.

Though O'Connell's election for County Clare in July 1828 is sometimes taken as the cause of emancipation, it was no more than the episode which brought things to a head. It had been clear to informed observers for years that resistance to Catholic emancipation was crumbling. As early as 1813 a motion for an enquiry into Catholic claims had passed the Commons with a handsome majority, only to fail by one vote in the Lords. In 1823 Nugent's bill to grant the parliamentary vote to English Catholics was supported by Peel, and passed by 59 votes before being wrecked in the Lords. In 1825 there was discussion that Wellington might replace Liverpool as prime minister and carry a measure of emancipation. In May 1828, after the repeal of the Test and Corporation Acts, the pro-Catholics obtained a majority of six on a Commons vote.[31] The following month, before O'Connell had declared his candidature for County Clare, Greville treated the matter as a foregone conclusion:[32]

> I do not believe he (Wellington) means to do anything until he is compelled to it, which if he remains in office, he will be; for the success of the Catholic question depends neither on Whigs nor Tories. . . .the march of time and the state of Ireland will effect it in spite of everything, and its slow but continual advance can neither be retarded by its enemies nor accelerated by its friends. . . .

Though the concession of Catholic emancipation may appear to be a choice example of the politics of pressure, the reality was less simple. English public opinion was overwhelmingly hostile to the measure. Two pressures were therefore in juxtaposition: Irish pressure proved superior since it carried the threat of civil war. But it is too cynical to presume that the governing classes gave way merely to the threat of force. Many members of both Houses were genuinely convinced that the exclusion of Catholics from parliament was an unjustifiable anachronism and had expressed this point of view years before the threat of Irish revolt could be perceived.

Lord Winchilsea and Lord Eldon sounded the note of defiance as soon as the king's speech, announcing measures of Catholic relief, had been read. Our revered constitution, Winchilsea declared, 'the national boast, the envy and admiration of the world, the ground-work of our liberties' was now to be subverted: the union of Church and State, insisted Eldon, was 'intimate and indissoluble.' In the Lower House, General Gascoyne accused Peel and the other ministers of truckling to the Catholic Association: the advocates of change 'need no longer despair of obtaining universal suffrage and parliamentary reform: they had nothing to do but to get up an association, and straight the alarmed ministers would come down to the House with a proposal to grant all they wanted.'[33]

Pro-Catholic speakers denied the sacrosanct nature of the constitution. Lord Milton argued on 5 March 1829:

> What was called the present constitution took its date, not from 1688, but from 1678. . . . That Act was passed by a House of Commons reeking with frenzy at the perjuries of Titus Oates. . . . He could not bear to hear it asserted that it was contrary to the constitution of 1688 to open the two houses of Parliament to Catholics.

Properly understood, Catholic emancipation was neither a surrender nor a catastrophe: 'if the ministers had been defeated,' declared Charles Brownlow, member for Armagh County, 'it was by time, by circumstances, by the progress of knowledge, and the extension of liberal and enlightened principles.'[34]

*   *   *   *

It is difficult to write about the remaining two groups without such savage abridgement leading to serious distortion. When we are dealing with Catholic Irish or Protestant dissent, we have reasonably defined units. But 'lower orders' and 'middling classes' are distressingly vague terms and their existence as anything like coherent groups has been denied by some historians.

That the lower orders were excluded from a share in power under the old régime was strenuously denied during the debates on the Reform Bill. One of Peel's strongest objections to the ten-pound franchise was that it would produce a one-class electorate, 'severing all connection between the lower classes of the community and the direct representation in this House.'[35] Certainly there were examples under the unreformed system of boroughs such as Preston, Honiton and Hindon where the right to vote included very humble persons.[36] But as a general political observation, Peel's claim seems contrived, sentimental, and, perhaps, disingenuous. In none of the counties, where the franchise was the forty-shilling freehold, could persons without property vote. Only in a comparatively small number of boroughs could men in humble circumstances vote, and even then they were normally disqualified if they were in receipt of poor relief. Consequently, those members of the lower orders who had the vote were few in number and isolated. The conditions did not exist in which they could use their vote as a purposeful political weapon and it is not surprising that they came to regard it mainly, if not exclusively, as a marketable commodity. Some of the most vociferous objections to reform came, therefore, from these voters. In Wallingford, they regarded reform as 'an attack upon their vested interests, deserving of determined, if not vindictive opposition', and when Cobbett canvassed Honiton in 1806 as a non-bribing candidate, he was told that he ought to be ashamed of himself for taking the bread out of the mouths of the poor.[37]

In order to explain the growth of a reform movement, it is not necessary to assume that the lower orders were unanimous in demanding change. It is enough to show that a substantial proportion of them had become politically aware and that they had some prospect of finding political allies. Comparing the 1810s with, say, the 1760s, it can hardly be doubted that more of the lower orders were interested in political affairs, that they were less respectful towards their social superiors, and that they showed a greater capacity to organize their protests effectively.

There are many ways in which the increasing participation of the lower orders in public affairs might be demonstrated. One can point to the organization of Hardy's London Corresponding Society and its counterparts in the provinces in the 1790s, the spread of trade unionism, the considerable organization behind Luddism, or the setting up of the Hampden Clubs in the 1810s. Let us take the examples of petitioning and the press. Petitions to parliament had grown enormously in both size and number since the early years of George III's reign. The agitation over Catholic relief in 1778 had provoked 15 petitions: the economical reform campaign that followed was supported by 38 petitions. By the 1820s, petitioning was on a totally different scale. Five thousand petitions are said to have been submitted about repeal of the

Test and Corporation Acts and 20,000 in relation to Catholic emancipation. In 1784, Bristol and Glasgow had submitted what were regarded as gigantic addresses with 5,000 and 4,000 signatures apiece: by 1829 the same constituencies were sending up petitions of 39,000 and 37,000 respectively. Though in detail the petitions may be suspect, with opportunities for impersonation and fraud, there can be little doubt that they represented a substantial extension of the political nation.[38]

Not everyone who signed a petition or address was from the humbler ranks of society. But the sheer size of some of the petitions – 81,000 names on an anti-Catholic petition from Kent, for example – means that many poor people must have signed. Other petitions stated specifically that they came from the less prosperous groups. More than 11,000 were said in 1817 to have signed a petition from Birmingham within 48 hours – 'nearly the whole of the labouring population'.[39] Three thousand petitioners from Newcastle described themselves as 'for the most part mechanics and artisans' and pointed out that they were deprived of the vote in their own town.[40] Bolton – like Birmingham, an unrepresented town – produced 10,000 signatures against Catholic relief in 1828.[41]

The increase in the number and circulation of newspapers is also evidence that by the early decades of the nineteenth century a considerable proportion of the lower orders must have had some knowledge of contemporary events. At the accession of George III there were four London dailies: by 1793 there were at least 13; in 1760 there were some 35 provincial newspapers: by 1836 there were said to be 175 published outside London. Estimates of circulation are more difficult since the fortunes of a particular newspaper could fluctuate wildly over a few years. But the sale of newspaper stamps rose from nine million in 1760 to thirty-nine million by 1837. In the 1760s, Woodfall's *Public Advertiser* was selling 3,000 copies, with a few hundred extra when a letter from *Junius* came out.[42] Cobbett claimed 44,000 for the first cheap edition of the *Political Register* in 1816, rising to 60,000 later. Hetherington's *Poor Man's Guardian* was reported in 1833 to have an average circulation of 16,000, and Carlile's *Gauntlet* some 22,000.[43]

Nor was the increase in circulation everything. The tone of many of the papers was quite different from that of 1760. Wilkes's and *Junius's* criticisms of George III, though considered audacious in their day, were expressed in veiled and deferential language. No such inhibitions muffled writers in the 1810s. It is true that the papers and caricatures of the Pelham period contained sharp criticisms of the leading politicians, and great quantities of scurrilous abuse were heaped upon the luckless Bute and the princess dowager in the 1760s. But the attacks, however painful, were rarely informed by a coherent political philosophy; 50 years later the comments were more sustained, better directed, and carried a clear radical and democratic message. The propaganda of such newspapers as *The Poor Man's Guardian, The Gauntlet, The Gorgon* and *Black Dwarf* was aimed specifically at the labouring classes. In 1812, goaded by the *Morning Post*'s simpering flattery of the Prince Regent, Leigh Hunt wrote his celebrated summary in *The Examiner*:[44]

> In short, that this delightful, blissful, wise, pleasurable, honourable, virtuous, true and immortal prince, is a violator of his word, a libertine over head and heels in debt and disgrace, a despiser of domestic ties, the companion of gamblers and demireps, a man who has just closed half a century without one single claim on the gratitude of his country or the respect of posterity.

Wooler's *Black Dwarf* in 1817 was equally savage:

> Put George Canning in the workhouse of Bethnal Green, and allow him half-a-crown a week (and that is more than he is worth to the state) and hear then what beautiful tropes and similies he would find for the Constitution.

*   *   *   *

Much attention has been paid by historians to the growing political awareness of the lower orders in the early nineteenth century. Less work has been done on the middling classes, yet it is arguable that the conversion of many of them to the cause of reform was of even greater moment.

The phrase 'middling orders' or 'middling ranks' is not a very precise one. It must be remembered that, in the 1800s, a very large proportion was in fact rural – farmers and landlords, or professional men such as attorneys, bailiffs, auctioneers, clergymen, dependent on the land and part of the local community. Though the urban middling classes had undoubtedly grown in numbers in the course of the eighteenth century, it would be wrong to think of the middling classes as exclusively bankers, traders or manufacturers.

It would also be misleading to imply that the middling ranks as a whole were excluded from influence by the Hanoverian settlement. Many of them qualified for the parliamentary vote as forty-shilling freeholders in the counties, or as freemen, inhabitant householders or members of the corporation in the boroughs. In corporate towns they might serve as councillors or aldermen, act as JPs, or fill some of the large number of local offices – trusts, charities and commissions for improvement – which provided opportunities for enterprising and public-spirited men. Some men of comparatively humble origins also made their way into parliament: Sir Joseph Mawbey had been a vinegar manufacturer, George Medley a wine merchant, John Calvert a brewer, while Robert Mackreth had started life as a waiter. But the most remarkable feature of the unreformed system was its haphazardness. A wealthy farmer who was a tenant would have no vote: his neighbour with a smaller farm had a vote if he held it freehold. Liverpool, Bristol, Newcastle and Norwich had their own representation: Birmingham, Manchester, Leeds and Sheffield did not. Malmesbury had its two MPs: Tetbury, its neighbour, had none: Morpeth was represented, Hexham was not. A man of substantial property might live in an unincorporated town and have no part to play in its affairs: even if the town had a corporation, as Bath, Salisbury and Bury St Edmunds did, he might have little influence if he was out of favour with the self-electing council. Nor did it necessarily follow that those who had representation were satisfied. Thomas Foley, in a farewell speech to his Herefordshire constituents in 1819 pointed out how absurd it was that their opinion could be nullified in the Commons by the representatives of the pocket borough of Weobley.[45]

There were few indications in the eighteenth century that this state of affairs was much resented. The middling classes of Birmingham and Manchester seem to have taken to heart *Junius*'s advice that they should count their blessings: 'you will find the interruption of business in those towns . . . by the riot and cabals of an election too dear a price to pay for the nugatory privilege of sending members to parliament.'[46] Neither town responded to Wyvill's appeal in 1780 to seek reform, and the bailiffs of Manchester wrote specifically to disavow his initiative: 'it is by no means proper to raise disputes and dissensions about altering and amending our excellent constitution.'[47] Nor did the inhabitants seem dismayed at their rudimentary local government. The authors of the *Birmingham Directory* of 1777 thought that the absence of a corporation contributed 'not a little to the increase of its trade, buildings and inhabitants',[48] and the author of a description of Manchester was in full accord: 'nothing could be more fatal to its trading interest, if it should be incorporated and have representation in Parliament.'[49]

Forty years later, the situation was very different. The petitions for reform from Manchester and Birmingham in 1793 and again in 1817 and 1818 were from the lower orders and were radical in tendency. But in the course of the 1820s, the middling classes took up the running. The boroughreeve, constables and ratepayers of Manchester petitioned in 1827 of the 'very great advantage which would, in the opinion of the petitioners, be experienced from the opportunity of direct communication with Members representing the town, and intimately acquainted with its interests.'[50] A petition from Sheffield in February 1830 was sober and respectful: expressing admiration for the constitution, it argued that a flourishing town of 80,000 people had 'a just claim to be directly represented in the House by deputies of its own choice, to whom its extensive and increasing interests may be particularly and confidently intrusted.'[51] Another petition, three months later, from Leeds specified that it came from the 'bankers, merchants and manufacturers' of the town.[52]

This remarkable change of attitude on behalf of the middling classes owed little to direct propaganda. It represented, of course, a growing awareness of their numbers and a growing self-confidence as producers of wealth. Petitions for representation dwelt with pride on the importance of the local community and the contribution it made to the nation: Birmingham, declared Sir James Mackintosh in 1828, was an unrepresented community of 120,000 inhabitants 'abounding with men of property, character and intelligence'.[53] But, more specifically, many bankers, merchants and industrialists had come to feel that their special interests needed direct representation if they were not to be overlooked in the clamour of voices. The introduction of tariffs to protect corn prompted the suspicion that the government used *laissez-faire* arguments only when they served its purposes, preaching patience and non-intervention to the lower orders and the business community while protecting the farmer. The new business class was less satisfied with the old arrangement whereby its affairs were looked after by the county members. The petitioners from Sheffield specifically made the point that the knights of the shire had 'such laborious duties to discharge that they cannot reasonably be expected minutely to attend the local interests of any particular place.'[54] The old argument that representation brought with it riots and orgies was not the deterrent it had been. The middling classes were confident that with parliamentary representation, a reformed local government and, perhaps, the introduction of a new police force on the metropolitan pattern, they could handle their own rowdies.

Nor had the attitude of the rural middling classes remained unchanged. The prolonged agricultural recession after the war prompted many farmers to take more interest in political questions. Defenders of the old order were dismayed at the reception given to Cobbett on his visits to market towns and farmers' clubs: their minds, wrote one Tory newspaper, had been 'soured and alienated by inflammatory harangues'.[55] In 1822, Sir Robert Heron presented a petition for reform from Lincolnshire, telling the House:[56]

> The population of Lincolnshire was almost exclusively agricultural. Formerly, contented with their lot, they were little inclinded to interfere in political questions . . . But now they were convinced that no relief was to be expected but from substantial and effective reform.

No longer could it be presumed that farmers were the automatic and unquestioning champions of the *status quo*. Their hardships made them more receptive not only to proposals for parliamentary reform, but to

arguments against tithes and to denunciations of aristocratic extravagance and corruption. It has been suggested that their enthusiasm for
reform was not lasting but melted with the return of agricultural
prosperity: 'never again would reform have much popularity with
farmers', wrote T. L. Crosby.[57] That is a serious misreading of the
situation. The solid support given to reform candidates in the shires of
England at the general election of 1831 testifies that a large proportion
of the freeholders remained convinced of the need for change.

*　*　*

The exposition so far is open to the objection that, since the upper
classes retained their parliamentary domination and never lost control
of the situation, it pays too much attention to those excluded from
power. A balanced assessment demands that we make some evaluation
of the attitude of the ruling classes.

The first thing to establish is that their opinions were no more mono-
lithic than those of other groups in the country. The point is of more
than passing importance. The lack of unity of the upper classes was a
factor of tactical significance: the existence among the upper classes of a
group which was positively favourable to reform was essential if the process of change was to remain peaceful and constitutional.

We may try to identify four attitudes. First, there was a group which
was little interested in politics. It is worth mentioning them since·
historians tend, on the whole, to be earnest and to presume, in the face of
much evidence, that most people in the past were as concerned with
governmental problems as they are. In fact, many members of the upper
class were content to spend their time breeding horses or planting trees,
looking after their families and running their estates, just as many
members of the lower orders had little inclination for anything after
work than ale, a pipe or a game of dominoes or backgammon. Among all
the petitions for and against Catholic emancipation or parliamentary
reform were others, no doubt as keenly felt, deploring the poor quality
of beer.[58]

There were three basic attitudes among upper-class politicians. An
important section of the aristocracy sympathized with the claims of the
middling class, and even of the lower orders, welcoming the construc-
tion of a more liberal régime. A second group, though unenthusiastic
about the direction some developments were taking, preferred to make
concessions rather than run the risk of a direct confrontation between
rich and poor. Thirdly, there was a vociferous group, strong in the
House of Lords, opposed tooth and nail to changes in the old social and
political order. It is easy to exaggerate the size of this backwoodsman or
ultra group. Its members were often remarkably vocal, they felt deeply,

and they argued the persuasive line that any concession merely prepared the ground for more. They make good copy for historians and are temptingly quotable: yet, judged by the final test of votes in parliament, they were never within reach of success. From the repeal of the Test and Corporation Acts to the Municipal Reform Act, they fought every inch of the way and, on every occasion, they lost.[59]

Even this analysis exaggerates the coherence of the upper-class response. The Acts of Parliament which I have lumped together came, not as a reform package, but spread over seven years. Some of the ultra-conservatives grasped the full significance of what was likely to happen from the first moment – indeed, they were inclined to overstate it. But others responded to each mini-crisis as it came. Moreover, though I have tried to explain the internal logic connecting these pieces of legislation, it was quite possible to accept some and reject others. Thousands of people, for example, petitioned against Catholic emancipation yet voted in favour of reform of parliament. And, of course, it was possible to have reservations in detail. A phrase like 'parliamentary reform', though convenient to historians, begs a whole battery of questions about the precise nature of the reforms intended.

One factor which undoubtedly contributed to upper-class disunity was party rivalry. Two circumstances made this of particular importance in late Hanoverian England. In a political struggle between groups of aristocrats and their allies, there was always a strong temptation to seek support from less privileged groups. For most of the time, the ruling class was well aware of this danger. But at times of crisis, when the stakes were high, the temptation to break ranks was almost irresistible. Hence eighteeth-century politics came to resemble tag-wrestling, where the combatants, if hard-pressed, can summon auxiliaries into the ring – with the risk that it is not always easy to get rid of them afterwards. The second circumstance is that, by the 1820s, the Whigs had established a powerful claim to be considered the least effective party of modern times, doomed to permanent opposition. It is not surprising that some of them should begin to question the merits of a system under which they did so conspicuously badly and that, in their desire to attain office once in a lifetime, they should grow reckless about the methods employed to discredit their political adversaries.

The Whig dilemma can be seen in relation to the policy of economical reform. The attractions of such a policy to any opposition are obvious. In a period with two long and expensive wars against America and France, economical reform was bound to appeal to tax-payers. It was hard for the government to resist without appearing to shield inefficiency, extravagance and corruption, and by weakening the government's command of patronage, it reduced its chances of survival. Economical reform could be squared with Whig traditions by representing it as a policy aimed essentially at curtailing the powers of the Crown. Yet it contained two concealed dangers. The most immediate was that, should the opposition succeed in turning out the government, they would have weakened the defences of the bastion they hoped to occupy. The second was that the long-term logic implied the abolition of all the privileges of the aristocracy, which must mean, ultimately, a different political system.

Some Whigs were more aware of the danger than others. Lord Grey was uneasy about the attacks launched by his more militant supporters on the Duke of York and army corruption in 1809, while the campaign against the government in 1810 for electoral malpractices he disliked as 'fighting with poisoned weapons'.[60] But if Grey had become squeamish and even his early enthusiam for reform had waned, a new generation of Whig politicians was prepared to work with radicals like Burdett, Wardle and Waithman and to force the pace. Several of this advanced group were scions of aristocratic families – Althorp, Russell, Milton, Tavistock and Ebrington.[61] The combination within the ranks of the Whigs of the nervous with the confident explains some of the ambiguities of reform in this period and makes it hard to say whether the Whigs, as a party, faced forward or backward.

It is sometimes presumed that the upper classes were resolute and unflinching during and after the Napoleonic wars. That is not altogether my impression. Indeed, it would be strange had their nerve not been shaken by some of the more lurid events of the times they lived in. At the time of the dagger plot, in 1792, Pitt was reported to have said that by tomorrow 'they might not have a hand to act nor a tongue to utter.'[62] Burke, as was his wont, outdid him easily in hysteria: to Windham he wrote in 1795 that it would be shameful not to put up a struggle before 'Mr Fox's guillotine' came to their door.[63] In 1809, Grey wrote that his forebodings were 'of the most melancholy nature' and that the attacks upon the Duke of York reminded him of the campaign against Marie Antoinette on the eve of the French Revolution.[64] In 1819, the Home Secretary admitted that the state of the country was 'frightful'.[65] Peel wondered a year later whether parliamentary reform could possibly be resisted for another seven years.[66]

Of course this is an impressionistic selection, and I am far from suggesting that the upper classes lived in a state of permanent panic. Nevertheless, the French Revolution had introduced a new dimension of terror, and I am not sure that it would be easy to compile a comparable anthology of apprehension from the period of Walpole and the Pelhams. It was a somewhat jumpy garrison in the 1820s that awaited the attack, and Russell had already noted that Peel, far from demonstrating any marked determination to die in the last ditch for the old constitution, was 'a very pretty hand at hauling down his colours'.[67]

*   *   *

In the late 1820s there was still widespread recognition of the benefits that the old order had conferred. It had given Britain a good deal of internal peace and security, and a measure of religious toleration. It had helped to raise British power and prestige in the world to unprecedented heights. In addition, it had assisted that industrial development which, in the course of time, was to transform the living standards not only of Britain but of much of the world. Indeed, it is at least arguable that the old order died of its own success in promoting or permitting such sweeping changes.[68] Perhaps that is why Bentham and the philosophical radicals were not more effective at this stage. They never quite succeeded in polarizing the argument into utility or antiquity, because the defenders of the old order maintained that it had shown itself to be a very effective working system. They did not defend it purely in terms of tradition.[69] It was not a regime that was hopelessly decrepit or demonstrably ineffective that was under scrutiny, and its defenders could appeal to more than naked class interest. The reputation of the Hanoverian settlement ensured its survival long into a changing world and meant that its demolition was bound to be accompanied by much heart-searching and bitterness.

The root cause of the overthrow of the old order seems to have been the growing political awareness of large sections of the nation. The spread of information through books and newspapers, the protracted economic difficulties at the end of the long war, and the growth of great new towns produced a society in which group after group was less patient, less prepared to suffer unheard, less willing to leave government to its betters. The activities of parliament were subjected to a far more sustained examination than had been the case in the past.

The 1688 settlement had, after all, been designed to deal with the twin dangers of Catholicism and royal despotism. By the 1820s each looked very remote indeed. But it was less clear that the settlement could cope satisfactorily with the economic and social problems of an emerging industrial society. In the first debate on the Reform Bill, Peel taunted Lord John Russell with a moderate speech he had made in 1819, in which he had advocated only piecemeal changes and extolled the virtues of the ancient constitution – that 'Aladdin's lamp' which had raised up a smiling land and wanted only a polish to work its miracles once more, that constitution which Montesquieu had referred to as the most perfect in the world.[70] No doubt Russell listened in some embarrasment, but for

Peel it was a debating victory only. The Aladdin's lamp needed more
than a clean-up, and for the angry Dissenters, hungry labourers and
distressed farmers of 1831 it was no great consolation that Montesquieu
had once praised their ancient constitution.

Colloquy on chapter 5
William Speck

The discussion began with a lively attack upon the central thesis itself. McCord argued that the proposition was so baldly stated, especially in the opening paragraph's assertion that the old political order was 'destroyed', that it needed modification. He would have preferred to use the traditional word 'reformed': 'those who participated in the reforms did not have any intention of, or understanding that they were, destroying the constitution, but rather that they were purifying and improving it.' O'Gorman agreed, finding merit in the notion that the ruling classes engaged in tactical regrouping in order to accommodate other interests in the system rather than surrendering to them. Although this resulted in a new polity, 'the continuities were enormous': the collapse of the *ancien régime* did not come about until the 1880s or 1890s. Dickinson suggested that the reforms removed a few bricks from the edifice of the Hanoverian constitution, but that, though shaken, it was not demolished.

Cannon conceded that he would go almost half-way to meeting these objections, admitting that he had experienced difficulty in focusing the problem: despite his own warning not to overstate the case, he had expected that some people would find the formulation melodramatic. He had certainly not meant to imply that the old order was destroyed *in 1832*. Nevertheless, the period had seen a rapid transition from one kind of constitution to another: 'a particular kind of constitution, based upon landed supremacy, Anglican domination, and monarchical participation in government' had been established by the Revolution settlement, and 'those three aspects were so very seriously challenged and eroded in the course of the nineteenth century that the old Hanoverian constitution was fundamentally changed.' Of course the advocates of reform had denied that they were destroying the old constitution, but some of the opposition insisted that the very essence of the constitution *was* at stake. But even if the formulation was open to criticism, the problem remained: the contrast between the respect expressed by most people – not all – for the constitution in 1760 as a priceless heritage to be preserved – and the contempt in which it was held by some people – not all – in the 1820s as 'old Corruption'. This change in public attitude needed to be explained.

The stages in this process attracted attention. Holmes introduced the topic by suggesting that stability was a plant slow to grow and, while it blossomed quickly in the 1720s, equally slow to wither. O'Gorman argued that instead of seeing the process of decline as a steady progression, it should be regarded as a series of spasmodic threats to the old order, starting in the 1750s and reaching peaks in the late 1760s, 1815 to 1820, and finally 1828–32. The earlier spasms were contained by the established order; collapses of confidence were repaired; but the last could not be absorbed. Among the reasons why previous challenges were contained, he adduced the weakness of radicalism, the sensitive response of the government, and the diversions of the American and French revolutions. Holmes added economic fluctuations. Dismissing the disturbances of the 1750s as not presenting a serious threat to stability, he observed that the mid and later 1760s, the early 1790s, and the late 1820s were all periods of economic recession, during which radicalism grew, only to shrink when conditions improved. Cannon considered that the crucial element was the change in the attitude of the middle classes during the 1820s. Derry, while agreeing that the 1820s were the important decade, argued that the changing attitude of the government and the middle classes came not from a breakdown in confidence but the very reverse: 'a feeling that a judicious readjustment was possible, safe, and practicable'. Cannon accepted that they were more confident than immediately after the war, but insisted that many, including Grey himself, were alarmed at the possibility of revolution if reform were not achieved.

This raised the question whether reform came about more because of outside pressure on the government or from the enlightened attitude of the Whigs. McCord insisted that contemporary politicians were not all that influenced by radical agitation: 'we must distinguish between the capacity to make a great deal of noise and the capacity to influence events, and it is arguable that the most important radical of the 1820s was not Orator Hunt, or Place, or Hume, but the Earl of Durham.' Dickinson protested that the 1832 Reform Bill would never have been passed without disturbances in the country which 'helped to stiffen the nerve of the Whigs.' Cannon contended that all the component parts had to be considered: 'to argue that reform was purely the product of popular pressure is just as inadequate as to argue that it was purely the product of an enlightened, sensible, moderate and liberal aristocracy. You have to put these things together.'

Discussion then turned to the four elements which Cannon had identified as the most significant in undermining the old system: Dissenters, Irishmen, the lower orders and the middling orders (p. 104). He had placed Dissent first because it seemed that the religious institutions were 'in the front line and crumbled before the other institutions'.

Holmes denied that the Dissenters were held to be unreliable, and pointed out that the Whigs had trusted them with the vote and with the effective control of a number of corporations throughout the Hanoverian period: 'many of the Whigs felt that the Dissenters *had* redeemed themselves.' Derry suggested that at the time of the French Revolution the Dissenters had become suspect once more. Dickinson detected a parallel in the fortunes of the Protestant Dissenters and the Catholics: both had been granted concessions from the 1770s to the 1790s, but then 'the clock was put back in a big way' when the former were suspected of political radicalism and the latter were implicated in the Irish rebellion of 1798. On the contribution of Irishmen, Dickinson contended that 'bringing the Irish into the constitution actually unbalanced it'. McCord pointed out that two kinds of Irishmen were admitted, the Catholics and the militant Protestant Ulstermen as well.

Opening a discussion on the role of the lower orders (p. 109), McCord stressed the practical obstacles to organizing them politically when most lived in scattered rural communities. Moreover, not all those who were politicized became radicals: on the contrary, many petitioned against Catholic emancipation. Cannon pointed out that, despite difficulties of transport, Cobbett, Hunt and even Major Cartwright did travel a good deal. Certainly liaison was difficult, but the essential point is that it was getting less so. Whether the lower orders adopted radical or reactionary politics did not really matter: 'if, for whatever reasons and on whatever side of the political fence, the lower orders are increasingly interested in politics, how long are they going to be content not to have direct political influence?' McCord suggested that the recourse to massive petitioning in 1817 and 1818 was, in itself, an indication that the lower orders retained considerable confidence in parliament. Cannon retorted that one could hardly argue that without looking closely to see what the petitions actually said: when a petition from Glasgow in 1817 demanded 'a complete change in the political system', it could scarcely be called in as a vote of confidence.[1] Dickinson agreed that there were at least some members of the lower orders who were losing confidence in the system – those, for example, who took part in the highly regimented marching and drilling, or the people at Birmingham in 1819 who elected a legislative attorney as a deliberate challenge to parliament.

The middling orders, it seemed to Holmes (p. 111), changed in character between 1780 and 1830. The growing manufacturing interest was less inclined to accept that it could be virtually represented by a predominantly landed parliament than had been the professional and business interests previously. Cannon was inclined to agree, especially when the refusal of the government to intervene in the industrial economy while introducing the corn laws indicated that there was one law for the landed interest and another for the business world. McCord objected that in 1815 the majority of the middling orders still formed part of the landed interest. Dickinson thought that the work of Asa Briggs, John Money and Donald Read had demonstrated among the middle classes a growth of civic pride and a desire for reform: they had captured and used the local press to advocate, at least, moderate reform.[2] O'Gorman agreed with Cannon on the importance of the movement for municipal reform (p. 210 n. 52). There must have been many thousands of people in different parts of the country who felt excluded – either because they had no vote or because the exigencies of the unreformed system meant that they could never hope to win. This was a time-bomb that had been ticking away under the old system. They were not just bankers and merchants and industrialists, but people in Shrewsbury and Colchester who had for decades been excluded from any say in how their town was governed. It was resentment of local oligarchy.

Finally, Cannon's analysis of the views of the ruling class was considered (p. 114). Cannon confessed that it was 'a slightly absurd exercise' to group them in this way, but he had wanted to make the emphatic point that there was no single upper-class response, since this turned out to be of great tactical importance. McCord remarked that the members of both Houses of parliament were men who lived in the local communities: they were not full-time politicians, living all the time in a parliamentary world. If, as has been suggested, they showed a good deal of restraint and commonsense, it was not just altruism, but because they had to live in that society. A thrashing, flogging attitude would be stupid.

In conclusion, Cannon suggested that it was unhelpful to see modern British political evolution as so continuous a process that no valid distinctions could be offered between the political systems of the eighteenth, nineteenth and twentieth centuries. Of course there was great continuity, but to say that since 1688 we have been governed by a parliamentary monarchy is positively misleading unless one tries to identify the very great shifts of power within that blanket description. One difficulty is that the various parts of the Hanoverian system decayed at different times: the day-to-day participation of the monarch in government, for example, disappeared sooner than the influence of the aristocracy. It still seemed to him however that the critical change of attitude came after 1815 and that there was growing dissatisfaction with the old order. The suggestion that reform came because of 'growing confidence' was teleological and naive: very few people, then or now, have so clear an idea where society is going that they can judge when the time has come for a judicious step forward. Most reforms are the product of pressure, political, financial or military. But though they may be yielded for conservative reasons, the sum total may represent a very real shift in the distribution of power. Though he had himself drawn attention to the conservative character of the Reform Act, when coupled with the religious changes, the reform of local government and the changes in poor-law administration, it meant that the old landmarks of Hanoverian England were fast disappearing.

Note on further reading

The starting point for a discussion of the decline of the Hanoverian system must be some understanding of the factors which helped to produce a more stable society in the early years of the eighteenth century; readers should begin with J. H. Plumb, *The Growth of Political Stability in England, 1675–1725* (1967) and continue with W. A. Speck, *Stability and Strife: England 1714–1760* (1977) and H. T. Dickinson, *Walpole and the Whig Supremacy* (1973).

Of the four groups taken for discussion, dissent can be approached through Clyde Binfield, *So Down to Prayers: Studies in English Nonconformity, 1780–1920* (1977); A. D. Gilbert, *Religion and Society in Industrial England* (1976); R. Cowherd, *The Politics of English Dissent* (1956); W. R. Ward, *Religion and Society in England, 1790–1850* (1972). Catholic dissent is treated in J. Bossy, *The English Catholic Community, 1570–1850* (1975) and in G. I. T. Machin, *The Catholic Question in English Politics, 1820–1830* (1964). A good introduction to Irish problems is the work of R. B. McDowell, particularly *Irish Public Opinion, 1750–1800* (1944) and *Public Opinion and Government Policy in Ireland, 1801–46* (1952). A more detailed study is G. C. Bolton, *The Passing of the Irish Act of Union* (1966).

On the formation of public opinion, there is a vast amount of evidence in E. P. Thompson, *The Making of the English Working Class* (1963). John Money takes an important provincial city for his theme in *Experience and Identity: Birmingham and the West Midlands, 1760–1800* (1977) and other valuable studies are Donald Read, *Press and people, 1790–1850: Opinion in Three English Cities* (1961) and Asa Briggs, 'The Background of the Parliamentary Reform Movement in Three English Cities', *Cambridge Historical Journal* (1950–52). A recent summary of the newspaper press is G. A. Cranfield, *The Press and Society: from Caxton to Northcliffe* (1978).

On reform of parliament, the most recent works are M. G. Brock, *The Great Reform Act* (1973) and John Cannon, *Parliamentary Reform, 1640–1832* (1973). U. Henriques, *Religious Toleration in England, 1787–1833* (1961) discusses the repeal of the Test and Corporation Acts and Catholic emancipation. Recent work on the new poor law includes J. R. Poynter, *Society and Pauperism: English Ideas on Poor Relief, 1795–1834* (1969) and M. Rose, *The English Poor Law* (1971). On local government matters, see D. Fraser, *Urban Politics in Victorian England: the Structure of Politics in Victorian Cities* (1976) and E. P. Hennock, *Fit and Proper Persons: Ideal and Reality in Nineteenth-Century Urban Government* (1973). An important article is G. B. A. M. Finlayson, 'The Politics of Municipal Reform, 1835', in *English Historical Review* (1966).

Lastly, an admirable bibliography, covering most of the period, is Lucy M. Brown and Ian R. Christie, editors, *Bibliography of British History, 1789–1851*.

6

Governing temperament under Pitt and Liverpool
John Derry

One of the most pervasive platitudes of eighteenth-century constitutional theory was that governments ought to be patriotic in character; that administrations should be broadly based, seeking to embrace the widest possible range of political support; and that loyalty to the Crown and to the establishment in Church and State should be an assumed prerequisite for office. Governments were supposed to be coalitions of men of good will, motivated by a desire to serve the State, rather than the agents of faction or party.

Practice never fully lived up to these lofty principles, but most eighteenth-century governments were coalitions, and arguably during the crisis provoked by the French Revolution and by the wars against the French Republic and Empire practice approximated more fully to theory than at earlier periods. Under Pitt and Liverpool governments had the support of a remarkably broad range of opinion, both within parliament and in the country at large, and, with the glaring exception of Pitt's attempt to grant Catholic emancipation, these governments could usually rely on the support of the Crown, which was still a decisive factor in the formation and survival of governments. Of course there were times when Pitt and Liverpool found the king or prince regent difficult to deal with, and despite their longevity their administrations experienced times of difficulty and internal dissension, but on the eve of the first fundamental changes in the constitution as it had been established by the Glorious Revolution—the repeal of the Test and Corporation Acts, Catholic emancipation, and the reform of parliament – governments still reflected those assumptions which had formed the conventional wisdom of the political nation for so long. Resistance to change was expressed in familiar terms, and necessary change was justified in traditional language. What has often been denounced as an age of reaction was characterized by a remarkable flexibility as well as by resilience in familiar patterns of thought and conduct. Although the break-up of the Tory party, which was such a dramatic feature of the years following Liverpool's resignation and Canning's death, opened up the possibility of more radical innovations, the era of Pitt and Liverpool was one of astonishing achievement.

The period from the triumph of George III and Pitt at the 1784 election to the death of Liverpool is still marked by several distortions in interpretation. Historians eager to trace the origins and development of Victorian political parties were prone to speak of a second Tory party, and this meant that the nature of the government which came into being in 1794 was misrepresented. The younger Pitt never thought of himself as a Tory and to the end of his days called himself an independent Whig. When Portland and his friends finally acceded to the government in 1794, after much private agony and political heart-searching, they did not see themselves as abandoning the Whig creed in which they had been reared. Nor did they lose their longstanding distrust of Pitt. They joined the government because they believed that the threat of revolution, both from the French abroad and the radicals at home, necessitated a combined defence of the constitution and traditional liberties against the forces of disorder and sedition. The government formed in 1794 was not a party ministry. Rather, to use a somewhat overworked phrase, it was a government of national unity, and it was a natural response to an unprecedented crisis. Even more insistently, the need to wage war effectively imposed unity upon a government whose ranks contained men who had been bitterly at odds only a few years earlier. As time went on the term Tory came to be applied to such an administration and it was within office, and within the constraints of waging war, that the tradition was formed which came to be called Tory in the early nineteenth century. But it was the familiar Whig constitution which was being defended. It was limited monarchy, not absolute or personal monarchy, which was being safeguarded, and it was a parliamentary system of government which was seen as the greatest bulwark against levelling ideas and social and political chaos. The government was conservative, but it was the Whig achievement which was being conserved, and in so far as the government had anything resembling an ideology it was one which any classic Whig would have found acceptable. Contrary to legend, Pitt was not the exponent of an ideology of counter-revolution. To the annoyance of Burke he was pragmatic and insular when the storm broke in the 1790s and he remained so to the end. The government's basic posture was a defensive, not an offensive one.

Much of this can be seen in Pitt's famous speech on public finance in the House of Commons on 17 February 1792. This speech has long been notorious as giving evidence of Pitt's complacency, since his forecast of 15 years peace in Europe was soon exposed as fallacious. But even here his language was rather more cautious than has sometimes been implied:

> I am not, indeed, presumptuous enough to suppose that when I name 15 years I am not naming a period in which events may arise, which human foresight cannot reach, and which may baffle all our conjectures. We must not count with certainty on a continuance of our present prosperity during

such an interval; but unquestionably there never was a time in the history of this country when, from the situation of Europe, we might more reasonably expect 15 years of peace than we may at the present moment.[1]

Pitt needed peace if his commercial and financial policies were to be as beneficial as he hoped. Nothing would throw out his calculations more savagely than war. Until a clear and unmistakable threat was posed to British interests in Europe he intended to follow a peaceful foreign policy. But his speech was interesting in that it included an explanation for the growing wealth and prosperity of the country which revealed the assumptions fundamental to Pitt's political outlook.

Although his speech was primarily devoted to financial questions Pitt affirmed that the progress of the country was the result of two main causes: first, a century of civil peace, and secondly, the benefits of the constitution, whose principles had been ever more fully understood and practised since the Hanoverian accession. Instead of seeing the constitution as itself resting on economic foundations he believed that the experience of free government had contributed decisively to growing wealth and opulence: 'It is this union of liberty with law which, by raising a barrier equally firm against the encroachments of power and the violence of popular commotion, affords to property its just security, produces the exertion of genius and labour, the extent and solidity of credit, the circulation and increase of capital; which forms and upholds the national character, and sets in motion all the springs which actuate the great mass of the community through all its various descriptions'.[2] He affirmed that all classes derived their well-being from the free form of government, and he urged the House always to remember with pride and affection the root cause of the nation's prosperity:

> The laborious industry of those useful and extensive classes (who will, I trust, be in a peculiar degree this day the object of the consideration of the House) the peasantry and yeomanry of the country; the skill and ingenuity of the artificer; the experiments and improvements of the wealthy proprietor of land; the bold speculations and successful adventures of the opulent merchant and enterprising manufacturer; these are all to be traced to the same source, and all derive from hence both their encouragement and their reward. On this point, therefore, let us principally fix our attention, let us preserve this first and more essential object, and every other is in our power! Let us remember that love of the constitution, though it acts as a sort of natural instinct in the hearts of Englishmen, is strengthened by reason and reflection, and every day confirmed by experience; that it is a constitution which we do not merely admire from traditional reverence, which we do not flatter from prejudice or habit, but which we cherish and value, because we know that it practically secures the tranquillity and welfare both of individuals and of the public, and provides, beyond any other frame of government which has ever existed, for the real and useful ends which form at once the only true foundation and only rational object of all political societies.[3]

This is not the language of panic or extremism, and Pitt saw the constitution as a source of vigour and vitality in the community. The British form of government was justified by its results, and if it were to be destroyed then the welfare of the nation would be destroyed with it. Although the reverence for the constitution which was so prominent a characteristic of eighteenth-century life may seem exaggerated to modern susceptibilities, Pitt and his contemporaries believed that it was validated by experience, and when they sought to secure the constitution against French ideas they believed that they were defending a way of life, not some cold abstraction.

This helps to explain why the government tended to follow opinion rather than to anticipate it, and why under both Pitt and Liverpool there was a general reluctance to make innovations in constitutional law and practice. Men who were obsessed by a reverence for the constitution, and who were convinced of its unique nature, were as reluctant to make innovations of a reactionary character as they were to yield to radical demands. They preferred the initiative to be taken by loyalist associations, rather than by direct legislative action. Initially they hoped to stem the tide of French influence and radical activity by exhortation rather than by intervention. They connived at the birth of loyalist associations, believing that public opinion was more likely to respond to voluntary pressures than to official interference. Only when they felt that such an approach was no longer adequate to meet a changing situation did they introduce laws such as the Treasonable Practices and Seditious Meetings Acts, or suspend Habeas Corpus. By their very nature these acts of government were seen as temporary and regrettable expedients. They were never intended to be permanent.

Pitt made this clear when replying to Fox during the debate on the suspension of Habeas Corpus on 17 May 1794:

> The honourable gentleman had carried his argument so far as to say that, if the Bill passed, all the rights of the people, and all the privileges of parliament, would be at once destroyed – a doctrine which he could never admit, by whatever ability or eloquence it might be supported. On that point it was important for the consideration of the House. . . . that the Bill was limited in its duration; that it was but a temporary measure, adapted to a present existing evil, and was to continue in force for little more than six months; and that it invested the executive government with a temporary discretionary power, to imprison suspected persons for that limited time, without bringing them to trial – all the rights of the people, and all the privileges of parliament, remaining uninterruptedly the same.[4]

When debating the Seditious Meetings Bill on the occasion of its second reading in the House of Commons on 17 November 1795, Pitt combined an appeal to precedent with reassurances about the temporary nature of the legislation proposed:

One great recommendation of this temporary measure was that it strictly adhered to the examples of former times; and while it added to the general security, made no innovation in the constitution, nor in the smallest degree weakened the spirit of the laws. Our ancestors, in times of danger, and even in that interval which took place between the deposition and restoration of the monarchy, adhered, as much as so peculiar a situation would admit, to ancient forms, and conducted the public business by means of both Houses of Parliament, if that assembly could properly be called a parliament, when it was actually deprived of one of its component parts.[5]

He denied that the government intended to deprive the people of the right to petition parliament for the redress of grievances, but he criticized those who seemed intent on stirring up agitation and goading people to bring forward irresponsible petitions. It was essential that the country should always look to parliament, and to parliament alone, for the redress of grievances, and it was also necessary for the mass of the people to have the confidence that if their complaints were proved to be well founded and 'practically remediable' parliament would act on their behalf. What was being debated was not a matter of right, but rather of how judiciously such a right might be exercised in difficult and unusual circumstances: 'It behoved them to take care that menaces were not conveyed to parliament under the pretext of petitions, and that they were not made the vehicles of indirect libels, fabricated at meetings convened under the pretence of very different objects, by men whose real purpose it was to undermine and subvert the constitution'.[6]

What was at issue between Pitt and Fox was whether the situation in the country was sufficiently grave to warrant even a temporary limitation of traditional privileges: both were agreed on the virtues of the constitution. There was a strong element of political calculation in the way they fenced for supremacy in debate and in the arguments they used. What was not in dispute was the unparalleled grandeur and utility of the British constitution.

This same determination to preserve the British pattern of government was as strongly evident during Liverpool's ministry as it had been during Pitt's tenure of office. When Liverpool spoke on 16 June 1817 during the debate on the suspension of Habeas Corpus his arguments were similar to those of Pitt, though he lacked Pitt's eloquence. With considerable regret he affirmed that the power of detention without trial was necessary to cure 'existing evils', for it had a deterrent effect: 'It operated not merely in the case of the persons detained, but also on all persons who were conscious that they ought to be suspected'. It was therefore 'a measure of mercy' which 'every good man should hail as the safeguard of his property and his freedom'. To identify the security of property with the enjoyment of freedom was a wholly eighteenth-century assumption, but Liverpool had earlier made a crucial distinction between crimes against property, which were devoid of any political significance, and those which were politically motivated. It was important not to apply a stronger remedy than a particular evil required, and where disturbances consisted of 'nothing more than an unlawful conspiracy for the destruction of frames and machinery' the government had not called for the suspension of Habeas Corpus.[7] Similarly, when Sidmouth was defending the Seditious Meetings Bills on 28 April 1817 he denied that the government wished to stifle all public debate: 'He had no objection to state that, according to his belief, neither the framers of the Act, nor those who supported it, ever intended that it should put an end to all political discussion whatever.'[8]

The distinction between the right to petition for the redress of grievances, and the way in which this right was exercised, was one which was never more clearly put than by Sidmouth when he was discharging Samuel Bamford after his examination before the Privy Council. In Bamford's own words:

> Lord Sidmouth said, 'Mr Bamford, I hope you are now before me for the last time. You will be discharged on conditions which will be read over to you; the same conditions which others of your fellow prisoners who have been discharged have accepted. I assure you I feel great pleasure in thus restoring you to your family.' I said, I hoped nothing would be proposed to me which was at variance with my political principles, as I could not forego any rights to which, as an Englishman, I was entitled. His Lordship could not desire me to give up the only right I had exercised; namely, the right of petition.
>
> His Lordship said; 'Nothing will be proposed to you which an honest and a good man need object to. We are not averse to the subject petitioning for a redress of grievances; it is the manner in which that right has been exercised which we condemn; a right may be exercised in such a way that it becomes a wrong, and then we must object to it. Mr Bamford, there are three things which I would have you to impress seriously on your mind. The first is, that the present distress of the country arises from unavoidable circumstances; the second that His Majesty's ministers will do all they can to alleviate such distress; and, thirdly, no violence, of whatever description, will be tolerated, but it will be put down with a very strong hand. I wish you well; I assure you I wish you well; and I hope this is the last time I shall ever see you on an occasion like the present.[9]

The extent to which the government faced a real revolutionary threat, or panicked in the face of the unknown, or cynically exploited uncertainty and confusion for their own partisan purposes, are questions which are still hotly debated. At one time it was common for historians to claim that the governments of Pitt and Liverpool over-reacted. The dominant mood among English radicals was thought to be so law-abiding that the suspension of Habeas Corpus or the introduction of the six Acts were seen as evidence of government hysteria. More recently, with at least some indication that a genuinely revolutionary tradition may have been more influential among the minority of extreme radicals than was once thought, the debate has shifted to slightly different ground. Although the consensus among historians is that there was no imminent danger of revolution in England, either in the 1790s or the post-Waterloo years, the reaction of the government is seen as more credible. The ministers were often ill informed about the state of opinion in the country, and it was easy for men who feared the worst to take radical agitators too seriously or, in the 1790s, to see French spies everywhere. There were times when the ministers' nerve seemed strained almost to breaking. When Pitt heard of the famous 'dagger plot', which Burke exploited with melodramatic effect in the House of Commons, he confessed that 'by this time tomorrow we may not have a hand to act or a tongue to utter', and in 1820 the Cato Street Conspiracy seemed to confirm the most lurid suspicions of the day. Nevertheless, too much should not be made of instances such as these. To suggest that Pitt and Liverpool conducted public affairs in a mood of permanent terror is as misleading as the imputation that Castlereagh was out of his mind in 1819. Whatever belief the ministers may have had in the likelihood of any revolutionary outburst they were politically astute in exploiting such a belief, especially in their relations with the House of Commons. Since the propertied classes were fearful of threats to property the governments of the day had to recognize that such fears were a potent force in forming opinion, and any failure to come to terms with the feelings of the political nation would have eroded the governments' own standing.

Probably no single generalization is adequate to meet all the facts, and it is difficult to know just what the facts were in many of the situations that pressed so intensely on the governments' attention. Although the majority of English reformers were constitutionalists, some radicals behaved with a lack of discretion which seriously damaged their own cause, as the Reverend Christopher Wyvill had foreseen, and no government could afford to ignore information which indicated any possibility of disorder. The famous 'insurrection' of 1792 has recently been examined, and Mr Clive Emsley has concluded that in November 1792 some members of Pitt's government probably believed that something was planned for December. When the expected trouble in London did not occur Pitt and his colleagues became more sceptical about the information they had received, while remaining aware of the utility of feeding such information to the press. In this way the spirits of the loyalists could be enhanced and the dangers of Jacobinism underlined, and Portland and the conservative Whigs found it convenient to allow such reports to be widely disseminated, since they were convinced that the government should take action to secure the country against 'the threats which they perceived from Jacobinism both at home and abroad'.[10] The governments of Pitt and Liverpool may be defended, not because of the existence or otherwise of an objective threat to public order, but because their decisions were judicious on the basis of the information available to them, even when a fuller knowledge of the facts reveals the defective nature of the evidence submitted to them.

But even during the so-called anti-Jacobin scare Pitt was not opposed to all change. Certainly, he set his face against all institutional changes (at least in England) during the war with France, but the strange episode of his abortive Poor Relief Bill is a reminder that he was not insensitive to the social problems of the day. In February 1796, when replying to an attempt by Whitbread to fix minimum wages, Pitt dealt with the problem of poverty in a spirit which was neither reactionary nor hard-hearted. 'The present situation of the labouring poor in this country was certainly not such as could be wished upon any principle, either of humanity or policy. That class had of late been exposed to hardships which they had all concurred in lamenting, and were equally actuated by a desire to remove.'[11] He assured the House that in general writers on political economy and the political experience of the most advanced societies warned against any artificial attempt to interfere with commerce, industry and trade. There had been instances where interference had shackled industry, and where the best intentions had produced pernicious effects. He went on: 'It was indeed the most absurd bigotry in asserting the general principle to exclude the exception; but trade, industry and barter would always find their own level, and be impeded by regulations which violated their natural operation, and deranged their proper effect.'[12] What he advocated was not some incidental interference with wages, but a reform of the poor laws. He believed that they fettered the mobility of labour, and that they had substituted a system of abuses in the place of the evils which they were meant to redress. He favoured the encouragement of friendly societies, so that when men were in work they could use their savings to provide for future distress. He argued the case strongly for the establishment of parish schools of industry: 'experience had shown how much could be done by the industry of children and the advantages of early employing them in such branches of manufactures as they are able to execute'. In this way relief to the poor would be converted into an encouragement to industry, instead of being a premium to idleness and a school for sloth. He also favoured abolishing the law which prohibited relief where any visible property remained. 'That degrading condition', he said, 'should be withdrawn. No temporary occasion should force a British subject to part with the last shilling of his little capital, and compel him to descend to a state of wretchedness from which he could never recover.' Small capital sums might be advanced to the industrious worker, in order to help him to provide for himself, the loans being repaid in two or three years. If the system of poor relief were to be changed he favoured an improved method of inspection by parishes or hundreds, with an annual report being submitted to parliament: 'There should be an annual budget opened, containing the details of the whole system of the poor laws, by which the legislature would show that they had a constant and watchful eye upon the interests of the poorest and most neglected part of the community.'[13] In November 1796 Pitt introduced a Bill giving effect to these ideas. As well as child allowances and the supplementation of wages it provided for primitive old-age pensions and the establishment of schools of industry, even for the provision of a cow to the destitute. The Bill was ferociously attacked and was withdrawn for amendment. It never reappeared. Although it would be a gross exaggeration to claim that it was an enlightened scheme of social reform, or a viable alternative to the Poor Law Amendment Act of 1834, it suggests that Pitt was less fearful of change than the prevalent image of the 'anti-Jacobin' implies.

Similarly, although Liverpool's government has sometimes been depicted as if the ministers were as deferential to new economic theories as they were fearful of reform, considerations of political expediency counted for more than doctrinal consistency. In general Liverpool was sceptical about government intervention. He believed that in normal circumstances it was best to allow trade and industry to find their own level. Sidmouth was convinced that man could not create abundance where Providence had inflicted scarcity: hardship and distress could not be abolished by Act of Parliament. But this does not mean that the ministers were lacking in compassion for the poor. Sidmouth was in many ways sympathetic to the economic grievances of the striking seamen in the northeast in 1815, and the ministers were prepared to make exceptions to their general rule about legislative interference.[14] The Poor Employment Bill of 1817 advanced money for the carrying on of public works and for the relief of the parish poor rates. In the debate on the Bill in the House of Lords on 10 June 1817 Liverpool made clear his own devotion to the principle of non-intervention and his belief that it was judicious to make intelligent exceptions to the general rule.[15]

The advancement of money for public works would be of particular benefit by affording employment to those for whose labour there was no current demand. If relief was provided in only a few cases the Bill would serve a useful purpose. The country was in an especially difficult economic situation because of a combination of circumstances – the depreciation of landed property, a depression in manufactures and trade, and a very bad harvest – and this 'peculiarly called for the special interposition of parliament'. Though time was the only effectual remedy a measure of temporary relief would perform an essential service. Whatever the limits of their legislation – and the ministers were aware of them – there is no evidence here of either callous indifference to suffering or any inclination to exploit economic distress as a means of keeping the poor in their place.

The Catholic question throws an interesting light on the complexity of attitudes taken by members of the Pitt and Liverpool governments to one of the major issues of the day. Where political necessity and national security demanded changes in the established political structure Pitt was prepared to act, and although at the time of the passing of the Act of Union he was careful to dissociate the measure from any broader consideration of parliamentary reform the Union's significance as a constitutional innovation should not be overlooked. Under the pressure of events Pitt was prepared to contemplate changes which the majority of his contemporaries regarded as fundamental. Pitt had long believed that timely and judicious concessions would make the Irish Catholics less vulnerable to the impact of Jacobinical ideas. It was chiefly because of the insistence of the Westminster government that civil rights and the parliamentary franchise were granted to the Catholics of Ireland in 1792 and 1793. The Act of Union was primarily a response to the rebellion of 1798 and its aftermath. Pitt was convinced that the Anglo-Irish ruling class was no longer capable of governing Ireland. With the Scots Union as his model he believed that a parliamentary union would be conducive to the more liberal consideration of the Irish problem. In Pitt's mind the Union was part of a comprehensive policy which involved religious concessions and commercial reforms.

Pitt had made this plain in his speech in the House of Commons on 31 January 1799. He was explicit in indicating the constraints within which the government worked, but there was no mistaking the general drift of his argument:

> Without anticipating the discussion, or saying how soon or how late it may be fit to discuss it, two propositions are indisputable. First, when the conduct of the Catholics shall be such as shall make it safe for the Government to admit them to the participation of the privileges granted to those of the established religion, and when the temper of the times shall be favourable to such a measure – when these events take place, it is obvious that such a question may be agitated in an imperial United Parliament with much greater safety than it could be in a separate Legislature. In the second place, I think it certain that, even for whatever period it may be thought necessary after the Union to withhold from the Catholics the enjoyment of those advantages, many of the objections which at present arise out of their situation would be removed if the Protestant Legislature were no longer separate and local but general and imperial; and the Catholics themselves would at once feel a mitigation of the most goading and irritating of their present causes of complaint.[16]

Those who opposed Catholic emancipation regarded it as a betrayal of the Glorious Revolution. But Pitt and Castlereagh believed that

Catholic relief was a fulfilment of the Constitution, not a denial of it. Castlereagh emphasized that the exclusion of Catholics from public life was a temporary expedient which the circumstances of the seventeenth century had made necessary. He argued that the constitution was capable of further development, its principles being given more appropriate expression in a changing environment. After the defeat of emancipation in 1801 Castlereagh wrote a long paper which expounded his own understanding of the Catholic question, and it provides us with a valuable summary of the Pittite attitude to constitutional reform.

Castlereagh admitted the force of several of the main objections to relief: that the repeal of the Test Act would constitute a breach in the Revolution Settlement; that essential safeguards to the Protestant Establishment in Church and State would appear to be surrendered; and that the admission of Catholics to Parliament and to most of the higher offices of state would make the limitation of the succession to the Crown to Protestants all the more of an anomaly. His reply was to draw a sharp distinction between the principles of the constitution and the particular securities which had been necessary to defend these principles at certain times:

> Although our constitution reverences the principles which have governed, and the provisions which had effected, the establishment of our liberties at certain memorable eras, and at none more than the Revolution, yet . . . nothing in our system is absolutely unchangeable; that the public good being the only consideration, the entire question of means must always be open to the supreme power of the legislature; that the principle of Catholic exclusion, as acted upon at the Revolution, was only the means – the liberties of the people and the preservation of the Constitution in Church and State the end – to which that measure was directed. If that exclusion has ceased to be necessary to the security of our liberties and to the stability of the State, inasmuch as the necessity of exclusion at all is in itself a misfortune, it may be laid aside without shaking the principles then contended for, as it may, and must be resumed, should circumstances again render it of the same expediency as it was at the period alluded to. [17]

Since many Catholics had benefitted from the growing wealth of the country, as well as from the relaxation of various old-fashioned laws, Castlereagh urged that it was all the more reasonable to admit them to the political nation. To do so would unite all men of property in defence of the constitution. To deny Catholics a legitimate means of political activity would heighten the risk that they would identify with Jacobinism: comprehension within the State would eliminate this danger. Here Castlereagh was resorting to an argument which some Whigs were later to use for admitting new forms of property to the political nation by timely parliamentary reform. The basic concern was the same in both cases: the preservation of the traditional constitution by making it harmonize with contemporary developments.

Pitt and Castlereagh never considered the Catholic question in terms of natural right. In May 1810 Castlereagh assured the House of Commons that the Union had been designed to put an end to what he described as the 'anomalies' of distinct legislatures in Britain and Ireland. It had been intended to open up the way to 'a more comprehensive and liberal system of government'. He regretted the premature and irresponsible agitation of Catholic claims. He remained opposed to the continued exclusion of Catholics from public life, but Catholics must recognize that they would have to make concessions in their turn if the goodwill and consent of Protestants were to be achieved: 'without sentiments of mutual conciliation and confidence previously established he feared a precipitate incorporation would only tend to excite political contention and animosity.'[18] Castlereagh saw *both* Protestant and Catholic as making concessions for *mutual* security. On 4 June 1815 he complained to Edward Cooke of the difficulties facing any measure of Catholic relief. Sadly, Catholic attitudes had contributed to the defeat of their cause: 'The tide is now turned strongly against them, nor will it be arrested in its course without activity on their part to make a character. They must positively determine to make love to the Protestants—making war will not do, nor will secession and inactivity reinstate the cause where it was.'[19]

But Pitt and Castlereagh represented a minority opinion, both within their own party and in the country, on the Catholic issue. More typical was the robust, no-nonsense approach of Lord Eldon. On 17 May 1819, in a debate in the House of Lords on a motion calling for an inquiry into the laws imposing religious disabilities, Eldon made a speech which summed up the Protestant case. He warned against the divided loyalty which afflicted all Catholics because of their allegiance to the pope, and reminded the House that in the past Catholics had systematically sought the destruction of the national Church. There was no evidence that they had changed their principles. He affirmed the inviolability of the Revolution Settlement, but he was anxious to make a distinction between securities for the political establishment and anything which smacked of religious persecution: at the time of the Revolution it had been resolved 'that this country should have a Protestant king, a Protestant parliament and a Protestant government', and, Eldon continued,

> Such was the great principle which parliament ought always to have in view, holding in due reverence that right of all men, derived to them from God, that they should not be persecuted for religious opinions. When religious opinions were attended with political effects injurious to that society to which their professors belonged, that society had a right to exclude them from offices of trust and emolument. Under a conviction of the absolute necessity of securing a Protestant establishment to these kingdoms in order

to render them free and happy, their Lordships' ancestors had enacted that no king who was either himself a Catholic, or who was married to a Catholic princess, should ever sit upon the British throne. The other disqualifying laws served only as a part of the mechanism . . . of which the constitution was composed.[20]

The question was whether the House would stand by the constitution which had secured liberty, or whether they wished to revert to a previous state of affairs.

It was not the mere name, but the substance of the Protestant religion that he wished to preserve. Indifference to religion generally led to great temporal evils, and if for no other reason, at least for this, ought the Protestant religion to be supported, that it would be always a barrier against oppression, and a nursing mother to liberty and freedom. . . . He repeated that any admission of supremacy not within the realm, but out of the realm, was ecclesiastical usurpation, and precisely that against which it was the object of the law to provide. It was that species of tyranny as well as usurpation which must terminate fatally for the liberties of the people.[21]

Eldon denied that any of the proposed securities were adequate. The laws as they stood provided for the interests of Anglican and Dissenter alike: 'The civil and religious liberties of the one were best maintained by the Establishment, and the civil and religious liberties of the other by a toleration as free as the safety of the State would allow.' However rigid Eldon's defence of the constitution was, he believed that the English constitution was unique in preserving liberty with order. Where he differed from Pitt and Castlereagh was in his understanding of how best to secure the constitutional liberties which both they and he valued so highly. Since Eldon is usually seen as the typical High Tory it is significant that the threat posed by the Roman Church to both political and religious liberty counted for so much in his opposition to it. Nor were those who opposed Catholic relief necessarily bigoted. The anti-Catholic case is so reminiscent of an age whose assumptions are entirely foreign to those of the twentieth century that a special effort of imagination has to be made to understand it. Liverpool shared Eldon's distrust of the Catholic's divided allegiance, but though he opposed Catholic emancipation he was willing to give Catholics the vote and to admit them to the magistracy. He had passed a Relief Bill for Dissenters in 1812. He believed that judicious toleration was an intelligent means of securing the interests of the Church of England. Just as the supporters of Catholic relief founded their case on political arguments, so its opponents were primarily concerned with political considerations. Sharing a common desire to preserve the Constitution, they differed in their understanding of the best mode of doing so.

The Catholic question is revealing, not only because it throws into greater prominence Pitt's concern for Ireland and his understanding

of the way in which the defence of the constitution could be associated
with the initiation, not the mere acceptance, of change, but also because
it demonstrates the continued importance of the Crown, and the com-
promises and tensions which were an inescapable accompaniment of a
broadly based administration. The place of the Crown in government
was still a controversial issue. Deference to the king and a respect for the
constitutional rights of the Crown had brought Pitt to power in 1783.
Like Shelburne, Pitt had defended the king's prerogatives, and particularly his right to choose his ministers, against the ideas of party and
collective responsibility, which had been advocated, for reasons of conviction and convenience, by Fox. Despite the controversial nature of
George III's intervention over the India Bill and the subsequent dismissal of the Fox – North Coalition, the election of 1784 had been a
remarkable vindication of the king's political judgment, and in some
respects it was even more of a victory for George III than for Pitt.
Although the opposition Whigs exaggerated the dangers of the
influence of the Crown, and although the influence of the Crown
declined during the first 20 years of George III's reign, the attitude
adopted by politicians towards the prerogatives of the Crown continued
to be a primary test of political alignment until the end of George III's
reign, and even beyond it. As an advocate of the traditional notion of the
rights of the Crown, and a minister who was respectful and deferential
towards the king, Pitt was compelled to resign because of George III's
hostility to Catholic relief. The defender of the rights of the Crown
became a victim of the prejudices of the king. But there can be little
doubt that most of his subjects concurred in George III's conviction that
Catholic emancipation was a dangerous step. Some historians have
claimed that Pitt ought to have handled the affair more deftly, but it is
hard to see that there was any real chance of carrying Catholic relief in
1801, given the intensity of the opposition which it aroused. If George
III had not had a viable alternative minister in Addington it would have
been harder for the king to have pushed the issue to the point of com-
pelling Pitt to resign. Although the king exaggerated the extent to which
his Coronation Oath ruled out any possibility of his consenting to
Catholic relief, his sincerity was unquestioned, and possibly he hoped to
retain Pitt in office if the minister could be persuaded to yield on the
Catholic question. But the depth of the king's opposition was equalled
only by his determination not to contemplate any wavering on the issue,
and the affair is a reminder that even a government of national unity,
comprehensive in its membership, dedicated to the preservation of the
constitution, involved in the waging of the greatest war in the nation's
history, and headed by the most experienced minister of the time, could
break up if the essential prerequisite of royal confidence were removed.
In 1807 the defeat of the Ministry of All the Talents on a more limited

proposal for Catholic relief was a further instance of the uncanny way in which George III's prejudices mirrored those of the nation.

The Catholic crisis also revealed the limits which still operated upon the functioning of the cabinet government. By George III's accession to the throne the membership of the cabinet had come to be identified with the major offices of state: First Lord of the Treasury, the Lord Chancellor, the Chancellorship of the Exchequer, the Secretaries of State, the Lord Privy Seal, the Lord President of the Council. The old struggle between the nominal and the efficient cabinet had ended in the victory of the notion that the cabinet should be limited to those who held the most eminent public offices. But this did not mean that cabinet government in the sense generally understood in the twentieth century, or even in the Victorian period, had come into being. Only during Liverpool's administration did it come to be firmly established that collective resignation would normally follow the dismissal or resignation of the prime minister. The younger Pitt had not been able to rely on the loyalty of his colleagues to this extent – as the Catholic crisis showed in 1801. In this sense Liverpool's ministry marks an important stage in the development of cabinet government. But the range of collective responsibility on matters of policy was limited, just as it had been throughout the first of Pitt's administrations. Pitt had found it necessary to allow his colleagues to take differing views on the reform of parliament, the abolition of the slave trade, and Catholic relief. His ministry would not have survived had he not done so. In 1801 he had hoped that the majority of the cabinet could be persuaded to support Catholic emancipation before he raised the issue with the king. Loughborough's behaviour rendered this tactic irrelevant, but all the Lord Chancellor did was to exploit the known realities of the situation to his own advantage. He did not create the divisions within the cabinet any more than he created the king's prejudices or his devotion to the letter of the Coronation Oath.

Likewise, Liverpool found it necessary for the Catholic question to remain 'open' during his own ministry. This was advantageous to the conservative side in the controversy, for a divided cabinet could hardly take the initiative, and the examples of 1801 and 1807 were hardly encouraging even for those who desired a positive approach to the problem. When Castlereagh and Canning cooperated with Grattan in seeking an agreement which would make a compromise solution possible they could do so only as individuals, much as Pitt had supported the reform of parliament in the 1780s. Several important members of the government – Liverpool, Eldon and Sidmouth – were opposed to Catholic relief, and among the promising younger men Peel made a reputation for himself as an unflinching 'Protestant'. It was Catholic relief, not the reform of parliament, which was the really dangerous issue for the Tory party, and the Tories eventually foundered over the

Catholic question. Wellington's insensitive handling of the Canningite and Huskissonite elements in the party had already eroded the broadness of the base on which Liverpool's long predominance had been built up, and the apparent about-turn executed by Peel and Wellington on Catholic relief outraged the Ultra Tories. But if comprehensiveness was part of the reason for Liverpool's success his ministry had come under stress whenever the delicate balance between the friends and foes of Catholic relief was likely to be disturbed. This may have been one reason for Castlereagh's anxiety over the promotion of Peel in 1821, and certainly the chief reason for Goderich's failure to form a viable ministry after Canning's death was the difficulty of keeping the balance between 'Catholics' and 'Protestants'. Goderich sought to follow Liverpool's example by making approaches to some of the Whigs, of whom Lord Holland was the most congenial. But when this provoked the opposition of Herries, the Chancellor of the Exchequer, and roused the suspicions of George IV, the fate of Goderich's ministry was sealed. Finance, foreign policy and public order were the issues on which something like habitual collective responsibility could be expected, but confidence in the first minister was still the fundamental condition of ministerial success.

Some caution is necessary when assessing the development of the premiership during this period. Pitt exercised a remarkable dominance over his cabinets. He tended to depend on a small circle of colleagues with whom he felt particularly close. In the 1790s the most important ministers were Dundas and Grenville, while towards the end of his life younger men such as Canning and Castlereagh were becoming more closely identified with Pitt. But this personal pre-eminence was not wholly synonymous with the development of the premiership. In 1803 Pitt had a famous conversation with Dundas, in which he stated

> not less pointedly and decidedly, his sentiments with regard to the absolute necessity there is in the conduct of the affairs of this country, that there should be an avowed and real minister, possessing the chief weight in the council, and the principal place in the confidence of the king. In that respect there can be no rivality or division of power. That power must rest in the person generally called the first minister, and that minister ought, he thinks, to be the person at the head of the finances. He knows, to his own comfortable experience, that notwithstanding the abstract truth of that general proposition, it is noways incompatible with the most cordial concert and mutual exchange of advice and intercourse amongst the different branches of executive departments; but still if it should come unfortunately to such a radical difference of opinion that no spirit of conciliation or concession can reconcile, the sentiments of the minister must be allowed and understood to prevail, leaving the other members of the administration to act as they may conceive themselves conscientiously called upon to act under such circumstances.[22]

This statement had often been assumed to be a description of Pitt's attitude and conduct during his first administration. This is misleading. In some ways Pitt was commenting on those defects of conventional practice which had become cruelly evident during the crisis over Catholic emancipation. Pitt had revised his position in the aftermath of Loughborough's behaviour. He was now preoccupied with preventing any repetition of such conduct and he was willing to put on a more regular basis what he had previously been content to exercise in a personal manner.

But Pitt remained deferential to the Crown. He allowed George III to extract from him a promise never to raise the Catholic question again in his lifetime, and in 1804, despite his own wish to construct a broadly based, all-party government – a government more comprehensive in its scope than that of 1794 – he found it impossible to persuade the king to accept Fox; this, in turn, meant that he could not persuade men such as Grenville and Grey to take office without Fox. Pitt's response was not to decline George III's invitation. Faced with disappointments and difficulties he became all the more determined to prove his critics wrong. He had not changed his opinion on the necessity of allowing to the king a real choice in the appointment of his ministers. The prime minister might propose names, might argue for them as vigorously as he could, but it was still for the king to make the final decision. The influence of the Crown had declined, but the king's will was of primary importance in the making of ministries.

In some ways Liverpool was in a stronger position than Pitt. He had the advantage that George IV was less skilful, less determined and less perceptive than even the ageing George III had been. Nevertheless, George IV shared more of his father's prejudices as he grew older, and he was equally committed to defending and upholding the rights of the Crown. But he found it harder than his father had done to thwart his ministers and even when he writhed under Liverpool's tutelage he knew that he had no alternative minister. He had antagonized his old friends, the opposition Whigs, in 1812, and his detestation of them was exceeded only by their contempt for him. The knowledge that George IV was opposed to Catholic emancipation put heart into the Protestant camp, but when the Clare election brought matters to a head George IV discovered that, unlike his father, he had to give way. This is not to say that the attitude of the Crown was without political import. George IV's unease helped to push Goderich out. During the controversy over the passing of the Great Reform Bill William IV proved an invaluable aid to Grey, despite the king's unhappiness about such matters as the proposed mass creation of peers to pass the Bill. But when William IV got rid of Melbourne in 1834 he found that he could not do for Peel what his father had done for Pitt in 1783. Between 1800 and 1830 the prime minister had become more powerful in his relations with the monarch than had been the case even in the closing years of Pitt's career.

This is to reveal the immense contribution made by Liverpool to the development of the premiership. As long ago as 1941 Professor W. R. Brock wrote, 'Liverpool ended his long career as prime minister in a position as strong as any holder of that office: he fought for the dignity of his position and, though his victories had not always been swift, they had been sure.'[23] The cabinet was a 'more solid body than it had been at any time previously', and this was almost entirely Liverpool's achievement. More recently, Professor Norman Gash has laid even greater stress on Liverpool's firmness, dominance and decisiveness.

> To his public life . . . he brought qualities which in aggregate few prime ministers have equalled. In grasp of principles, mastery of detail, discernment of means, and judgment of individuals he was almost faultless. Cautious and unhurried in weighing a situation, he was prompt and decisive when the time came for action. In debate he was not only informed, lucid and objective, but conspicuously honest. . . . Though his colleagues might occasionally disagree with him, he never lost their respect or their trust. He repaid them in full. He never dismissed a minister; he was never ungrateful or disloyal. Kindly by temperament, he had an instinctive tact in dealing with others.[24]

Despite the number of talented men who served under him – Castlereagh, Canning, Wellington, Peel, Robinson, Palmerston, to name only the most obvious – Liverpool was master in his cabinet. The catastrophe which overtook the Tory party after his retirement is a measure of his achievement. This achievement was all the more astonishing when the unprecedented range of problems facing the government during the Liverpool years is borne in mind, and when it is recalled that Liverpool lacked the resources of patronage which had been available to eighteenth-century ministers and the disciplined party organization which was to be so significant in the hands of his nineteenth-century successors.

Although Liverpool had a special regard for the landed interest, believing that its welfare was essential for national prosperity, he was capable of recognizing the importance of other interests and part of his success lay in convincing financial and commercial interests that his government was as sympathetic to their problems as to those of agriculture. Anxiety about agriculture, and the government's vulnerability in the House of Commons, explained the Corn Law of 1815. Similarly, the defeat over the income tax in 1816 exposed the government's weakness when it antagonized backbench MPs, and despite Castlereagh's justifiable complaint about the House of Commons' ignorant impatience of taxation, Liverpool knew that he had to accept the decision of the House, even when it went against him. Peterloo, the Six Acts, and the Cato Street Conspiracy also seemed to confirm that the ministry was an aristocratic caste, repressing legitimate agitation with the ferocity of frightened and myopic reactionaries. But recent work on these questions has thrown into greater relief the restraint of the government. Peterloo was precisely the sort of incident the government sought to avoid. Sidmouth was of the opinion that the magistrates should try to disperse crowds only if they committed acts of violence, and Donald Read has made it plain that Liverpool and his colleagues never desired or precipitated anything like what happened at Peterloo: 'If the Manchester magistrates had followed the spirit of the Home Office there would never have been a "massacre".'[25] In private the ministers were critical of the Manchester magistrates; in public they felt they had to support them, since they knew how dependent they were on the magistrates for the maintenance of public order. Dr J. E. Cookson has emphasized the restraint of the Six Acts, and the way in which the government deftly appealed to dominant opinion within the political nation, making the Whigs appear uncertain in their own understanding of the situation:

> Great care was taken to preserve the right of assembly as much as possible. Only meetings deliberating on 'any public grievance or any matter in Church and State' was to come within the act's purview, and though notice of time and place was made obligatory so that the magistrates might alter both at their discretion, the power was very limited, just sufficient, it was hoped, to make insurrection through simultaneous meetings next to impossible. Bills prohibiting unauthorized military training and permitting the seizure of arms 'dangerous to the public peace' were the natural corollary.[26]

Dr Cookson has made the acute observation that Liverpool and his colleagues were charged with reaction because they seemed to be opposing those popular forces – presumably those calling for the reform of parliament and the repeal of the Corn Laws – which eventually triumphed. But what this attitude overlooks 'is that, on the whole, they managed to keep the support of those popular forces which were triumphant in the immediate future.'[27] It is surely one of the ironies of historical interpretation that success ensured future misrepresentation.

The truth is that to see late eighteenth and early nineteenth-century governments in terms of a 'reactionary' versus 'progressive' alignment is wholly inappropriate. It imposes a false scale of values on the understanding of past events. The approach is false whether one applies the standards of Cobdenite Liberalism or late Victorian imperialism or modern ideas of Social Democracy or welfare economics. Liverpool's government believed in keeping expenditure down: so did Whig administrations. Economy, the purification of the political system, the defence of the constitution, the maintenance of law and order, the pursuit of peace – these were the preoccupations of both Tories and Whigs. If they differed about parliamentary reform or Catholic emancipation the differences were often ones of emphasis. The fact that Ripon, Palmerston and Melbourne learned their trade as Tories and later served under Grey is evidence that no unbridgeable ideological gulf separated the two parties. The disagreements were often about the most judicious means of preserving the inheritance which had been bequeathed by the heirs of the Glorious Revolution. When politicians invoked new ideas, this was often because they happened to confirm the wisdom of what they intended doing anyway. If Boyd Hilton is right even those Liberal Tories who condoned the move towards free trade were more concerned with getting a static model of the economy working 'without friction' than with economic growth: 'like mercantilists they saw the main task as being to preserve wealth.'[28] The new science of political economy could conveniently be quoted whenever a government had decided to do nothing as the best way of playing safe. The interplay between theory and practice was an ambiguous one, but for politicians their experience of proven political realities was always a surer guide. The famous ambivalence of the Liverpool era – looking backward to the eighteenth century in some ways, looking forward to the great days of Victorian England in others – is more subtle and more elusive than was once thought.

But again contemporaries would have put a different stamp on their evaluation of Liverpool's achievement. They would have recalled victory in war as the most dramatic and glorious of the ministry's accomplishments. They might have recalled bold new initiatives in foreign policy under Castlereagh and Canning as deserving of more attention than the speculations of theorists or the speeches of demagogues. They would have valued the preservation of the country's traditional institutions, and the sense that both Pitt and Liverpool followed the national interest, rather than more sectional claims, in what they achieved and what they sought to do. When they resisted reform Pitt and Liverpool were fond of citing the idea that the time was not ripe. By winning the war and laying the foundations for prosperity in peace they ensured that one day reform would again become a practicable policy, posing no threat to the country's institutions.

Liverpool and his colleagues knew that their roots lay either among the country gentry or the commercial or professional classes. Liverpool's father was a civil servant; Sidmouth's a country doctor; Eldon's a coal merchant, who had once been an apprentice. Canning's father was an impoverished and disinherited barrister, and his mother an actress. Castlereagh, usually regarded as the most aristocratic of them all, was the offspring of Ulster merchants and country gentlemen. They earned the privileges of power by effort, dedication, intelligence and public service. They were themselves products of the constitution they revered, and in serving it they believed that they served not mere self-interest but the public good. Eldon was fond of claiming that if men of humble origins such as his brother and himself could rise to eminence this was proof that in England the liberty of the individual counted for something. After the battle of Trafalgar, Eldon told Henry Legge that Collingwood and himself were 'memorable instances of the blessings to be derived from the country of our birth and the constitution under which we live'. He went on:

> He and I were class-fellows at Newcastle. We were placed in that school, *because neither his father nor mine could afford to place us elsewhere*; and now if he returns to this country to take his seat in the House of Lords, it will be my duty to express to him, sitting in his place, the thanks of that House (to which neither of us could expect to be elevated) for his eminent services to his country.[29]

Men such as these knew all too well how tenuous were the bonds which held anything like a civilized society together. They knew, much more surely than any historian, just how much brutality, squalor, greed, envy, cruelty and violence there was in eighteenth-century society. They did not think it any part of the politician's task to create an earthly paradise; their knowledge of human nature was too sure for that. As men who had lived through the period of the French Revolution they felt that they had peered into the abyss, and with such an awareness in their minds they could pardonably feel satisfaction in their own achievements. To have secured liberty and property was a worthy life's work for men who, whatever party designation they bore, were the heirs and guardians of the eighteenth-century achievement, believing that liberty and order were compatible, and that in England liberty under the law had become a reality, part of life's tangible experience. They believed that experience was a better guide in politics than abstract speculation, and in much of what they did they demonstrated the truth of this conviction as well as the vitality of the country's representative institutions.

Colloquy on chapter 6
Norman McCord

Holmes inaugurated the discussion by questioning Derry's statement (p. 126) that it was 'the familiar Whig constitution which was being defended' by the governments of Pitt and Liverpool. Could not the constitution be better seen as a kind of consensus which had been reached by the two main parties? After all, the Tories themselves had done a lot to limit monarchy with the Act of Settlement of 1701. Perhaps the Walpole period had seen the emergence of the consensus and by the 1740s the Tories had been able to come to terms with the constitution in Church and State?

Derry replied that Pitt could best be understood as a conservative Whig, and that in 1794 the Portland Whigs saw themselves as rallying to the defence of the Whig constitution during the French wars: 'in the sense that it is a balanced constitution, a limited monarchy, but with a recognition that the Crown had a real role to play, together with the emphasis on parliament as representative of places and interests, it is very main-stream Whig.'

Dickinson brought these two lines of argument together. 'In Walpole's years, the Tories came to terms with a Whiggish constitution, making concessions on limited monarchy, the Hanoverian succession, limited toleration, and sovereign parliament rather than sovereign monarch.' The Whigs too made some concessions: they retreated a bit on the right of resistance because of their fears of Jacobitism, and they did not go as far in toleration of Dissenters as, left to themselves, they might have done. Although the Tories passed the Act of Settlement in 1701, it was not an intrinsically Tory measure, but represented a tactical move because the Tories were scared stiff who was to be on the throne, when William III died. So they adopted almost a Country Whig attitude. If the monarch had been the one they really wanted, they would not have added all those terms limiting the monarch's powers. When the Whigs took over after 1714, the Tories had to choose between Jacobitism and some kind of Whiggish consensus. The consensus once accepted, divisions arose within the consensus, with Pitt, Portland and Liverpool representing the more conservative wing and the Foxites the more liberal wing. The radicals came to form the most important group outside the constitutional consensus.

Holmes agreed with much of this, but pointed out that in their years of power during Anne's reign, the Tories did not seek to modify the Act of Settlement, even though they realized that the Hanoverians were coming – perhaps that was why? Instead of the Tories in the 1790s and 1800s defending a Whig constitution, he saw them as defending the achievements of the governing class as a whole. Dickinson accepted this, provided one recognized that, within the consensus, the Whigs had won more of the battles on constitutional issues.

Holmes also noted that by the 1780s the terms Whig and Tory had come to mean different things from what they had meant earlier. Derry preferred the term 'emergence' of the Tories rather than 're-emergence', since there was much to distinguish the Pitt – Liverpool group from earlier Tory traditions. Pitt never thought of himself as a Tory but always as an independent Whig. Used as a term of abuse in the 1780s and 1790s, 'Tory' came back into the political vocabulary around 1810 as applied to government and the conservative policies of the time.

Discussing the difference of opinion over Catholic emancipation, Speck cited a possible parallel with Strafford and Pym in the 1630s, suggesting that very different concepts of the constitution could be embraced by men who used very much the same language about it. Cannon agreed, adding that it was not enough to say that someone defended the constitution unless one asked what he meant by the constitution he was defending. On Catholic emancipation, Derry and Dickinson agreed that it was perfectly possible for both sides to support the general idea of a Protestant constitution but to differ on how it should be interpreted. (pp. 136 – 7). The pro-Catholics within the Tory party did not advance a case based upon natural rights, but on practical grounds of expediency. Dickinson noted that it was possible to argue that part of the received constitutional tradition was a toleration of Dissent, provided that it did not threaten the state: by the late eighteenth century the Catholics were no longer a threat to the state – indeed, during the period of the French Revolution they were a buttress.

Discussion then turned to the influence of the Crown in the period after 1780 (p. 141). Derry thought that in a broad political sense the influence of the Crown remained strong during the years in which George III was capable of playing an active political role, but that there was a decline in royal influence thereafter. O'Gorman drew attention to two factors of importance here – the rapid development of cabinet procedures from the 1790s onwards, and the emergence of a strong Tory party. By the mid 1790s, Pitt's cabinet was acting much more independently of the monarch than previous ministers had done. From this point of view, an interesting aspect of the royal interventions of 1801 and 1807 was not that the interventions took place, but that they had to come in the form and timing that they took: '1801 and 1807 were

George III's last stand against the encroachments of the cabinet. After 1807 there was little further resistance.' Derry differed somewhat here, if only in emphasis: in 1801 and 1807 the king could claim that Catholic emancipation was a fundamental constitutional question rather than a matter of routine administration, and this allowed him much more of a comeback. O'Gorman stressed the difference between the position of ministers in the latter part of George III's reign and that of persons like Bute and Grafton at the beginning. The government itself had acquired a much greater coherence and more independence: 'Pitt treated the king much more severely than Fox would have done.' Moreover, 'ministers had a Pitt or Liverpool to relate to, to show loyalty towards, rather than the service of the Crown. There was a much wider, more broadly-faceted notion of the politics of government. It was a sort of de-personalization of the very intimate relationship which Bute, Grafton and North had had with the king – and perhaps that Pitt himself had had with the king in his early years in office. The king was no longer 'the first of the party leaders'. Derry and Dickinson thought that the long period of Tory rule and the unprecedented strains of the struggle against France had also helped to forge party and ministerial loyalties.

The later part of the discussion concentrated on Derry's generally sympathetic attitude towards the Tory administrations under survey, with special reference to the questions of reform and repression (pp. 128–32). Dickinson thought that the account given amounted to an apologia and questioned the claim that the Liverpool government was actuated by a desire to serve national rather than sectional interests (p. 144). Speck observed that earlier governments had actively intervened to prevent distress by attempting to control prices and by similar expedients: Stevenson had shown that there was a major change in the government's attitude in this respect.[1] Dickinson pointed out that the Assize of bread and the regulation of apprenticeship collapsed at just this time. Derry did not deny that the government in general moved away from intervention, but this was because it genuinely believed such a policy to be in the national interest: 'how far their perception of the national interest was accurate may, of course, be more open to dispute.' Although there was certainly contemporary criticism of government policies in social and economic matters and alternative strategies were put forward, government policies were broadly supported by the bulk of the nation.

Cannon asked whether it was really in the national interest that the British government had done so little to encourage any major expansion of education in the period? Was it in the national interest to lag so far behind France, Russia, Austria, Prussia, Denmark, all of which had laid the foundations of a State educational system? Holmes and McCord doubted the validity of these continental parallels, noting the limitations enforced by a tax-paying electorate in Britain, while Derry observed that many radicals were strongly opposed to any extension of the functions and powers of the State. McCord remarked that British society was not refusing to build schools in that period, but did not choose to do so through the agency of the State.

Dickinson also attacked Derry on the question of government repression, claiming that restrictive powers against political agitation were more sweeping and more prolonged than they need have been. A government that tried to make traitors out of Horne Tooke and Thomas Hardy, whose sole offence was to advocate parliamentary reform, must be open to severe criticism. Derry, in reply, distinguished between the 1790s and the Liverpool period: if, for example one looked at the Six Acts of 1819 what is surprising is not their savagery but their restraint in the light of the situation. There was less 'panic' in 1815 to 1820 than in the 1790s. While Dickinson claimed that the government's repression was often strenuously criticized at the time, Derry stressed that the government's policies were supported by dominant opinion within the country. McCord asked if the treatment of political offences should not be compared with the other penal practices of the period: compared with the brutal treatment of ordinary offenders, political offenders were rather lightly punished. Dickinson maintained his attack, expressing the view that 'any society ought to cherish its Richard Prices and its Thomas Hardys'.

Derry remained convinced that it was essential to consider the Pitt and Liverpool administrations in a more flexible spirit than that which represented the period as one of unrelieved reaction, seeing everything in terms of a reactionary Tory government confronted by a liberal Whig opposition. In some respects the Tories were more open to new ideas than the Whigs. Tories and Whigs shared common assumptions about society, property and government: the real challenge to the prevalent consensus came from radicals who were either outside the system or impotent within it. But there was a fluidity about political alignments and a range of response on both the Whig and Tory sides which contributed to a complex interplay of opinion on such issues as Catholic emancipation, the poor law, the slave trade and parliamentary reform. While taking the point about society cherishing its critics such as Price and Hardy, it was hardly surprising that the radicals suffered from popular hostility after 1792, and if relations between British radicals and French Jacobins were frequently misunderstood, the radicals themselves contributed to this misunderstanding. British governments between 1790 and 1830 have suffered, far more than their opponents, from the prejudice of historians. Not everything that was done was admirable or defensible, but almost everything was explicable, and what was remarkable was the degree of political skill which was shown in dealing with unprecedented problems, both in winning the war and in adjusting to economic and social change. Britain was victorious in war and able to cope with the problems of peace in such a way as to avoid the revolutions which afflicted so many continental countries. Whatever their limitations, at least some of the credit for this must be given to those who shouldered the burdens of public office at a period of unique difficulty, and whose outlook was so firmly rooted in the heritage of the eighteenth century.

Note on further reading

There is no single work which covers the themes referred to in this essay and, so far as the younger Pitt is concerned, we still await the second volume of John Ehrman's biography, which promises to be definitive. In the meantime, a good deal may still be learned from J. Holland Rose, *William Pitt and the Great War* (1911), while for Pitt and the Poor Law the same author's *Pitt and Napoleon* (1912) should be consulted. A new biography of Liverpool is also badly needed, but Norman Gash's essay in volume one of *The Prime Ministers*, ed. H. van Thal (1974) is useful. Three works are essential reading on the Liverpool ministry: W. R. Brock, *Lord Liverpool and Liberal Toryism* (1941); J. E. Cookson, *Lord Liverpool's Administration, 1815–1822* (1975); and B. Hilton, *Corn, Cash and Commerce: the Economic Policies of the Tory Governments, 1815–1830* (1977). The most balanced treatment of Peterloo is still D. Read, *Peterloo: the Massacre and its Background* (1957). C. Emsley, *British Society and the French Wars* (1979) provides a helpful synthesis of much recent work. For the Catholic issue, G. I. T. Machin, *The Catholic Question in English Politics* (1964) is indispensable. R. J. White, *Waterloo to Peterloo* (1957) deals with both the government and its critics with wit and insight. A number of recent biographies provide much illuminating detail on several of the main issues: D. Gray, *Spencer Perceval* (1963); Elizabeth Longford, *Wellington: Pillar of State* (1972); W. Hinde, *George Canning* (1973); J. W. Derry, *Castlereagh* (1976); P. Ziegler, *Addington* (1965); N. Gash, *Mr Secretary Peel* (1961).

7

Economic and social developments between 1780 and 1830
Norman McCord

The economic and social history of the late eighteenth and early nine-teenth centuries in Britain poses particular problems of interpretation, and it may be helpful to begin with some discussion of the approach to these problems which this essay represents. The 1780–1830 period is complex in itself because of the demographic, economic, social and political changes but in addition study of this period is affected by factors which have little to do with history itself. The absence of trade unions from neolithic society, or the failure of Anglo-Saxon England to develop a national health service, may be regarded as causes for regret, but no competent student would regard such an approach as likely to aid understanding. The dangers of anachronism are less obvious for periods which appear to have more in common with our own; it is important to remember how much the processes of political, economic and social change have accelerated during the century and a half which separate us from 1830.

The problem is compounded by the widespread assumption that some of the important changes under way in the 1780–1830 period possess a continuing relevance to the political and ideological preoccupations of our own society. During those years the economic and social changes summarized in the term 'industrial revolution' made significant pro-gress, including the development of manufacturing and kindred sectors organized on a capitalist basis. The temptation to regard the history of this period as a convenient magazine of ammunition with which to fight our contemporary political battles is one which exists for students of history who belong to varying political camps. A wider temptation is a willingness to regard oneself as a kind of superior court before which the past is haled for judgement. It is often easy to argue that some distasteful past event ought not to have occurred and that something different should have happened. It is healthier, and no less interesting, to accept that the essential task of the student of history is to understand and explain the past as far as the available evidence allows.

It is unlikely that a historian will ever be in possession of a complete range of knowledge relating to the context which he is studying, unlikely indeed that those involved in that context were themselves in such an ideal situation. We may however reasonably assume that what did happen represented the sum of the factors involved, so that to argue that what happened ought not to have happened is merely to advertise a deficiency in understanding.

If we are to try to understand the experience of those who lived during that period, there are a number of key elements which we ought to look for. Certainly we will want to appreciate the individual personal characteristics of those concerned, but they must be considered in the light of the context into which these individuals were born, and the influences to which they were exposed. There is little point in criticizing late eighteenth-century dukes for an absence of egalitarian tendencies, or early nineteenth-century industrialists for a lack of sympathy towards workers' cooperatives. If we wish, for example, to understand the career of Sir Robert Peel, we need to know what kind of individual he was, the nature of the *milieu* into which he was born, and the actual influences to which he was exposed during his career.

In trying to analyse and describe the nature of British society in the 1780–1830 period we are dealing with a complex society containing millions of individuals. Obviously it is necessary to resort to a variety of categories if any meaningful description is to emerge. Yet the problems here are considerable, and the conceptual equipment at our disposal remains seriously defective. A common form of categorizing is to group very large numbers into broad social classes, but it is important to remember that such an approach has serious limitations. The terminology of class can serve as a crude social shorthand, but more detailed applications often involve grave difficulties of interpretation. Even a limited knowledge of recent writings will indicate that historians differ very considerably in their views of the nature and extent of class allegiance in this period. One of the most influential of all the books written in this field during the present century, E. P. Thompson's *The Making of the English Working Class*, laid great stress on the development of working-class solidarity, yet it is not difficult to find other writers less willing to accept this conceptual approach. Consider, for example, this passage from a recent book, dealing here not with the working class, or even with handloom weavers in general, but with handloom weavers in cotton:[1]

> This lack of homogeneity among the cotton handloom weavers was to crop up again and again among other groups of outworkers, and was to have many important consequences, not the least of which is the impossibility of making generalizations about large groups which had such diverse experiences and values.

If we choose to define someone as a member of a working class or a middle class that in itself may tell us very little about him, and a category which will serve for one purpose may be inadequate for another. For example, if we want to know how much of British society was influenced by the religious revival of the early nineteenth century, the vocabulary of social class will not supply adequate categories, since it is clear that this development influenced significant numbers of people of varying social status without effecting the complete conversion of any one social class. Similarly the extent to which individuals were interested in political matters cannot be adequately covered in terms of social class, since it plainly varied considerably within such broad categories. Nor should this difficult problem of categories be avoided by a coy resort to such expressions as 'the middling classes' or 'the lower orders', borrowed from contemporary usage, unless it can be demonstrated that contemporaries understood those terms with a sufficient precision for the purpose to which the historian seeks to apply them.

In our present state of knowledge and understanding, any form of over-generalized simplicity ought to be regarded with suspicion. One useful guideline may be to avoid pressing categories further than the available evidence will sustain them. If, for instance, we can be reasonably sure that a given mode of thought or action was shared by the overwhelming majority of workers, then an expression like 'the working class' may usefully be employed. In other contexts it may be more helpful to employ expressions such as most workers, many workers, some workers or a few workers, depending on the implications of the available evidence.

Although we may recognize elements at work in the Britain of 1780 – 1830 which were to be of continuing importance in later periods, we must also be aware of the major differences which separate that society from our own. To take one simple but important element, if we wish to compare the Britain of 1801 with modern society, we may usefully begin by removing from the scene something like four out of five of our present population.

In the last decades of the eighteenth century there were varied opinions about contemporary population trends, an indication of the paucity of available evidence on the issue. The first national census came in 1801 and did much to resolve these doubts. The resultant evidence suggested that the population of England and Wales had grown by about a million since 1780. Successive decennial censuses provided surer ground, with the total for England and Wales estimated at nearly nine million in 1801, over ten million in 1811, 12 million in 1821, nearly 14 million in 1831. For the whole of the United Kingdom, the 1831 census gave a total of almost 21 million. This substantial increase within half a century was of fundamental importance.

The distribution pattern of this increasing population was also changing, but we must not anticipate the emergence of a predominantly urban society. The 1851 census was the first to show a majority of town dwellers, and this majority still included many country towns as well as industrial centres. Most towns were still quite small; in 1831, for instance, the three main towns of Bedfordshire – Bedford, Luton and Leighton Buzzard – had only 14,000 inhabitants between them.[2] In 1831 the great majority of British people lived in much smaller communities; for example, the 1821 census showed that more than 60 per cent of the inhabitants of Northumberland and Durham lived in communities of less than 2,000 inhabitants.[3] Within this pattern of predominantly small communities life was normally dominated by local affairs and local interests.

The exceptions to this established pattern were growing. In his 1780 *Essay on the Population of England*, Dr Price noted that it was

> allowed on all hands, that the principal manufacturing and trading towns have increased, and some of them, as Manchester, Leeds, Birmingham, Sheffield, Liverpool, and Bristol, most amazingly.

Price died in 1791; if he had survived much into the next century his cause for amazement would have been even greater. Manchester's population grew from 75,000 in 1801 to 182,000 in 1831 (if more nearby satellite communities are included the figures are 95,000 and 238,000), Bradford from 13,000 to 44,000, Oldham from 12,000 to 32,000, Halifax from 12,000 to 22,000. Nottingham had some 12,000 people in the mid-eighteenth century; by 1801 this had grown to 29,000, and reached 50,000 by 1831. Sheffield had a population of nearly 46,000 by 1801, and this virtually doubled over the next 30 years.

Within this growing urban minority London provided a prodigious example. The city's population was well over a million by 1801, and almost doubled by 1831. In addition to being a centre of commerce and government, London remained a major centre of production. Much of this manufacture was carried on in a variety of small workshops, but as early as 1801 there were at least 112 steam engines employed there, while the *London Directory* of 1837 was to list 16,500 industrial enterprises in the capital.[4]

Although the urban centres of industrial Britain were growing at an accelerating rate, a great deal of industry was carried on in smaller settlements, as was necessarily the case with most mining enterprises. The distinctively urban areas were growing rapidly, but even in the 1830s held only a minority of the expanding population.

The resources with which this larger population was supported had to be found within the national economy. The most important single element within this economy was still agriculture. This provided the biggest source of direct employment and also supported a wide range of dependent economic activities. The half-century after 1780 saw considerable progress in agricultural improvement, but the process was patchy rather than general, and for many years after 1830 it was possible to find large areas of farming of a kind very different from the highly publicized centres of improvement. Nevertheless the pace of improvement did accelerate, with marked increases in productivity and profitability in many areas.

Improvements took place in the quality of cultivated crops and in modes of crop rotation, in the breeding of cattle, sheep and other livestock, and in the application of agricultural machinery and fertilizers. These processes attracted a high level of contemporary comment, but the causes were imperfectly understood. Some observers conjectured that improvement was connected with large estates with large farms, others saw an effective spur in the granting of greater security to farmers by lengthy leases instead of precarious annual tenures. For others the process of enclosure provided much of the explanation. However, it is not easy to correlate the known areas of improvement with any of these explanations, although enclosure could often be a necessary prerequisite for improved methods. Security of tenure did not always lead to significantly better techniques, nor were large estates always in the van of progress. Other factors, evident also in other sectors of the economy, played a major role which can be illustrated by a single impressive example.[5]

George Culley was born in 1735, a younger son of a Teesside farmer. The family farm was to be inherited by the eldest son, so George and his brother Matthew were endowed instead with a sound training; their father sent them to work with Robert Bakewell in Leicestershire. This brought the brothers an introduction to the advanced farming thinking and techniques of the day. In 1767 they entered upon the tenancy of a farm in North Northumberland. By 1800 the Culley brothers had prospered, by dint of hard work, technical skill and commercial acumen, and George especially had acquired a national reputation as an improving farmer. Their early contacts with reforming farmers elsewhere were sedulously maintained and extended; George was in Leicestershire and Scotland in 1771, the Midlands and East Anglia in 1784. Matthew was in Scotland in 1770 and 1775, in Leicestershire in 1794 and 1798.

The Culley brothers improved the efficiency and profitability of their farms in various ways. In manuring and liming, in improving the quality of cattle and sheep, a substantial investment of effort, skill and money reaped substantial dividends. Farming success brought the brothers reputation, status and influence, increased income and ready access to credit. Their hard work produced especially good results in the years of high prices during the French wars. In 1801 their profits amounted to well over £4,000, an income equal to that of many gentry families. With such resources they could go on to buy land. The first estate was bought for £24,000 in 1795, a second six years later cost £13,000, and the successful transition from tenant farmer to land-owning gentry culminated in 1807 with the acquisition for £45,000 of a substantial estate centred on the mansion of Fowberry Tower. Even such a hard-bitten business man as George Culley was moved by the social as well as the financial gain; in 1810, three years before his death, he told his son:

> Whenever I am at Fowberry, I am struck with astonishment, when I reflect on our beginning in Northumberland 43 years ago. To think of my son, now inhabiting a *Palace*! altho' his father in less than 50 years since worked harder than any servant we now have, and even drove a coal cart.

A society which provided this kind of reward for conspicuous success was well placed to encourage economic growth, and not only in agriculture.

A distinction between industry and agriculture is commonly made, but we should be chary of exaggerating the extent to which this can be applied to this early period. By the end of the nineteenth century it was much easier to make the distinction than it had been in 1830. The technology applied to many industrial contexts between 1780–1830 presented no great mystery to many rural craftsmen. Consider this recent judgment from Professor A. E. Musson:[6]

> It is not generally appreciated that in 1800 steam power was still in its infancy, that in the vast majority of manufactures there had been little or no power-driven mechanization, and that where such mechanization had occurred water power was still much more widespread and important than steam. And after 1800, the 'triumph of the factory system' took place much more gradually than has generally been realized.

If the application of steam power to a narrow range of mining processes was an important innovation, most early engines were simple devices and most colliery work was still carried out with simple hand tools, little different from those used in farming contexts. A millwright could be concerned with rural watermills or windmills as well as an early industrial plant.

Mixed employment was also common. A combination of mining with small-scale farming was normal in the lead-mining dales, and a similar pattern has been noticed in connection with mining and industry in the west Midlands.[7] An even clearer example of transferable skills in industry and farming comes from their mutual dependence on the horse. Consider the many groups of workers concerned here:[8]

> smiths, farriers, saddlery and harness makers; whipmakers, stirrup, bit and spur makers; wheelwrights, carriage- and coach-builders, fitters, painters, upholsterers and trimmers; cart, van and waggon makers; coachmen,

grooms, cabmen, flymen, carmen, carriers, carters and hauliers; horse-keepers, horse-breakers, horse-dealers, jobmasters and livery-stable keepers – not forgetting the knackers.

The skills needed for many jobs within this formidable list might be deployed in many contexts – a farm or a country house, a factory or a colliery.

Yet alike in contemporary comment and subsequent analysis, the growth of industry has appeared a prodigious achievement of the 1780–1830 period. Certainly this growth was a major element in providing the livelihood of an increasing proportion of the growing population, and the increase in productive power was often striking.[9] The coal industry increased its output from seven million tons in 1780 to 22.4 million tons in 1830. Pig iron production rose from 60,000 tons to 667,000 tons. In 1780 some 6,500 tons of paper were manufactured, well over 25,000 tons by 1830. In 1780 duty was paid on 36.5 million lbs. of soap, 105.8 million lbs. in 1830. The greatest prodigy of them all was cotton, with imports of raw cotton rising from 6.9 million lbs. in 1780 to 237 million lbs. by 1830. By 1820 there were 66 cotton mills in Manchester alone, and by 1832 this had jumped to 96.

Even the limited technical progress made could have significant results in increased efficiency. Some types of cotton yarn could be bought in 1830 for little more than a third of their 1800 price. In the late eighteenth century it took eight tons of coal to make a ton of pig iron, by 1830 only three and a half tons. With cost reductions on this scale, manufactured products were in a strong position to provide an increased share of the national income.

Industrial improvement was paralleled by improved communications. The coming of the railway was the most spectacular development here, but had not produced a marked effect by 1830, though the wider use of earlier forms of waggonway was important, especially in mining districts. Other forms of transport saw significant improvements before the railway age dawned. The growth of the system of turnpike roads, and the coming into service of the stage-coach network, are well known, but they did not stand alone. By the 1830s the country was largely covered by an intricate network of road freight services, mainly using the slow but serviceable stage waggons, heavy vehicles with broad wheels to minimize road wear. Associated with this was the increased sophistication of the coastal shipping services, often linked into the road transport system by chains of established collection points covering wide inland areas.

Increased productivity and improved communications led to better provision of a wide variety of goods and services.[10] In the 1830s Aldeburgh in Suffolk was a fishing village with a population of about 1,300; it had markets twice a week, large fairs twice a year, eight inns, six shoemakers, four grocers, three bakers, two chemists, four tailors, three milliners, five blacksmiths, a saddler and a hairdresser. Twice a week the village was served by a regular carrier of goods to and from the neighbouring town of Ipswich. Thirsk, a Yorkshire town of some 5,000 inhabitants, supported 30 public houses, 12 butchers, two fishmongers, four bakers, 25 shoe shops, 12 grocers, three confectioners, two tallow chandlers, four chemists, 18 general shops, 15 tailors, eight drapers, nine milliners, five hairdressers, four hatters, two clog-makers, six cabinet-makers, two china shops, four booksellers, three ironmongers, four clock-makers, three blacksmiths and a coal merchant.

Improvement in transport provides another useful example of some of the causes which encouraged technical innovation and economic growth. The building of the Stockton and Darlington Railway of 1825 was an important event, though there can be considerable controversy as to just which 'first' it represents. It was not the first railway or the first railway to use locomotives. It ought to be celebrated as a very early convincing demonstration of the commercial advantages which the building of a railway could confer. In the early nineteenth century the cost of road haulage was such that a ton of coal which cost 4s. at a colliery near Bishop Auckland cost 8s. when carted to Darlington and 12s. further on at Stockton, a total distance of 19 miles. The building of the early coal-carrying railways in County Durham reduced the carriage cost from about 4d. or 5d. per ton/mile to less than 1½d. Moreover, in addition to serving local towns like Darlington and Stockton, the new railways enabled coal from southwest Durham to compete effectively in the lucrative ship-borne coal trade.[11] A similar commercial motivation lay behind other improvements. On a reasonably well metalled road of modern type, a single horse might pull a load three times as heavy as on more primitive roads. If a load of two tons was about as much as any horse might be expected to move even on a well metalled road, a horse might pull a boat of 50 tons along a canal towpath.

It was unusual for the men who were responsible for the increase in economic resources in these years to be motivated by any disinterested zeal for improved technology. When George Culley bred an improved variety of sheep suited to local conditions he was not interested in producing an animal of attractive appearance or peculiar size. He wanted a breed hardy enough to withstand northern winters, with at least a decent fleece, and carrying a sufficient weight of meat, even if of moderate quality, to cater for the increased demand for cheap mutton which Culley's keen eye detected in the growing urban and mining areas nearby. We have seen how such acumen carried Culley into the ranks of the landed gentry. The same qualities could earn similar rewards in other sectors. When Robert Stephenson was born in 1803 his father George was a colliery workman, unknown outside a limited local circle.

In the latter years of George Stephenson's life he was a respected national figure, and the family address was now Tapton House, near Chesterfield. By 1850 Robert Stephenson enjoyed an income of some £30,000 per annum, equal to the patrimony of many an aristocratic family; part of this wealth derived from his father's work, much of it was of his own making. In the Britain of 1780–1830 it was possible for the innovator and the adventurer to come to grief, but for those who succeeded the rewards were great.

At the top of the social pyramid stood the monarchy and the aristocracy. The sovereign, as in the case of George IV, may not always have been held in high regard by those closely acquainted with him, but for most of the people the Crown was still invested with a high degree of respect. Not only were petitions about popular grievances commonly offered to the monarch as well as to parliament, but there is ample evidence for the survival of a genuine belief that this could be an effective course of action. The diminution of the sovereign's power in practice occurred well before this was generally appreciated among the less educated and less sophisticated sectors of society. The landed aristocracy exercised a high degree of authority, which was not significantly eroded in the period before 1830. Their basic economic asset was the ownership of land, which conferred substantial advantages. It seemed, and usually was, a safe and permanent form of wealth, while wealth derived from commercial and industrial activity could be highly precarious, as the lists of bankruptcies often eloquently testified. Ownership of a landed estate normally conferred a position of secure independence, likely to be jeopardized only by a singularly feckless course of incompetence or extravagance. The acquisition of a landed estate promised security and at the same time signalled arrival into the higher reaches of society. The advantages conferred by landed wealth were fully appreciated by many men in industry and commerce, however proud they might be of the progress made in those spheres. This appreciation was often given emphatic expression; in 1846 one of the organizers of the great Cobden testimonial fund – himself a manufacturer – had this to say:[12]

> Nor have I any notion of its being desirable that the public man whom his country shall have qualified to sit down on his own broad acres, should remain subject to the contingencies of an anxious trade, of watching, either personally, or by deputy, the processes by which 6d. a piece is to be gained, or 2/6 to be lost, in the production of beggarly printed calicoes.

Here too the distinction between land and industry must not be pressed too far, as the extent of aristocratic involvement in the period makes clear.[13] Coal-mining provides one of the clearest links between the old aristocratic élite and the developing industrial sector. In the Midlands, for instance, mining magnates included Lords Dudley and Hatherton, the Earl of Dartmouth, the Marquess of Hastings and the Dukes of Portland, Rutland and Cleveland. On the Great Northern Coalfield of Northumberland and Durham a list of coalowners provides virtually a roll of the nobility and gentry of the two counties; the Marquesses of Londonderry and the Earls of Durham remained directly concerned with mining for many years after most aristocratic entrepreneurs had dropped out. In the period 1780–1830 it was common to find a great aristocratic landlord as owner or part-owner of towns, mines, quarries, waggonways, harbours, shipping, canals, iron works and a considerable variety of other industrial enterprises relevant to the opportunities offered by their estates. Such direct intervention diminished in the period after 1830.

Many aristocratic magnates were becoming markedly richer as our period developed, with larger cohorts of dependents. Yet the position of even the greatest landed magnate included obligations as well as power. If in theory he could dispose of his own as he wished, in practice the position was less absolute. In most cases great noblemen wished not only to be the recognized head of local society, but for this recognition to be normal and willing, rather than an obtrusively enforced deference, and this could constrain the freedom of action of even the greatest magnates. An accepted part of the role was an obligation to take a leading, and often expensive, part in the provision of local amenities, to be a principal contributor to local philanthropic activities, a leading patron of a very wide range of local interests. While in theory able to dispose of his farm tenancies as he wished, in practice a landlord needed to attract and keep good tenants, and this involved some concern for their interests and their opinions. It was a common practice for land-owners to give substantial rent remissions to help tenants over bad seasons, and to provide stocks of food, fuel or fodder for poorer dependents in hard times.

The role of the aristocracy, with its complex web of political, social and economic influence, was reproduced further down the social scale by the landed gentry. If their influence rarely equalled that of a great magnate it was often significant, and collectively the gentry of a county were a group which a leading magnate must cultivate. Gentry families could also share the mixed economic interests associated with such aristocratic industrialists as the first Marquis of Stafford or the third Duke of Bridgwater. The Northumberland family of Ridley provides a good example here. Early in the eighteenth century the family acquired a substantial landed estate, mainly from confiscated Jacobite properties. Thereafter the Ridleys kept a watchful eye on the efficiency of their farms, but were careful also to exploit other opportunities offered by their estates.[14] The acquisition of a baronetcy did nothing to impair the family nose for a profit. In the 1780s Sir Matthew White Ridley, Bart, MP, owned collieries and a harbour, and was a partner in a major New-castle bank. In the mid-1780s he built a new brewery at Blyth and worked it directly for nearly ten years, making an average annual profit from it of about £400. When in 1800 the baronet leased a butcher's shop in Blyth, he prudently inserted in the lease a stipulation that if during the lease period the building became a public house then all the ale and porter sold there must be bought from the Ridley brewery. Such gentry families had their own corps of dependents, and their possessions commonly invested them with a useful combination of political, social and economic influence.

At first sight we ought to have no difficulty in accepting the presence within the society we are studying of a powerful, coherent and articulate middle class, for such a concept enjoyed a prominent place in contemporary evaluations of the society of the late eighteenth and early nineteenth centuries. In 1799, for instance, Canning attributed the defects of Irish society, as against Great Britain, to the absence from Ireland of[15]

those classes of men, who connect the upper and lower orders of society, and who thereby blend together and harmonize the whole. . . that middle class of men, of whom skill and enterprise, and sober orderly habits, are the peculiar characteristics. . . .

This middle class was commonly invested by contemporaries with striking qualities; consider, for instance, this lyrical description from James Mill:[16]

The opinions of that class of people, who are below the middle rank, are formed, and their minds directed, by that intelligent, that virtuous rank, who come the most immediately in contact with them, who are in the constant habit of communication with them, to whom they fly for advice and assistance in all their numerous difficulties, upon whom they feel an immediate and daily dependence, in health and in sickness, in infancy and old age; to whom their children look up as models for their imitation, whose opinions they hear daily repeated, and account it their honour to adopt. There can be no doubt that the middle rank, which gives to science, to art, and to legislation itself their most distinguished ornaments, the chief source of all that has exalted and refined human nature, is that portion of the community of which, if the basis of the representation were ever so far extended, the opinion would ultimately prevail. Of the people beneath them, a vast majority would be sure to be guided by their advice and example. . . .

Yet if we turn away from this kind of social mythology, and look instead at the realities of that society, the identification of a coherent middle class will not prove nearly so easy. A scratch collection of suitable candidates might include lawyers, doctors, ships' captains, teachers, bankers, factory and mine owners, tenant farmers. A very strong case could be made out for regarding the tenant farmers as the nearest approach to a coherent middle class in the Britain of 1780–1830. Farmers did vary in their status, attainments, interests and opinions, but in view of the continuing importance of agriculture any concept of a middle class which does not comprehend the farmers must be seen as distinctly dubious. Yet it is clear that the prevailing contemporary estimate of the middle class had something quite different in mind; where belief and reality fail to correspond to such a striking extent it is unwise to accept too readily this kind of contemporary evaluation.

We may conjecture that when Canning, James Mill and a host of others employed this kind of language about the middle class they were primarily thinking of an urban context, despite the fact that the towns only contained a minority of British society at that time. In the towns of this period, local oligarchies normally exercised a dominant influence. These groups often exhibited marked internal disagreements in such important spheres as commercial rivalries, religion and political opinions, but collectively occupied positions of strength in the social, economic and political structures of their communities. Local leadership normally rested with the 'principal inhabitants', usually including the biggest employers and the principal tradesmen and professional men. Such groups controlled whatever agencies of urban local government which existed, and also other local institutions such as schools, hospitals and dispensaries. In the old but expanding town of Newcastle upon Tyne, for instance:[17]

> Municipal office passed between the members of a limited range of families, of which the Brandlings, the Bells, the Andersons, the Cooksons, the Smiths and the Claytons were amongst the most prominent. Thus, in 1817 Nathaniel Clayton was Town Clerk; he had held that office since 1785 and was to be succeeded in 1825 by his son John; his brother Robert was mayor and Robert's son, William, was sheriff; in the following year, although Robert and William were out of office, Henry, another son of Robert's, was sheriff.

Where newer urban areas possessed no traditional municipal institutions, statutory improvement commissions were often provided in this period – 300 of these were set up between 1800 and 1830. These bodies, invested with limited rating and administrative functions, were normally dominated by similar forms of local oligarchy.

The effects of economic change on the condition of the workers and their families has given rise to one of the most interesting of modern historical controversies, the great standard-of-living debate. A recent study lists in its bibliography 49 significant contributions.[18] A main area of disagreement is whether industrial development in the late eighteenth and early nineteenth centuries improved or impaired living standards;

there is broad agreement that the later nineteenth century saw significant improvements. Much of the heat engendered springs from opposed concepts about capitalist industry which are not confined to the history of this period, but extend into wider areas of political and ideological controversy. We may usefully remember that in the 1780–1830 period industrial development only exerted a direct effect on a minority of the growing population, and that it was only in the later nineteenth century that industry came to occupy a dominant position, affecting the lives of a much greater proportion of the country's inhabitants.

The imperfect nature of the surviving evidence about the standard of living in Britain during the late eighteenth and early nineteenth centuries makes it unlikely that any very complete picture will ever be attainable. There are some aspects, however, in which it is possible to see some progress. In a recent study Professor Michael Flinn has compared the available indices which have been offered by various scholars in connection with trends in real wages between 1750 and 1850.[19] A generally high degree of correlation can be established between these studies, indicating a slow rise in real wages over the period 1780–1830 in aggregate terms. Such a generalization, however, is of limited value, since the overall pattern must take account of considerable variations in time and place. In addition, the level of real wages is an imperfect guide to the condition of the people, which can be affected by other factors which can influence the quality of life.

There can be little doubt that the condition of some group of workers, including many employed in declining occupations, deteriorated during this period; other groups of workers benefitted from new opportunities created by industrial expansion. In examining such conditions we must again beware of the limitations imposed by the available concepts of categories. For instance, an account of that society which classes the workers and the very poor together should be received with caution, if only because we can be sure that many workers of that period would have repudiated any description which assumed that they should be identified with contemporary paupers.

Factory workers were far from being the typical British workers of the 1780–1830 period.[20] When in 1851 the census was for the first time able to present a more sophisticated breakdown of occupations, the two largest groups were still agriculture with almost a million and a half jobs, and domestic service with more than a million. Large factories employing more than 1,000 were in 1830 rarities even within the unusually advanced cotton industry. Cotton employed around 450,000 workers in the early 1830s, a high proportion of them women and girls. At the same time the building industry probably employed about 350,000 men and boys in a very different work situation. Coal-mining probably employed less than 100,000, in contexts ranging from unusually large modern collieries with perhaps 500 workers through to the many small drift mines employing only a handful of workers, often on a part-time basis. A great range of crafts carried on individually or in small workshops provided a much more typical form of work in our period, and the dark satanic mills saw only a small minority of the work force of pre-Victorian England.

Even in this highly unequal society working people often evinced a capacity for vigorous protest. With a population still largely distributed in small locally orientated communities such protests could often be received with considerable restraint by the dominant groups in society, who usually had the wit to perceive that a policy of harsh repression was unlikely to be conducive to future comfort. There are some notorious exceptions to this generalization, none better known than the Peterloo Massacre of 1819 and the Tolpuddle Martyrs of 1834. Yet the very notoriety of these events should inspire caution; if the bloody dispersal of public meetings, or the transportation of workers for trade union activities, represented the normal working of that society, it is distinctly odd that these individual incidents appear so prominently in the historical record. It may well be that Peterloo and Tolpuddle should be regarded as extraordinary events, rather than manifestations of the dominant pattern of social relationships.

Let us consider a much more low-key, and perhaps more typical, instance of popular protest. During the Napoleonic War the quality of silver coinage in circulation deteriorated. In 1816 a re-coinage was imminent, and gave rise to rumours that debased coins would not be accepted as legitimate currency. Wage payments often included such coins, and shopkeepers might be unwilling to accept them in this uncertain atmosphere. This practical problem provoked a flurry of popular demonstrations. Events at Sunderland provide a typical example.[21] Here is part of a letter sent to the Home Office by a local magistrate in September 1816:

> On Wednesday last a riot began in Sunderland about nine o'clock at night, when it was very dark. The mob, consisting of men and women, boys and girls, proceeded to acts of violence by breaking the windows of a grocer's house, who had become obnoxious to them by refusing to take some of their silver money, as had been hitherto done. Mr Davison and I, being informed of the tumult, attended as magistrates and expostulated with the crowd hoping to prevail upon them to disperse. A division of the 33rd regiment, now in the barracks here, had been sent for by another magistrate, who did not attend on account of illness. Mr Davison and I got these soldiers to march up and down the high street. The rioters, being there, made way for the soldiers and frequently cheered them, abstaining from violence in their presence; tho' one of them was hurt by a stone, or a piece of a brick, thrown

from a distance in the dark. Hoping that peace was nearly restored we suffered the detachment to return to the barracks before midnight. But soon afterwards the rioters became more numerous, and proceeded to break the windows of the Exchange and four other houses. Upon this it became necessary to send for the military again and proclaim the Riot Act. Then the populace began to disperse.

The next day the magistrates summoned a meeting of the town's principal inhabitants, which brought pressure on local tradesmen to accept all silver coins in current use. In common with magistrates facing similar trouble elsewhere, the Sunderland magistrates reported to the central government what had happened and urged the Home Office to hasten the impending re-coinage. The central government responded by issuing a royal proclamation guaranteeing the value of coins in circulation, and privately told the Mint to accelerate the process of re-coinage.

It is unlikely that this demonstration embodied any sustained desire for a remodelling of society; more probably it was intended to induce those in power to use their authority to remedy an immediate practical grievance. Such incidents also provide useful illustration of how unofficial influences could buttress the limited resources of official authority. The resources of central and local government were growing during our period, but this growth began from low levels of resources and sophistication. In local government, for instance, the key official was the justice of the peace, and with the exception of a very few stipendiary magistrates in London these men were unpaid amateurs. Nor did the appointment to a magistracy make a man important; that was not the way in which this society worked. A man who for other reasons, such as the possession of rank or property, was already important, possessed also a good claim to become a magistrate. This combination of unofficial influence and official authority provided a key element in local government.

The poor-law system represented the only administrative structure which covered the whole of England and Wales. It enshrined the hallowed principle of local responsibility, and in practice presented a kaleidoscopic variety of method and competence. During our period population growth did bring an increase in the number of paid poor-law officials; Lancashire provides a clear example, with about 230 paid Assistant Overseers in the early 1830s.[22] Even these men were in no sense trained professionals, but part-timers who varied considerably in competence, humanity, honesty, literacy and sobriety.

At central government level the situation was similar. When Sir Robert Peel went to the Home Office in 1822, that major department possessed a staff of 20 officials.[23] By the late 1830s the staff at the headquarters of the Board of Trade had crept up to a total of about 30 officials.[24] Nor were the arrangements for the recruitment and retirement of these civil servants calculated to produce miracles of administrative efficiency. Patronage remained the normal mode of appointment, arrangements for retirement and pensions were unsystematic. An example may be drawn from the Admiralty, at once a mainstay of national defences and one of the country's biggest spending departments; the key post of secretary there was held (with one brief interval) by Sir John Barrow from 1804 until his retirement at the age of 80 in 1845.[25]

The apparatus of government was not highly regarded by contemporary opinion. The patronage system, with the accompanying suspicions of nepotism and political jobbery, was not likely to inspire confidence among the wide range of taxpayers who were in no position to benefit from the perquisites of office. Instead of any sustained demand for the expansion of government to cope with contemporary problems, there was a much more pervasive demand for cheap government. Even in radical propaganda demands for reductions in public spending were much more vocal than any proposals for the beneficial extension of government intervention. Such attitudes were widespread, but perhaps received their most effective expression within the ruling élite itself. The Whigs entered office in 1830 with the slogan 'Peace, Retrenchment and Reform'. For many of their followers peace meant a reduction in the cost of the armed forces, retrenchment meant what it said, and a principal aim of reform was to eliminate those parts of the constitution which were regarded as not only corrupt but also costly. Nor were these hopes disappointed. When the Whigs came to power revenue was running at about £55½ million *per annum*, and by 1835 about £5 million had been lopped off this modest total. Only demonstration of a very clear need was likely to persuade parliament, or the taxpaying electorate, to sanction the tax increases necessary for an increase in government resources.

Other features of the Britain of 1780–1830 imposed further limitations on the capacity of governments. When the Whigs took office in 1830 there had been only three national censuses, all of them imperfect and limited in the amount of basic statistical information which they could provide. There were not even reliable maps covering the country's terrain in any systematic fashion. Arrangements for the drafting of legislation were still imperfect and limited. Some of the major reforms of the 1830s provide striking illuminations of the problems accompanying innovations.

The Great Reform Act of 1832 was not of course intended as a democratic measure, and there is no good reason why it should have been. The aim was to produce a restricted electorate, including those worthy of the franchise and firmly excluding those who were regarded as unfit or dangerous. But just how was this distinction to be attained? If the reformers had wished to use age as a test of fitness, this was impracticable in a society without a system of registration of births. A common way of expressing the aims of the reformers of 1831–32 was to assert the need to secure a better representation for the property and intelligence of the country. 'Intelligence' here was not used in our more common modern sense, but in its older meaning of information, as in the gathering of intelligence or the Intelligence Corps. In a society in which access to sophisticated education was commonly dependent upon the possession of property, the coupling of property and intelligence in this way appears less absurd than it may seem at first sight. The property qualifications employed in the 1832 Act represented not only the contemporary high regard for property, but also an appreciation of practical possibilities. All of the qualifications could be tested by reference to evidence already in existence, such as rate books, leases, rent receipts, tax certificates. The celebrated £10 household qualification in the boroughs was not dreamed up by the reformers of 1831–2, but represented the borrowing for electoral purposes of a yardstick already employed in assessments for the house tax.[26]

In 1833 an important Factory Act was placed on the statute book. At first sight its stipulation prohibiting the employment of children under nine in certain factories seems clear enough, but what in the Britain of 1833 was a child of nine? The formal registration of births did not begin until some years later, and would obviously take some time to become an effective test of age. The drafters of the Act sought to meet this difficulty by devising a system whereby surgeons would give certificates specifying children's ages for this purpose. The available criteria were less than precise, and in the opinion of the Law Officers of the Crown the surgeons must be guided by their opinion[27]

> that the child had the ordinary strength and appearance of a child *at least nine years* of age, or *exceeding* nine years of age, as the case may be.

This rough and ready response, however, dealt with only part of the problem, for who, in the Britain of 1833, was a surgeon? The development of the medical profession into an established pattern of qualification and registration was very far from complete, and the best opinion which the Law Officers could give here was that

> any person acting as a Surgeon although not a Member of any College of Surgeons is a Surgeon entitled under the Factory Act to grant certificates.

During the 1780–1830 period there were improvements in the quality of public servants and the processes of administration but, as in the contemporary fields of science and technology, the progress was limited. The expansion of the population and the development of the economy produced social problems which the machinery of government was not well equipped to tackle. The horrendous accounts of social conditions in the early nineteenth century are sufficiently well known, but we should be cautious in assuming either that they were new or that they can be attributed simply to the consequences of unregulated industrial growth. Consider two examples from the well known series of early Victorian sanitary reports:[28]

> Great filth of every description may always here be found, and it has long been noticed as much subjected to fever. An open sewer, containing all kinds of putridity, which is seldom or never cleansed, runs from the Green Batt so far down the yard, and, where it becomes covered, its place is supplied by a large midden, into which all the blood and offals from the slaughterhouses are thrown, and frequently for a considerable time to retain.

> I enquired for the return of mortality, and found that, for the last seven years, it was actually some 27½ in the thousand, but with 'cooked' returns it was 24 in the thousand. . . . I then traced disease to crowded room tenements, undrained streets, lanes, courts and crowded yards, foul middens, privies and cesspools. The water I found was deficient in quantity and most objectionable in quality, dead dogs being lifted from the reservoir. . . . I am staying at the best hotel in town, but there is no water closet, only a filthy privy at some distance.

These descriptions are not drawn from Manchester, Leeds or Liverpool, but from Alnwick and Hexham, two country towns which could scarcely be seen as in the van of the industrial revolution. A perusal of Cobbett's *Rural Rides* as well as much other evidence will also demonstrate that social problems were not the monopoly of industrial or urban communities. It remains true of course that the rapidly growing industrial towns provided additional and serious concentrations of bad conditions; they did not introduce such problems but aggravated long-standing difficulties which contemporary resources were not well equipped to solve. For example, problems of urban sanitation and water supply could only be tackled effectively after public health engineering had reached higher standards of skill and reliability than existed in 1830.

The limitations placed upon corporate and official activity by the resources and beliefs of contemporary society were real enough, but they were less harmful during the 1780–1830 period than might appear at first sight. The energies of that society were primarily deployed in unofficial activity, and this was as true in the field of social amelioration as in the economy. Society was still largely organized on a local basis, and within the locally coherent communities this period saw significant growth in a wide variety of philanthropic activities, made possible in part by the increased wealth generated by economic development. Voluntary agencies provided many communities with new resources such as hospitals, dispensaries and schools on a scale which far out-stripped anything attained by official agencies.[29] Here again, however, limitations such as the extent of contemporary medical knowledge were significant factors. The growth in philanthropic activity accelerated in the later nineteenth century, and provided one of the main lines leading into the twentieth-century welfare state, but even by 1830 the trend was clearly established.

The period 1780–1830 saw significant changes in many aspects of life, especially in population growth and economic development. Many of the trends and developments involved represented an acceleration of changes which had long been under way and which continued to accelerate for many years after 1830. During the remainder of the nineteenth century, population growth, economic expansion and the development of political and administrative institutions moved further and faster than they had done from 1780–1830; however, the experience of those decades provided a crucial transitional stage in the complex processes which transformed Britain from a decentralized, thinly populated, largely rural society into the highly governed, largely urban and industrial society characteristic of later periods. The 1780–1830 period demonstrated that it was possible to support a much larger population without catastrophic consequences, provided that human ingenuity was harnessed to the task of expanding the economic base on which the greater numbers must be supported, and provided that a reasonable level of social and political stability could be maintained.

Colloquy on chapter 7
John Cannon

Discussion on Norman McCord's paper was dominated by methodological considerations. McCord's opening section, warning against the dangers of anachronism, attracted comment (p. 151). Speck suggested that McCord was attacking a straw man and that no reputable historian held such extreme views: 'you have obviously suffered at the hands of lunatics.' Cannon argued that in emphasizing the differences between that society and the present day, McCord had exaggerated them: dukes, after all, were not notoriously egalitarian today, nor did modern industrialists commonly rub their hands with joy when government money was used to support workers' cooperatives. There was, certainly, a sense in which Regency England was very different, but it might have been more helpful to say that it was becoming increasingly like our own society. Derry strongly supported McCord in resisting the suggestion that, in the early nineteenth century, modern England in its essentials came into existence. The beginnings of fundamental change might have been there, but the decisive shift came much later in the century. Not until then did religion, for example, begin to lose its dominant place in the national life: the development of the educational system throughout most of the century could only be understood in the context of the religious rivalries. The growth of modern political parties, with their powerful central and local organizations and mass support, was essentially a late nineteenth-century phenomenon. Even in industry, the tendency of recent scholarship had been to place the crucial changes in the second half of the century.

The difficulty of seeing historical change in its right perspective was illustrated again by an exchange of views over town growth (p. 154). Derry pointed out that the development of great agglomerations such as Merseyside came surprisingly late: Donald Read in *Edwardian England* had quoted remarkable figures on the growth of towns *after* 1870. Dickinson retorted that, on McCord's own evidence, the growth of Birmingham and Manchester by 1830 was considerable, and was already having an impact on society. McCord replied that the great industrial towns were still very unusual in the period up to 1830 and certainly did not set the pattern for most people's lives: most industry, even in Manchester, was on a small scale – even in cotton, which was the pace-maker, the degree of mechanization was still very limited. Cannon pointed out that these towns were growing less unusual decade by decade and that, in any case, the unusual was quite capable of having important historical consequences. Speck drew attention to the figures (p. 157) showing a very impressive growth in the economy: 'are you trying to tell us that this kind of achievement had only a limited social impact?' He detected a paradox in McCord's paper: 'you revel and glow in the economic achievement of that society, but play down the social and political implications.'

On the historian's attitude towards the past (p. 152) there was agreement that it was as foolish to slide into defending whatever had happened as to deplore what had happened. McCord thought that it was necessary to stress the folly of deploring the past since this attitude was still prevalent – Derry remarked that, even by 1830, economic developments were beginning to bring considerable prosperity to certain groups while destroying the traditional way of life of others: an older generation of historians such as the Hammonds, still widely read, had tended to the view that somehow the process ought to have been painless.[1] But nobody, after all, would seriously argue that modern British textile production should still to be based on hand-loom weaving. Dickinson, while agreeing that a 'bleeding-heart mentality' was not particularly useful, felt that the historian had nevertheless a duty to register the amount of distress and resentment produced: he was not convinced that this side of the period was adequately represented in McCord's paper. Holmes and Speck argued that McCord might have noted a key change which took place in the period – the shift from traditional riots against food prices to strikes for higher wages. As industrialization grew, workers could not actually seize grain and sell it off cheaply, as they had done in the past, so they switched to industrial action against their employers. McCord admitted an increase in political protest during the period but did not regard it as dominant.

The next skirmish took place on the use of class terminology (p. 153). While not denying that class terminology was inexact and might be mis-employed, Dickinson, O'Gorman, Speck and Cannon regarded it as a helpful method of analysis. Cannon pointed out that no description in two or three words could be other than approximate: since the objections to the use of the word 'middle class' might also be levelled at 'Catholic' or 'British', the historian was in danger of finishing up with no vocabulary of analysis at all: 'after all, if you say a person is "British", it does not tell you whether that person is alive or dead, male or female, young or old, proud of being British or ashamed of being British. It is a very vague description indeed. But we do not say that the historian should not employ that word.' What was the alternative to employing class terminology? Contemporaries – Durham, Huskisson, Russell,

Grey – were always using class categories. It would be almost impossible to describe Grey's political intentions in 1830 without using the language of class since his avowed intention was to bring the middle classes into the constitution. McCord and Derry reiterated the limitations of class concepts and the many exceptions with which they bristled: 'all the categories we have available leak like sieves.' It is true that you could describe people as middle class if you wished, but what could you then use the category for? Certainly not to presume their political or religious beliefs? O'Gorman replied that a man's occupation and status, while by no means determining his political behaviour, had usually a considerable relationship to it. Dickinson supported him: 'if you say that someone in that period is a member of the working classes, you can say that he is likely to be poor, that he is likely to be dependent on his employer, that his housing will probably be bad, that his education may be non-existent, that he will have very little direct political power, that he may be faced by the prospect of unemployment, and so on . . . you can go on inferring things about his probable life style.' This McCord denied: 'every one of those things you mention may be challenged and may well not fit. At every stage you will drop bits out of the category. The extent to which he will be poor, or badly educated, or badly housed is a variable, not a characteristic.' Moreover, the fact that contemporaries used such categories does not mean that they were valid or that historians should endorse them or use them: 'the middling classes that the reformers talked about in 1832 were not the middling classes as they actually existed.'

The discussion of the 'scratch-list' on p. 161 carried the methodological argument a stage further. Why had the clergy, an important social group, not been included? McCord explained that the clergy, as a profession, spread *across* classes: the archbishops and bishops, for example, could hardly be placed in the middle classes. Speck asked whether this was not, in itself, an admission that classes did mean something? McCord thought that to have added 'the clergy' to the list without a long explanation would merely have confused. Holmes asked whether one could not have distinguished upper and lower clergy – or even have made a tripartite division into bishops, upper and lower clergy – as most social analysts from Gregory King to Colquhoun had done? Speck argued that to place factory owners between bankers and tenant farmers 'jumbled them promiscuously together': the factory owner, as a category in society, was relatively new whereas the other two groups had been in existence long before 1780: though there were factories and factory owners in Defoe's day, as a category they emerged in the later eighteenth century and that was evidence of the way society was changing.

The question of balance came up yet again in the discussion over protest and discontent (p. 164). Dickinson accused McCord of being cavalier in dismissing Peterloo and Tolpuddle lightly. They represented the peaks of huge mountains of strikes and demonstrations maintained over many years. McCord, in reply, thought that the protests had been intermittent, coinciding usually with economic recession: though no one could doubt the existence during the period of groups of dedicated radicals, the continuity of *mass* support for radicalism could not be demonstrated. Even when large-scale protest was taking place, the masses were not likely to be motivated by ideological considerations. Cannon thought that the distinction between bread-and-butter issues and ideological protests was false: 'your ideology might well be to say that as long as we have this kind of system, we shall get this kind of economic crisis and this kind of unemployment. I wouldn't know whether that was a bread-and-butter grievance or an ideology. In any case, does it matter? If one can prove that people were not actually in possession of a coherent ideology, this does not somehow remove their grievance or remove their protest.' McCord disagreed totally: 'there is a significant difference between the kind of protest that aims at redistributing power and the kind that is primarily intended to obtain redress of specific grievances.' Cannon did not deny that if one had a riot about turnpikes this did not necessarily mean profound dissatisfaction with the political arrangements of the country: 'but I would have thought that in the area we are talking about – the radical movements of the 1820s – it was peculiarly difficult to disentangle bread-and-butter grievances from ideological ones.' Holmes, while admitting that there had always been fluctuations in the economy, asked whether those from 1790 onwards were not on a far more dramatic scale, involving far more people? McCord replied that the long periods of comparative tranquility, between 1822 and 1828 for example, suggested that the commitment to radical change did not run deep. Speck thought that the allusion to Peterloo and Tolpuddle had been misunderstood: the argument was not that protest was intermittent, but that savage repression of popular demonstrations was by no means the rule.

In conclusion, Cannon put to McCord a summary of some objections to his paper: 'You are telling us that we must not, of course, exaggerate the protests and the discontents of this period. You are telling us that governments were, on the whole, sensible and moderate and responsive; that there was no organized coherent middle class to take the lead in challenging the old order; that the lower classes were, by and large, getting better off, and that the aristocracy was still widely respected. You remind us what a localized society it still was. Surely that leads to difficulties? The first is that it seems not to catch the mood of the period. And I'm not sure how it links up with the great political struggles that were taking place. Are you not in danger of removing the dynamic, of finishing up without any explanation of why these great political developments were taking place?'

McCord, in reply, agreed that the weight of protest may not have been fully expressed: 'I accept that I have not caught all the moods in a society that was far from having just one mood.' But one of the most illuminating aspects of the discussion had been the nature of the topics which had dominated it. Although his task had been to discuss economic and social history from 1780 to 1830 the discussion had fastened instead on the political developments.

Although several colleagues had criticized what they considered his neglect of popular politics, no one seemed much concerned that he had not explored the political views and activities of the aristocratic minorities who controlled the country. Perhaps these men, rather than the radicals, stand most in need now of rescue from, in E. P. Thompson's splendid phrase, 'the enormous condescension of posterity'. Given the realities of that society, he could not consider that radicals provided a very important element, and it was by no means clear that their prescriptions offered any very constructive response to contemporary problems.

Criticism had been directed at the cautionary expressions with which his paper began, but much of the discussion had served to underline them. Historians tend to have an abnormally high interest in political and ideological matters, and the history of this period in particular is much obscured by political noise, partly generated at the time, and partly contributed subsequently, which makes it more than commonly difficult to talk about 'the mood of the period'. Yet certain points seem reasonably clear. Throughout the period there was a hard core of devoted radicals, convinced that British society needed larger and swifter changes than contemporary governments and parliaments were willing to concede. From time to time this hard core was reinforced by a substantial degree of mass support, but this was intermittent. Mass support appeared in times of economic and social stress, and tended to evaporate in more prosperous times. Two deductions may reasonably be made. First, that it was the hard times which produced mass discontent, rather than any mass conversion to radical politics; second, the intermittent nature of mass support suggests that commitment to political interests was not very strong as far as most people were concerned.

The problem of finding adequate categories for description and analysis remains a crucial difficulty in studying this society, and our conceptual equipment is still defective. This is not simply a problem for students of history, but extends into the ambits of many other disciplines. While history has an important contribution to make to the complex matter of learning to understand how human society operates, it is also a matter of interest for those concerned with politics, economics, sociology and law. An optimist might hope that in future years our understanding will increase and our conceptual equipment improve, in the light of the contributions to be derived from all these varied approaches to this central problem. At present, however, there is much to be said for taking careful note of the limitations imposed by our problems of classification, and for avoiding the imposition on imperfect categories of an explanatory function which they are incapable of performing.

Note on further reading

Many general books cover the economic and social history of this period. *The Industrial Revolution, 1750–1850*, (1971) by Robin Reeve, provides one convenient source for much of the background evidence. Peter Mathias, *The First Industrial Nation, an Economic History of Britain, 1700–1914*, (1969), offers a good example of modern text book coverage. Among older books J. H. Clapham, *An Economic History of Modern Britain; the Early Railway Age, 1820–1850*, (1930), is still useful for the latter part of our period, especially in the warnings given against anticipating the transformation of Britain into an urbanized and industrialized society.

For the impact of technological change D. S. Landes's *The Unbound Prometheus: Technological Change and Industrial Development in Western Europe from 1750 to the Present*, (1969) is full of interest and well written. For changes in British agriculture, a key work is *The Agricultural Revolution, 1750–1880*, by J. D. Chambers & G. E. Mingay, (1966). *Land and Industry*, edited by J. T. Ward & R. G. Wilson, is a volume of papers of varying scope, but the contributions by David Spring and J. T. Ward are important studies of the relationship between the dominant landed interest and industrial development.

Three articles contributed to the *Economic History Review* can be singled out. In 1974 Professor M. W. Flinn offered a comprehensive paper on 'Trends in Real Wages 1750–1850', which discusses the various wage indices for this period and also includes a bibliography of elements involved in the debate on the standard of living. Two years later Professor A. E. Musson contributed an article on 'Industrial Motive Power in the United Kingdom, 1800–1870', which applied an invaluable corrective to older views of the extent of industrialization in the early nineteenth century. Also in 1976, Professor F. M. L. Thompson, in a short paper on 'Nineteenth-Century Horse Sense' provided a brilliant assessment of the continued importance of the horse in the industrializing economy of the nineteenth century.

Two influential works which represent in somewhat different ways a Marxist approach to the period are E. P. Thompson, *The Making of the English Working Class*, (1963), and John Foster, *Class Struggle and the Industrial Revolution: Early Industrial Capitalism in Three English Towns*, (1974). While neither of these books has won general acceptance among historians working in this field, both of them succeeded in bringing about significant re-thinking on the topics with which they dealt.

8

Final discussion

John Cannon

Contributors: John Derry
                    Harry Dickinson
                    Geoffrey Holmes
                    Norman McCord
                    Frank O'Gorman
                    Bill Speck

Cannon: In this final session, we want to try to do two things – to see whether we can reach any agreement about a framework in which eighteenth-century history can be discussed and, if we can, see how the various issues which we have reserved from our previous discussions relate to that framework. In the past, people who have had to teach eighteenth-century history have sometimes complained that it seemed a rather incoherent period, that it was, if you like, atomized. Though in recent years all manner of fierce academic combats and controversies have been going on, it is not easy for the general reader to link them together and to see any overall pattern. Now the last thing I want to do is to suggest a framework of interpretation if there really isn't one. But the first question is whether you see any such pattern emerging.

O'Gorman: It seems to me that, fifty years after Namier, the Namierite thesis is no longer adequate. If we are all agreed that Namier's England was a period of unusual calm, compared with the decades before and after; if we are all agreed that Namier's treatment of the monarchy and of party was appropriate only to a fifteen-year period in the middle of the century, then clearly we do stand in need of some alternative framework.

Cannon: I'm glad you have raised the point about Namier immediately, because although it has often been regarded as Namier's century people have objected that Namier himself did not try to hold it together, and that he was better at destroying interpretations than at offering counter-proposals.

O'Gorman: Namier did not attempt to offer a detailed synthesis. There are all sorts of hints and assumptions but it wouldn't be true to say that Namier worked out any kind of overall interpretation.

Cannon: Well, can I offer three quick points? Although there seems to be general agreement that Namier achieved a great deal, even in the area on which he concentrated he needs a lot of revision. Secondly, Brewer has very adequately summarized the feeling that Namier's approach was far too narrow – it was not only narrow in the sense that he was almost purely a political historian, a parliamentary historian, but even within those narrow limits he was still narrow – and at the very least we have to broaden the idea of the 'political nation' in the Namier period.[1] Thirdly, I want to ask a question – whether you feel that Namier's method of approach is now played out? Structural analysis, after all, was regarded at one stage as a revolutionary breakthrough in historical technique. Do you still feel that it has a lot of mileage in it?

Dickinson: Can I take structural analysis first? I still admire Namier for this. I think we all use it. But you have to remember two things. One is that structural analysis will only answer certain questions. This is where it comes back to the differences between Bill and myself, on one side, and people like Linda Colley, on the other, as far as Whigs and Tories are concerned.[2] If you analyse structurally, as she tends to do, you come up with one kind of answer; but if you look at other forms of evidence that can't be considered structurally – pamphlets and sermons and parliamentary debates and the like – you get another answer. So to think that structural analysis is a solution to all our problems is a mistake. Secondly, it is rather a conservative way of looking at politics and at human motivation, and because it is conservatively-biased, it seems to me that it comes up with conservative answers about that society.

Speck: I would like to expand on Harry's distinction between Namier's method and Namier's conclusions. First of all, the notion that Namier's conclusions would inevitably emerge from any collective biographical enterprise has bedevilled the study of the period. I don't think that Namier himself went along with that – he was pretty cool, pretty guarded in his reception of Walcott, who claimed to have applied the technique to Anne's reign.[3] As for his method, it is an essential starting-point, not only for parliament, but also for the electoral behaviour of the voters. We have got to establish how people voted before we can go on to offer explanations why they voted.

Holmes: Obviously I agree with both Harry and Bill on this. No, Namier's methodology is not played out, and never will be as long as there are new periods of politics to be studied or existing periods to be studied from a different direction. My reservation is the way the technique has been used by certain historians. You can gather any amount of biographical evidence, but if you see people basically as puppets (and I don't say that Namier held such a crude view as this), if you see them as robots, instead of as people of flesh and blood, as individuals, with passions, with imagination, with ideals – yes, even in 1760 at the accession of George III – then you are in danger of serious distortion, you can produce desiccated history.

Speck: But, of course, Namier himself could be extremely sophisticated in his treatment of character – I'm thinking of the biography of Charles Townshend, in which he applied Freudian analysis, arguing that the domination of Townshend by his father accounted for a lot of his later political activity. . . .[4]

Dickinson: Yes, I should like to praise some of his work. He has a reputation of being desiccated, as though methodology dominated the whole of his work, as though it was all tables and statistics. But, in fact, the books are beautifully written, the style is marvellous, and his interest in people, in human psychology, though limited, makes them a delight to read. I think we have all been influenced by his views on Newcastle, even if we don't agree with them: somehow the man comes alive – and the same is true of George III.

Cannon: Now, can I try to summarize this? There is obviously vast respect for Namier, but one couldn't say – if one is a sixth-form history teacher or an old-fashioned college tutor – 'Go off and read Namier, my boy, and you'll understand the eighteenth century!' So, whatever the merits of Namier, it isn't totally adequate today. That brings us on to Frank's second point, that if Namier is not adequate, are there other interpretations we ought to look at? Can we now move on to look at some alternative ways of organizing the material, of regarding the eighteenth century?

When Plumb, in 1967, published his *Growth of Political Stability*, it looked very much as though this was a concept that had a good deal of historiographical life in it, and we have, in fact, leaned on it a great deal in our discussions here. I wondered though – there have been reservations expressed in the course of our discussions about what we mean by stability – I think that Frank felt rather strongly that stability was a rather doubtful concept – and I wondered whether it did not look as promising as an over-all interpretation as it did, say 48 hours ago when we began these colloquies. Frank, are you very worried at using stability as a concept?

O'Gorman: Not particularly. I think it is a little artificial to divide the century into stable and unstable periods, but that may be something we have to do. What worries me more is that the concept has never been really worked out except for the period 1675 to 1725. What happens after that to stability? Where does it go after 1725? It's not so much that I am con-cerned about the ambiguity of the concept, but that I don't think that for our purposes it has been sufficiently refined, it has not been sufficiently tested.

Speck: I was going to ask Geoff to come in, because the definition Plumb offers for stability does seem to be one that can be tested decade by decade, and I think Geoff would agree that Plumb's definition would hold good for the 1730s, 1740s and 1750s, but perhaps not for the 1760s.

Cannon: Let's see if Geoffrey does agree?

Holmes: Well, it is odd that during the discussion of my paper and John's, we never did get round to mentioning what Plumb's definition was. It is as follows: 'By political stability, I mean the acceptance by society of its political institutions and of those classes of men or officials who control them.' The important thing about the definition is its duality. We have to remember the distinction Plumb makes between the institutions and what he calls, perhaps rather loosely, the classes of men or officials who control them. Plumb himself, in the introduction to his book, tried to set it against the sixteenth and seventeenth-century backcloth. I think, on reflection, one needs to add 'religious' to the phrase 'political institutions', and then one has a very good working definition.

Cannon: I think that is very helpful. The difficulty of course is that 'society' doesn't really accept or reject in quite that way. As we have been assuring each other interminably, some people do and some don't, the balance changes, and it doesn't change in a regular and predictable way, but in a fitful sort of way.

Speck: If we start off with the highest office in the land – the monarch – I don't think the acceptance of the person of the monarch could be said to be complete before the accession of George I had been safely accomplished. But that, in turn, brings up the subject of Jacobitism again. Is there a large section of the political nation that does not accept George I? My own strong feeling is that there is not. But we need to do justice to other historians of the period – and particularly to the *History of Parliament* – who take a very different view.[5]

Dickinson: I like this definition as a means of holding the period together. I agree that stability is a relative matter, but the eighteenth century is held together by a political and constitutional emphasis much more than other centuries. The critical factor is the acceptance of the existing social hierarchy and the acceptance of the distribution of property. And the breakdown of stability begins when some people start to challenge that.

Derry: I endorse what Harry says, provided that we do not interpret stability in such a rigid way that it excludes change and development. There is no doubt that the eighteenth century did see a greater confidence in the country's institutions, a feeling that they had settled some of the seventeenth-century problems that were so bitter and divisive. But it was not a static stability: it was a dynamic, a developing stability. It's a success story. . . .

Dickinson: Oh! (turmoil)

McCord: I would just enter a note of dissent about the extent to which the situation became unstable in the period dealt with in John Cannon's paper. I take all that Harry said about the growth of protest and discontent – and, of course, after the end of our period we have Chartism coming up – but nevertheless, all these things were *contained*.

Cannon: But, Norman, can I press you on this? So, we agree that Plumb was right that there was a growth of political stability up to, say, 1725 or so. Does that just go on for ever? Right up until 1979? Has there never subsequently been a period of instability?

McCord: This is one of the problems about the meaning one attaches to the term 'stability'. If you are talking about the mechanisms of the political system, about the rise and fall of party, that is one thing: if you are talking about the nature of society itself, that is another. On the whole, I am convinced that evolution has dominated and I don't think one could find an enormous destabilization of British institutions.

Cannon: Well, in the sense that there never was a subsequent revolution you are indisputably correct. . . .

Holmes: But this is surely where Plumb's definition is helpful. It is this distinction between the acceptability of the institutions and the acceptability of the classes of men who control them. You can have a considerable measure of instability when one *or* the other is under stress, and yet it can be contained. I do see the beginnings of instability in the 1760s, because one of the fundamental institutions – parliament – or perhaps the ability of parliament adequately to represent interests and people – is being questioned. Now it hasn't really been questioned since the 1640s. But the classes of men who controlled the institutions were still not being fundamentally questioned in 1760. It is when *both* institutions and classes are being questioned that the system really begins to crumble, as it had done in the early seventeenth century. We spent a lot of time on the question of Court and Country, and what seems clear is that there is a major difference between the conflict of Court and Country in the early seventeenth century – before the Civil War – and that in the Walpole period. The seventeenth-century conflict was fundamental: it amounted almost to a complete alienation of the two sides, two different moral outlooks. Now, although the conflict in the eighteenth century did spill over into the constituencies, it does not in any sense involve a loss of confidence in the classes of men who are running the country; Individuals, yes: classes, no.

Cannon: I think the time has now come to call in absent friends.[6] When we are talking about conflict and agreeing that eighteenth-century political conflict did not run as deep as in the previous century, we lay ourselves open to the retort that we are looking at the wrong conflict, that we ought to be looking at the conflict between the governing class and the lower orders, or the rest of the people. We have used phrases like 'acceptance by society' and John Derry has even talked about a 'success story'. But the absent friends might well point out that most people in the period didn't

have much alternative but to accept – they were not consulted, they had little or no political influence, and there
was the shadow of the gallows to remind them of the
penalty for not accepting. They would paint a society in
which many people were probably not in agreement with
the traditional institutions. So, I wanted to ask whether we
might look at a third framework – that of consensus or conflict – which is a framework in which, I suppose, E. P.
Thompson and his associates might prefer to work.[7]
Harry, would it present an alternative way of looking at
things? It has its similarities, of course, since there is not all
that difference between acceptance and consensus.

Dickinson: I accept that there was consensus among the governing
classes, but I think we are in danger of forgetting those
people outside it. The people outside it hadn't got the
education, the leadership, the experience to develop a
radical critique of the system. They can't see the economy
organized in a different way until industrialization shows
them that it is possible to organize things differently. I
suspect that Thompson is right that there was not just
deference – though many people certainly did feel that –
but also resentment against the system and resentment
against the people who dominate it – and this resentment
comes out at times in ballads, and threatening letters, and
arson and crime.[8]

Speck: I think that some people did show that they were not going
to cooperate with some of the machinery of govern-
ment – I'm thinking particularly of customs and excise.
The excise scheme, as Walpole presented it to parliament,
was prefaced by a long account of smuggling – hair-raising
stories – doubtless touched-up for the occasion – of how
many customs men had been attacked and in some cases
killed in the previous ten years, and of the amount of
revenue which had been lost. It seems as if smuggling was
really an organized connivance at evading the implications
of supporting this régime. . . .

Cannon: But, Bill, may I just point out that you were telling me
joyously the other day that Walpole himself was up to his
neck in smuggling, using admiralty barges for the purpose? Surely he cannot have been the chief architect of
stability and the man who was undermining it?

Derry: I don't go along with this portentous explanation of
smuggling as a protest against 'the system' – whatever that
was. Any more than I believe that the thousands of people

today who fiddle their income-tax really want to see the overthrow of all existing institutions. After all, in the eighteenth century, plenty of parsons like Woodforde joined in smuggling, but one would hardly point to the Hanoverian clergy as a group smouldering with discontent, a radical protest group.

Speck: But it's not just smuggling. There are riots on all sorts of issues. The Porteous riots in Scotland were not just a flash in the pan. They showed very deep resentment of certain features in Scottish society. Then there were the militia riots, press-gang riots, cider tax riots. . . . As for the lower clergy, I'm not at all sure that they were not, at least in the Walpole period, an alienated group. Many of them were High Church Tories and out of sympathy with the régime.

Holmes: Bill touches upon a very interesting example when he talks about the widespread hostility towards the exciseman in eighteenth-century England. It had always been regarded as one of the great strengths of the system that local government and local taxation were in the hands of local men. But at the beginning of the period we are discussing, this is starting to change. The exciseman is there in every county and the exciseman's walk and the exciseman's ride covered every yard of ground in the land. Now although there were in the 1720s perhaps only some four thousand excisemen and some three thousand customs officers – and although seven thousand officials may strike us as a tiny number – it was seven thousand more than it had been before, it may have seemed quite startling to contemporaries, and it may be another ingredient in explaining some of the resentment.

McCord: I agree with what Harry and Bill have said. Although there seems to be agreement among ourselves that, by and large, the dominant minority showed considerable adroitness, there were many exceptions to this. If you have a society organized as Hanoverian England was, then it is perfectly possible for someone who is squire and magistrate and landowner to be a very nasty piece of work indeed. They weren't all adroit, they weren't all considerate and pleasant.

O'Gorman: I don't deny the resentment and I am sure that there was, throughout the century, a massive popular interest in politics. But, for our purposes, these resentments never fuse, never come together, are not continuous enough to mount an effective challenge to the régime. There are occasional ominous hints of what might happen – the Excise crisis, the Jew bill riots, Wilkes, Wyvill, and so on.[9] But one has the feeling that, towards the end of the eighteenth century, they do begin to come together to pose a real threat, and in the end, the régime has to be thoroughly reformed. . . .

McCord: Yes, but reformed by whom? I agree that there was considerable resentment, but we do not have a beleaguered establishment garrison, isolated in an ocean of opposition. A large part of the garrison is the effective instrument of change. It is not a case of the governing classes flatly resisting all change. . . . The men who bring in the changes are to a great extent the men who are already in power.

Cannon: Bill, can you give us a last quick word on this subject? Consensus or conflict, stability or strife, to use your phrase?

Speck: I agree with Harry's acknowledgement that E. P. Thompson in *Whigs and Hunters* has introduced a new dimension in looking at the Walpole period. What impresses me, though, is this: the resentment, which is certainly there, does not take a political form. That raises the question, what political form could it have taken. There is no way in which it could have been radical, but it could have become Jacobite. Nicholas Rogers, looking at London in the early years of the Hanoverian regime, found rather more popular Jacobitism than we might have thought.[10] But it was a resentment with nowhere to go.

Cannon: We did agree that we would give ourselves the luxury of looking again at subjects which we hadn't discussed adequately. One of those subjects was Jacobitism, so we can now move on to that section?

Dickinson: Jacobitism wasn't a programme for the lower orders and I don't think the Jacobites wanted them. There isn't any link between them.

Cannon: No, but people are very good at latching on to a cause that doesn't really belong to them and moving the cause over to their own position. Isn't that what some people tried to do with Wilkes? I'm not sure that Wilkes was really a radical cause in himself but people like John Horne Tooke tried to turn him into one. Is it impossible to think of the lower orders supporting Jacobitism in order to try to exploit it?

Speck: Walpole certainly thought that. One sees it in the Mother Gin riots of 1736 – there is an obsession with 'Are these people Jacobites?' when clearly they were just against the gin duties. But the government was always frightened when there was a popular disturbance that the Jacobites could exploit it.

Dickinson: There is a difference between anti-Hanoverian or anti-government feeling and pro-Jacobitism. The reason that resentment didn't get very far is first, that the governing class was united, secondly that they couldn't develop a programme, and thirdly that they had no effective weapons. Where are the economic weapons for these people to use?

Holmes: I was very happy to accept, when my paper was being discussed, the suggestion that popular radicalism, in order to be dangerous, had to have leadership. What struck me about Rogers's article on London was the contrast between what I found when looking at the Sacheverell riots of 1710 with what he found when looking at the disturbances of 1714–16. In 1710, I had shown that there was open incitement of the mob by High Church parsons and perhaps by the Tory gentry in London: in 1715, he found very little, if any, direct incitement. I think he has slightly underestimated it but, by and large, I accept it. The significance is that in 1710 nobody could have believed that the irruptions in London or in any other town could possibly have produced an overthrow of the dynasty – Queen Anne was by no means unpopular. In 1715 it could have led to much more serious consequences had it been channelled.

Cannon: Can I ask a question? We have repeatedly talked about the deep-seated dislike of Catholicism in the country at large – the Gordon riots, the tremendous volume of protest against Catholic emancipation in the 1820s. Was it primarily the anti-Catholic sentiment that prevented people supporting Jacobitism? Or was it, as Harry said, that there was nothing in it for them – it would just be a change of dynasty and why should they bother?

McCord: Anti-Catholic feeling didn't stop in 1832. The Ecclesiastical Titles controversy of 1851 shows how long it continued.

Cannon: The Old Pretender ought (a) to have changed his religion and (b) to have anticipated Tom Paine with a social programme to have a decent chance of success?

Dickinson: Jacobitism had nothing to offer for most people. I agree that a handful of excluded Tories could have come back and we would have changed the royal family – but at the risk of Catholicism, civil war, French intervention – it just didn't have enough to offer people for them to take the risk.

Cannon: We have been discussing Jacobitism as one movement which might, conceivably, have threatened stability. Can we now go on to discuss another movement? We've used the word 'radical' repeatedly. We've assumed a growth of radicalism in the eighteenth century, though we argue about the extent and chronology. But what do we mean by it? Can we offer one definition or is it so relative that we have to define it for every decade?

Dickinson: Well, radicalism can be defined as wishing to overturn the whole system, but that seems a rather extreme definition; or it can merely mean those to the left in a particular political debate or context, so that one could talk about radical Whigs in the Walpole period. But that would be very different from the radicalism of the 1820s.

Cannon: Well, that is what I wanted to ask. If you take a Tory in the 1730s, who says that when he gets into power he is going to repeal the Septennial Act, root out the placemen from government, and change the political settlement, can you claim him as a radical? Bill, do you see him as a radical?

Speck: No, I don't. In so far as a label of any kind is useful, other than Tory, perhaps one sees him as a reactionary, wanting to get back to a seventeenth-century system.

Derry: But surely there can be a strong reactionary element in radicalism, particularly when it is tied up with the mythology of the ancient constitution. So much eighteenth-century radicalism was put forward in terms of restoring the pristine purity of the old constitution. That is what makes it such a diffuse movement.

Speck: If you take a very broad definition of radicalism, it must, of course, encompass very different people. I think myself that in radicalism there is a forward-looking notion.

Dickinson: If I were talking about real radicalism, I would draw attention to two very different strands. First there were the men who wanted so to amend the franchise that it would have changed the constitution far more significantly than the Reform Act of 1832 ever did. The second type is Paineite – concerned with social welfare, demanding more government involvement with the conditions of the poor. And by about the 1820s one sees the beginning of the concept that you might actually restructure the whole of society. That is only just beginning, but it is a very different form of radicalism to that of the Horne Tooke or Cartwright variety.

McCord: You don't exhaust the strands there by any means. You have the utilitarian radicals who certainly by contemporary standards would be regarded as a very important group of radicals and yet are clearly different from the ones you mention.

O'Gorman: I want to make a slightly different point and that is, how relatively disappointing the performance of radicalism is. You don't find it in very many places. At the general election of 1774, after the Wilkite movement, you have only eleven or twelve candidates whom you could regard as radical. At the general election of 1780, in the middle of the Wyvill uproar, there are not more than about fifteen to twenty. Of course, it is an unreformed electoral system and doesn't give all that chance to popular radicalism, but I am still astonished at the lukewarm reception radicalism gets.

Cannon: Isn't this partly because the radical programme of the 1760s was presented in a rather arid constitutional form? It wasn't very likely that the lower orders would be swept off their feet by the Cartwright approach, unless one could demonstrate that it meant something in terms of jobs and wages and education and houses. Which is why Paine adds such an important ingredient to the argument.

Dickinson: The comparative failure of radicals in the constituencies is understandable because the system didn't allow them enough representation. You have to look beyond that framework. I agree that the programme is so limited that it is difficult for the radicals to win widespread support. But I have done some work on the situation on Tyneside and what I have noticed is that in the clubs and the societies and the newspapers there is a great deal of discussion. It was not, perhaps, organized, committed, intense radicalism, but growing numbers of the middle orders and artisans were talking about the system and were not quite satisfied.[11] The press, I think, is of crucial importance – we haven't said enough about it – but it created the climate for more radicalism later.

Cannon: Yes, I agree with Harry about the press. It was of critical importance because it was the main way – almost the only way – in which ideas could circulate. And if I tried to explain the importance of the Wilkite agitation, I agree with Frank that it did not give much of a direct boost to radicalism, but it did help to promote the growth and freedom of the press – even if it was 40 years or so before that could be fully exploited by radical politicians.

McCord: We tend to make the assumption that what the radicals were arguing for, what they believed in, was congruent with the needs of the mass of the people. But some groups of radicals can be seen quite plainly in conflict with certain groups of workers involved in industrial disputes or restrictive practices. This is particularly true of those radicals who argued for a very strict non-interventionist political economy. In the case of the *Tyne Mercury*, for example, we see a radical newspaper often at loggerheads with groups of workers.

Holmes: Can I mildly suggest, John, that we have left behind the point on which you set us out – how do we define radicalism, how can we characterize it? I tend to apply a very literal definition, that a radical is someone who wants to effect a change in the institutions he is dissatisfied with, that he is not content to snip away at the foliage or even the branches, but wants to get down to the roots. It is a simple definition but it has its uses. Can I go on to make the further point that it is misleading to think that radicalism must always be forward-looking, or that it must always be backward-looking. In fact it very often combines both these things.

Cannon: Norman, would this ambivalence also apply to the Chartist movement? To someone like Henry Vincent, asking his listeners why they should have smoking chimneys when they could go back to fields of waving corn?

McCord: Oh, certainly, and to the anti-Corn-Law League as well.

Dickinson: The Utilitarians, perhaps?

McCord: The Utilitarians perhaps not. But this is one of the problems. We have had a lot of references to 'the radicals'. We have been a bit too simple about it. But we seem to be clearing things up now.

Cannon: We have indeed. We are going to move on now. Can we now turn to the theme of party and may I begin by addressing a brutal and rather offensive question, particularly to Frank and Bill – whether we have not paid too much attention to party? Is there not an accusation here that we have all succumbed to the dreaded Whig interpretation of history and because party became of such importance in Victorian and later times, we have spent a great deal of our own time chasing its origins in the eighteenth century? Frank?

O'Gorman: Well, I think I would agree with you. If we have not spent too much time, at least we may have looked at it too much as a narrow political phenomenon. I'm not all that worried now about the state of party historiography. Ten years ago

I didn't know where to look. Now at least I've got a vague idea. So, if you are saying that we ought not to become obsessive about party, I quite agree. . . .

Speck: Would that we could! The trouble is that other people in the profession keep coming back and telling us that the nice little pattern we have established isn't right, or doesn't fit. So we have Linda Colley and Eveline Cruickshanks and J. C. D. Clark putting forward very different views of party, and we have to defend ours or modify them in the light of their comments and their research.[12] And party is, after all, a very important branch of historiography. I think it is justified also because people in the eighteenth century – at least in the articulate classes – were rather obsessed about the nature of the political system and how party fitted into it.

O'Gorman: I don't think it matters that there is no general consensus among historians about party – there isn't much consensus about anything. But I remember that when I was a student, one could seriously ask whether there was such a thing as party in the eighteenth century. Compared with that, we have moved on. We can look at the popular contacts of the parties, at the relationship of party with radicalism, the development of a two-party system, and so on. We have a fairly firm base now.

Dickinson: Yes, but if one looks at party, the danger is that most of the people concerned are among the political élite anyway. I want to look at others outside that élite. That is where the press comes in. The press, and particularly the provincial press, is being developed mainly by people who are not among the political élite. They have to sell their newspapers, they have to find customers. And when you read the newspapers of the later eighteenth century, there is a great deal of political comment, and it grows and grows and grows. The Tyneside press of the 1790s is full of comment on the French Revolution, there are long quotes from Burke and Paine, discussions of what the London Corresponding Society and the Society for Constitutional Information and the Sheffield Society are doing. There are people intensely interested in all this, and they are not within the political nation in the strictest sense.

Holmes: I agree with Frank that there has been a good deal of progress about party in the last fifteen years or so, and I'm very thankful for it. But we ourselves have used party in various ways and over rather long periods, and it seems a valid question to ask whether we all mean the same thing by it. When, for example, we talk about the re-birth of party in the later eighteenth century, is this the same thing as parties – Whigs and Tories – in Anne's reign? We can't entirely shirk this question of definition. I've always found a useful definition was that given by J. R. Jones in his book on *The First Whigs*. He asked what were the distinguishing features of party and offered six criteria. I may be putting a gloss on some of his points. A party should have a recognized leader or leaders; it should have an organization, and that should not merely be a parliamentary organization, but should have some ramification in the localities and the constituencies; it should have a political platform, though that could clearly change from time to time; it should have some sort of central committee or directing body; it should have propaganda organs, however crude – some sort of press; and, finally, it should have some kind of political philosophy, some kind of ideological base, and that should be understood by its supporters, though obviously at various levels of sophistication. Now these are very stiff criteria. . . .

Cannon: They are indeed. I wanted to ask Frank and Bill whether they find these definitions too demanding, too sophisticated?

O'Gorman: I'm not particularly interested in definitions like this. I think it is the kind of criticism I would make of some of Donald Ginter's work – you get too involved in problems of semantics.[13] To impose a seventeenth-century definition on a nineteenth-century political party doesn't seem to me very appropriate. The Foxite Whigs may or may not meet these criteria: if they don't, I'm not much bothered – I shall still write a book on them. I don't think that there is an ideal type of party which developed from the seventeenth to the twentieth century. Party has developed different manifestations and forms at different periods.

Holmes: That is absolutely true, but it will be very confusing unless we can arrive at some sort of definition, some irreducible core.

Derry: I would strongly support that. Unless we suggest *some* criteria, the term becomes too vague to use. We have this problem particularly in the eighteenth century of differentiating between party and faction and connection. Contemporaries were very conscious of some distinction – it appears repeatedly in the literature of the period. We have

	to give some guidance. I like the Jones approach, except that we don't have to insist that each of the six elements is present all the time in every party. . . .
O'Gorman:	What's the point of the definition, then?
Derry:	Well, I think you can say, these elements were present, even if these were not. It gives us some way of distinguishing a party from a faction.
Speck:	I share Frank's suspicions of this kind of definition. I think it vitiated all of Walcott's work on Anne's reign, when he simply said that any division of the legislature is a party. I don't think that to take back wholesale a bag of definitions is very helpful.
Dickinson:	There are, I think, two essential characteristics from that list of six. One is organization. The other is that the party members must want to do certain things when they gain power – perhaps it may only be to protect the existing system. But if they haven't some aim, other than furthering their own careers, then they are purely a faction. If you haven't got at least these two characteristics, then you haven't got a party – it must be an interest or a group or a connection or something else. That is why I took the view that it is difficult to interpret the Walpole period on party lines. You have the mechanics, the organization, which Colley has identified, but there isn't enough of a platform or philosophy; on the other hand, there isn't a Country party because though you have the platform and the ideology, you haven't got enough of an organization. You have to have the two.
Speck:	I think I accept that this is the irreducible core.
Cannon:	Splendid. While we have agreement, however temporary, I shall move on to our last point. It is far too important to be left until last, but that, too, may be significant. I find it rather odd. I gave a religious explanation top priority in my paper, in the sense that I put it first among the explanations of why people became dissatisfied with the old settlement. We gave a religious definition to the constitutional arrangements, calling it the Protestant Ascendancy. Having paid lip-service to the importance of religion, we then abandoned it. Why did we abandon it? Is it because we are not really convinced that religion was so very important?. . . . You all look very shocked!
Derry:	I don't think you can read into our silence the assumption that we didn't think religion was of vast importance. It is true that we have devoted much of our attention to other

matters. But although we haven't had time to discuss religious developments, we would all recognize that this is a very important aspect of the period.

O'Gorman: I would support the hypothesis that religion is a de-stabilizing factor of great importance. The religious issues were always there, but at the turn of the century the religious revival was crucial in regenerating both parties – in the revival of popular Anglicanism, for example. The revival of religion as a divisive issue within the ruling class, as well as a popular issue in the country, was absolutely critical in the ending of political stability.

Speck: We have touched on religion in all our essays. I offered an explanation for the dimming of the glory of the Tory party in terms of a decline in religious intensity. Nevertheless, you are right that we have missed vast areas. We have missed Deism. We have missed Methodism. . . .

Dickinson: Yes, but it is because our discussions have centred on politics, so that there are huge areas of the history of the period that we have missed out in any case. But it is true that we have to connect certain aspects of religious life with what we *have* been doing. If you look at the late seventeenth and early eighteenth centuries, the religious aspects are crucial: if you look at the early nineteenth century, at the conflicts over the repeal of the Test and Corporation Acts and over Catholic emancipation, then again, religious issues are absolutely central. Whereas, in the middle of the eighteenth century, the religious differences are much more contained.

Cannon: So, we are saying that religious animosities were extremely important in producing political instability in Anne's reign, and we are saying that religious animosities were extremely important in the nineteenth century in producing instability: are we therefore arguing that one of the important causes of the comparative stability of the middle period was a decline in religious animosities and religious fervour?

O'Gorman: They were *contained*. It wasn't the disappearance of the fervour. It was the ability to contain it.

McCord: Yes. One of the things students must find most difficult – because this *is* an area of discontinuity – is to comprehend the decline in the importance of religion in society. Students who have lived all their lives in an overwhelmingly secular society must find it hard to think their way back into a period in which religion was as important as it was

in the eighteenth century. They have to make a very considerable imaginative jump. But if they do not make that
jump, they cannot really understand that society.

Holmes: Without wishing to be mischievous, let me suggest two
aspects of the problem which historians have got to come
to grips with. Perhaps one of the major reasons why
popular radicalism was so absent in the eighteenth century
is that it did not have the religious dynamism which
Puritanism had given it in the mid-seventeenth century.
Why it did not have that dynamism is something we can
hardly discuss now. Secondly, the most important popular
religious movement in the period between the 1650s and
the nineteenth century – the rise of Methodism – occurred
at precisely the moment when we seem to have agreed that
the political system and society was at its most stable.

Cannon: Can I come to a final point and put it captiously? We have
spent all this time discussing 'the eighteenth century'.
I wanted to ask whether there was such a thing as the
eighteenth century, as a significant unit of discussion. It
would be rather sad after ten hours or so of discussion to
decide that there was not, but we must be brave. We have
allowed ourselves the luxury of extending it at both ends
and pinching 12 years from the seventeenth century and 32
from the nineteenth. So, 1688 to 1832, does it make sense
and, if so, what are the characteristics of it?

O'Gorman: There's not much problem, is there? A certain type of
political and social system emerged in the later seventeenth
century and then changed itself considerably in the third
decade of the nineteenth century. It does seem to be a
régime about which generalizations can be made. I don't
see much of a problem.

Cannon: Norman, do you see any problem?

McCord: No, not really. It's part of the question of categories. We
can't spend two days just talking about history. We have to
define an area. But we have never tried to isolate it from
what came before or after, to apply a guillotine. It is as
useful a period as any.

Cannon: And you're not unhappy about ending in 1832?

McCord: No. I'm just a little unhappy about the extent to which
some people think the period of stability ended there. I
don't think it did.

Derry: 1688 to 1832 is the period of the Revolution settlement and
that does give it a certain coherence. I agree with Norman
that we have to be very careful not to suggest that in the

early 1830s there is a great upsurge of discontinuity.

Cannon: Does anyone feel that the world of Robert Harley was so far away from the world of William Cobbett that we are stretching it to get them both in? . . . I can't provoke you?

Dickinson: I thought William Cobbett wanted to get back to the seventeenth century.

Cannon: An unlucky example? On that happy note, we will stop.

Notes

Notes to chapter 1

1   E. P. Thompson, *Whigs and Hunters* (1975), Pt. 3, esp. Ch. 9.
2   J. H. Plumb, *The Growth of Political Stability in England, 1675–1725* (1967).
3   Plumb, *Political Stability*, ch. 3; J. Cannon, *Parliamentary Reform 1640–1832* (1973), pp. 33–41; W. A. Speck, *Stability and Strife: England 1714–1760* (1978), pp. 146–52, 160–3; G. Holmes, *The Electorate and the National Will in the First Age of Party* (1976) and *The Trial of Doctor Sacheverell* (1973), pp. 276–83; J. P. Kenyon, *Revolution Principles*, pp. 170–208.
4   H. T. Dickinson, *Walpole and the Whig Supremacy* (1973) pp. 93–101; W. A. Speck, *Stability and Strife*, pp. 155–8; P. G. M. Dickson, *The Financial Revolution in England . . . 1688–1756* (1967), pp. 199–204.
5   See *The Growth of Political Stability*, pp. xvi, xviii, 3, 4–9, 83, 86–92, 188.
6   I make a distinction here between this and the 'other' or 'alternative political nation' which John Brewer has illuminated in the mid-eighteenth century. Down to the 1720s at least the latter was still able to find an adequate and frequent outlet through the old electoral process.
7   See G. Holmes and W. A. Speck, editors, *The Divided Society* (1967); Holmes, *British Politics in the Age of Anne* (1967), ch. 1; Speck, 'Conflict in Society' in G. Holmes, editor, *Britain after the Glorious Revolution, 1689–1714* (1969), pp. 135–54.
8   Most systematically by the Cambridge Group for the History of Population and Social Structure, which has studied 404 'sample' parishes from the sixteenth to the eighteenth centuries, using sophisticated techniques, and more than 150 others. This paragraph could not have been written without the kindness of Dr Anne Whiteman of Lady Margaret Hall and Professor E. A. Wrigley of the Cambridge Group in making some of the Group's population estimates available to me. It owes a particular debt to Professor Wrigley, who read and commented on the first draft.
9   See, e.g., J. D. Chambers, *Population, Economy and Society in Pre-Industrial England* (1972), pp. 136–49 *passim*.
10 Even with renewed acceleration after 1736, the 6 million mark may not have been reached until the mid 1740s. The population curve described here corresponds closely with that depicted graphically in D. C. Coleman, *The Economy of England 1450–1750* (1977), p. 16, and to some extent with that presented in similar form in J. D. Chambers, *op. cit.* p. 19; although

Chambers now seems to have overestimated the scale of the recovery from 1690 to 1720.

11 J. Macky, *A Journey through England* II (1722), p. 239. Except in the 1690s meat prices remained remarkably stable throughout our period and those of the 1730s were the lowest for a century.

12 See A. H. John, 'English Agricultural Improvements, 1660–1765', in D. C. Coleman and A. H. John, editors, *Trade, Government and Economy in pre-Industrial England* (1976), pp. 48–9.

13 In just four of the thirty years from 1711 to 1740 less spectacular crop failures pushed the average price of a quartern loaf in London slightly above 6d. – a figure reached approximately every other year in the much lower-wage economy of the years 1629–61. For prices see Lord Ernle, *English Farming Past and Present* (1912), p. 440; M. Beloff, *Public Order and Popular Disturbances, 1660–1714*, table, p. 159; W. G. Hoskins, 'Harvest Fluctuations and English Economic History, 1620–1759', *Agricultural History Review XVI* (1968), p. 19.

14 As late as 1766 Charles Smith calculated that even in times of relative plenty only about 60 per cent of the population at large normally ate wheaten bread. Even so, it has been estimated that this represented a 20 per cent increase since the 1690s. Charles Smith, *Three Tracts on the Corn Trade and Corn Laws* (1766), cited in P. Deane and W. A. Cole, *British Economic Growth 1688–1959* (2nd edn., 1967), p. 63; T. S. Ashton, *Changes in Standards of Comfort in Eighteenth Century England* (Raleigh Lecture, *Proceedings of the British Academy* (1954–5), p. 173. The ratios of wheat prices to the prices of barley, rye and oats in a string of towns, published in the weekly tables of John Houghton, *A Collection for the Improvement of Husbandry and Trade* (20 vols, 1692–1703, repr. 4 vols, 1969) are often highly revealing. Cf., for example, those for 2 Feb. 1694, at the height of a serious wheat shortage, with those for 27 Feb. 1702, in a time of plenty. *Ibid.* iv, no. 79; xvii, no. 501.

15 Hoskins, 'Harvest Fluctuations', *loc. cit.* p. 21; M. Beloff, *Public Order and Popular Disturbances*, map opposite p. 68.

16 D. Defoe, *The Complete English Tradesman* (1745 edn.) I, p. 76; A. H. John, 'Aspects of English Economic Growth in the first half of the Eighteenth Century', repr. in E. M. Carus-Wilson, editor, *Essays in Economic History* II (1962), p. 366.

17 A. P. Wadsworth and J. de L. Mann, *The Cotton Trade and Industrial Lancashire* (1931), pp. 124–40.

18 *Complete English Tradesman*, I, p. 252.

19 P. Earle, *Monmouth's Rebels* (1977), pp. 4–5, 13, 16.

20 T. B. Howell, editor, *A Complete Collection of State Trials* (1809–14), XI, p. 881.

21 An operation brilliantly detected by the researches of Dr Blair Worden. See B. Worden, intro. to Edmund Ludlow, *A Voyce from the Watch Tower*, Camden Society 4th series, 21, 1978, p. 19. For 'Calves-Head' republicans, see *ibid.* p. 19; *The Secret History of the Calves-Head Club; or, the Republican Unmasked* (1703). For the Commonwealthmen, H. T. Dickinson, *Liberty and Property* (1977), pp. 105–6, 111–12, 164–6; Mark

Goldie, 'The roots of true Whiggism, 1688–94', *History of Political Thought*, I (1980), pp. 195–236.

22 Beloff, *Public Order*, pp. 25, 41–3; W. L. Sachse, 'The Mob in the Revolution of 1688', *Journal of British Studies* IV (1964).

23 G. Holmes, 'The Sacheverell Riots: The Crowd and the Church in Early Eighteenth-Century London', *Past and Present* 72 (1976), pp. 61–4.

24 Plumb, *Political Stability*, pp. 134–5; A. McInnes, 'The Revolution and the People' in G. Holmes, editor, *Britain after the Glorious Revolution*, pp. 84–90.

25 John Trenchard, in *The London Journal*, 15 June 1723. See H. T. Dickinson, *Politics and Literature in the Eighteenth Century* (1974), pp. 64–6.

26 McInnes, *loc. cit.* p. 91; Holmes and Speck, *The Divided Society*, pp. 2, 77–8. London itself was contested no fewer than 14 times between 1689 and 1715, Westminster 11 times, Southwark 12, Bristol 9 and Coventry 9. For these and many other examples see H. Horwitz, *Parliament, Policy and Politics in the Reign of William III* (1977), Appx. A; W. A. Speck, *Tory and Whig: The Struggle in the Constituencies, 1701–1715* (1970), Appx. E.

27 G. Holmes, *The Electorate and the National Will in the First Age of Party* (1976).

28 Hoskins, 'Harvest Fluctuations', pp. 22, 30.

29 *Ibid.* p. 29.

30 N. Rogers, 'Popular Protest in Early Hanoverian London', *Past and Present* 79 (1978), pp. 90, 100. See also pp. 92–3, 96–8.

31 T. H. Hollingsworth, *The Demography of the British Peerage*, supplement to *Population Studies* XVIII (1964), ch. 3–4.

32 P. Earle, *Monmouth's Rebels*, pp. 17, 28-33, 202-3.

33 Anon. letter, 12 Feb. 1722, quoted in G. V. Bennett, *The Tory Crisis in Church and State: The Career of Francis Atterbury, Bishop of Rochester* (1975) p. 240. *ibid*, chs. 11–12 and pp. 285–94 for Jacobite inertia. See also P. S. Fritz, *The English Ministers and Jacobitism between the Rebellions of 1715 and 1745* (1975).

34 *Angliae Notitia* (1694 edn.) pp. 442–3.

35 E. D. Heathcote, *An Account of the Heathcote Family* (1899), pp. 47, 63–7, 69, 75, 103, 105; 'A Paper signed by Sir Gilbert Heathcote', printed in *ibid.* appx. VI, pp. 238–9:

36 For Thomas and Sir William Scawen, see R. Sedgwick, editor, *The History of Parliament: The House of Commons, 1715–1754* (1970) II, 410–11; for Sir William, D. Defoe, *A Tour through England and Wales* (Everyman edn.), I, 158–9.

37 R. Grassby , 'Social Mobility and Business Enterprise in Seventeenth-century England', in D. Pennington and K. Thomas, editors, *Puritans and Revolutionaries* (1978), p. 357, confirms this – noting especially the increase 1650–90.

38 *Ibid.* pp. 364–5. Defoe protested in the 1720s against the 'unaccountable' rise in London premiums of relatively recent vintage; that the 'thirty or forty pounds' which was once 'sufficient to a very good merchant' was 'now run up to five hundred, nay to a thousand pounds with an apprentice'. *Complete English Tradesman* I, 112–13. His complaints are to some

extent borne out by the Stamp Office records for London from 1711 onwards. Yet It is possible to find examples of London merchants taking on gentlemen's sons for little more than £100, and in July 1712 Sir Herbert Croft, bart., of Herefordshire, indentured his son William to Jacob Hollidge, London merchant, for £215. P.R.O. I.R. 1/1/9, 1/1/120. Professor Hughes thought, on the basis of that evidence, that £130 in Liverpool was the highest provincial premium recorded *c.* 1718; but it has since been shown that a few exclusive 'gentlemen merchants' of Leeds were demanding premiums of from £150 to £300 for taking on the sons of baronets, knights and gentlemen for 7 years between 1712 and 1721. In the ports I have found gentlemen's sons bound to merchants for as little as £15 (Bideford, 1712) and as much as £200 (Hull, 1730). E. Hughes, *North Country Life in the 18th Century: the North-East* (1954), pp. 106–7; R. G. Wilson, *Gentlemen Merchants: the Merchant Community in Leeds 1700–1830* (1971), p. 24; P.R.O. I.R. 1/42/49, 1/12/75.

39 Wilson, *op. cit.* pp. 24, 246; G. Jackson, *Hull in the Eighteenth Century* (1972), pp. 104–6; T. Heywood, editor, *The Norris Papers* (Chetham Society, 1846), pp. xx–xxi and *passim*; F. E. Hyde, *Liverpool and the Mersey* (1971), pp. 13–14, 16; Hist. MSS. Comm. *Portland MSS.* IV, p. 623 for Anderson. See Wilson, *op. cit.* p. 25, Wadsworth and Mann, *Cotton Trade*, pp. 73–4, 94, P.R.O. I.R. 1/42/7 (2 Nov. 1711), for linen-drapers' and woollen-drapers' premiums in Leeds, Manchester and Bolton, much lower than those of merchants.

40 T. W. Innes Smith, *English-Speaking Students of Medicine at the University of Leyden* (1932); E. A. Underwood, *Boerhaave's Men* (1978).

41 This point will be substantiated in my forthcoming book, *Augustan England,* and in my Raleigh Lecture to the British Academy (1979), 'The Professions and Social Change in England, 1680–1730'.

42 See, e.g., *Lists of Attorneys and Solicitors admitted in pursuance of the Late Act for the Better Regulation of Attorneys and Solicitors* (by the Speaker's Order, London, 1729), pp. 3–5 and *passim*.

43 Five examples are Edward Russell, George Rooke, John Jennings, George Byng and Matthew Aylmer.

44 R. E. Scouller, *The Armies of Queen Anne* (1966), p. 327.

45 *Growth of Political Stability*, p. xviii.

46 *The Examiner,* No. 13, 2 Nov. 1710; Pakington's speech on the Bewdley election, quoted in G. Holmes, *British Politics in the Age of Anne*, p. 149.

47 Henry St John to Charles Boyle, Earl of Orrery, 9 July 1709, printed in H. T. Dickinson, editor, *The Letters of Henry St John to the Earl of Orrery, 1709–1711, Camden Miscellany* xxvi (1975), p. 146.

48 *The Examiner,* No. 37, 19 April 1711; Lord Bolingbroke, *A Letter to Sir William Wyndham* (1753 [written 1717]), p. 28; E. Chamberlayne, *Angliae Notitia* (1694), p. 583; P. G. M. Dickson, *The Financial Revolution in England . . . 1688–1756* (1967), p. 495; *The Supplement* No. 427, 6–9 Oct. 1710 (manifesto of the four Tory candidates for the city of London); D. W. Jones, 'London Merchants and the Crisis of the 1690s', in P. Clark and P. Slack, editors, *Crisis and Order in English Towns, 1500–1700*, p. 336.

49 *The Examiner*, No. 13, 2 Nov. 1710; John Macky, *A Journey through England* II (1722), pp. 41–2, 205; Defoe, *Tour* I, pp. 126–7.
50 For the latter, see *Complete English Tradesman* I, p. 247; R. Sedgwick, *op. cit.* I, pp. 479–80.
51 C. Morris, editor, *The Journeys of Celia Fiennes* (1949 ed.), p. 72; Hist. MSS. Comm. *Portland MSS.* II, p. 308. IV, p. 429; Defoe, *Tour* I, pp. 46, 222, 231, II, pp. 156, 268; Macky, *Journey* II, pp. 153–4, 172, 205.
52 See M. Walton, *Sheffield* (4th edn, Sheffield and Wakefield, 1968), pp. 104, 97–106 *passim*, 125–7, 142; C. Gill, *History of Birmingham* I (1952), pp. 60–9 *passim*; M. Rowlands, *Masters and Men in the West Midland Metalware Trades before the Industrial Revolution* (1975), pp. 114–18, for the social 'mix' in these two metal working towns in the early eighteenth century; R. G. Wilson, *Gentlemen Merchants*, pp. 208, 230, 231–2, for Leeds. For the mingling of substantial shopkeepers with professional men and prominent local landed families in the small cathedral city of Wells, see E. Hobhouse, editor, *The Diary of a West Country Physician* (1934).
53 Macky, *Journey* (1722) II, p. 211; *V.C.H. Yorkshire: The City of York* (1961), p. 531; P. Borsay, 'The English urban renaissance: the development of provincial urban culture c. 1680–c. 1760', *Social History* V (1977), p. 582.

Notes to colloquy 1

1 Particularly in *The Divided Society: Party Conflict in England 1694–1716* (1967, with W. A. Speck) and *British Politics in the Age of Anne* (1967).
2 There is an extensive note on the work of the Cambridge Group for the History of Population and Social Structure in P. Laslett, *The World We Have Lost* (2nd edn, paperback, 1971), pp. 254–7. An important article by Dr Anne Whiteman of Lady Margaret Hall, Oxford is in *Statesmen, Scholars and Merchants: Essays in Eighteenth-Century History Presented to Dame Lucy Sutherland* (1973) under the title 'The Census that Never Was: a Problem in Authorship and Dating.' For a summary of recent findings, see D. C. Coleman, *The Economy of England, 1450–1750* (1977).
3 A. J. Little, *Deceleration in the Eighteenth-Century British Economy* (1976).
4 Tony Hayter, *The Army and the Crowd in mid-Georgian England* (1978).
5 J. Stevenson, *Popular Disturbances in England, 1700–1870* (1979).

Notes to chapter 2

1 Robert Willman, 'The Origin of "Whig" and "Tory" in English Political Language', *Historical Journal*, xvii (1974), pp. 247–64.
2 See, e.g. Henry Horwitz, *Parliament, Policy and Politics in the Reign of William III* (1977); Geoffrey Holmes, *British Politics in the Age of Anne* (1967); W. A. Speck, *Tory and Whig: The Struggle in the Constituencies 1701–1715* (1970); G. S. Holmes and W. A. Speck, editors, *The Divided Society* (1967); B. W. Hill, *The Growth of Parliamentary Parties 1689–1742* (1976); E. A. Smith, *Whig Principles and Party Politics* (1975); Frank O'Gorman, *The Rise of Party in England* (1975); Frank O'Gorman,

The Whig Party and the French Revolution (1967); Frank O'Gorman, *Edmund Burke: His Political Philosophy* (1973); Michael Roberts, *The Whig Party 1807–12* (1939); and Austin Mitchell, *The Whigs in Opposition 1815–1830* (1967).

3 See, however, John Carswell, *The Old Cause* (1954), ch. 9–15; L. B. Namier, *England in the Age of the American Revolution* (2nd ed., 1961), pp. 179–202; and John Brewer, *Party Ideology and Popular Politics at the accession of George III* (1976), pp. 39–54.

4 G. S. Holmes, 'The Attack on "the Influence of the Crown" 1702–1716', *Bulletin of the Institute of Historical Research*, xxxix (1966), pp. 47–68.

5 In trying to define Whiggism I have not only used the type of book listed in notes 2 and 3, which deals primarily with Whig actions, but have had recourse to the type of book which seeks to relate political action and political ideology. The most useful of these are J. P. Kenyon, *Revolution Principles* (1977); Caroline Robbins, *The Eighteenth Century Commonwealthman* (1959); Isaac Kramnick, *Bolingbroke and His Circle* (1968), ch. 5; E. P. Thompson, *Whigs and Hunters* (1975), ch. 8–10; J. G. A. Pocock, *The Machiavellian Moment* (1975), ch. 12–14; C. C. Weston, *English Constitutional Theory and the House of Lords 1556–1832* (1965), pp. 112–214; and H. T. Dickinson, *Liberty and Property: Political Ideology in Eighteenth-Century Britain* (1977) esp. ch. 3, 4 and 8.

6 For the Whig view of natural rights and civil liberties see H. T. Dickinson, 'The Rights of Man: From John Locke to Tom Paine', in O. D. Edwards and G. A. Shepperson, editors, *Scotland, Europe and the American Revolution* (1976), pp. 38–48.

7 Peter Fraser, 'Public Petitioning and Parliament before 1832', *History*, xlvi (1961), p. 203.

8 For the power of the press see L. W. Hanson, *Government and the Press, 1695–1763* (1936); G. A. Cranfield, *The Development of the Provincial Press 1700–1760* (1962); R. M. Wiles, *Freshest Advices* (1965); Ian Christie, *Myth and Reality in Late Eighteenth-Century British Politics* (1970), pp. 311–58; and John Brewer, *Party Ideology and Popular Politics at the Accession of George III* (1976) pp. 139–60.

9 D. Hay, *et al.*, editors, *Albion's Fatal Tree* (1975), pp. 17–63.

10 See, in particular, J. P. Kenyon, 'The Revolution of 1688: Resistance and Contract', in Neil McKendrick, editor, *Historical Perspectives* (1974), pp. 43–69 and John Dunn, 'The politics of Locke in England and America in the Eighteenth Century', in John Yolton, editor, *John Locke: Problems and Perspectives* (1969), pp. 45–80.

11 'Instructions' were used spasmodically in the early Hanoverian period, but nearly all were organized by opposition MPs to enlist the support of their constituents against the administration. London was the only constituency prepared to send 'instructions' without being encouraged by its representatives in parliament.

12 See, e.g., the debate in *London Journal*, 23 June 1733, 5, 12 and 19 Oct. 1734; *Free Briton*, 18 Jan., 28 June 1733; *Common Sense*, 18 June 1737; and *The Craftsman*, 24 May 1735, 28 Feb. 1736.

13 See, e.g., the speeches of Governor Pownall in 1769 and of Chatham in

1775 in [T. C. Hansard,] *Parliamentary History of England*, xvi, 612 and xviii, 153–154 note.

14   See, e.g., the speeches of Grey, Fox, Pitt and Dundas, all of whom appealed to the Whig constitution, in *ibid.*, xxix, 1301, xxix, 1315, xxxii, 357–8, and xxxii, 467.

15   See, in particular, Burke's *An Appeal from the New to the Old Whigs* (1791), in *Works* (Bohn ed., 6 vols., 1854–8), iii, 1–115.

16   I am indebted to my colleague Dr F. D. Dow for her helpful comments on an early draft of this essay.

Notes to chapter 3

1   Sir Lewis Namier, *England in the Age of the American Revolution* (1961), pp. 179–80.

2   *ibid*, p. 191.

3   J. Brooke, *The House of Commons 1754–1790: Introductory Survey* (1964), p. 273.

4   Sir Lewis Namier, 'Monarchy and the Party System', *Personalities and Powers* (1955), p. 32.

5   *ibid*, pp. 21–2.

6   Sir Lewis Namier, *The Structure of Politics at the Accession of George III* (1957), p. xi.

7   R. Walcott, *English Politics in the Early Eighteenth Century* (1956), p. 160.

8   *ibid*, p. 155.

9   Professor Walcott made his cards available to other historians on micro-film which he kindly deposited in the Institute of Historical Research in London.

10   Walcott, *op. cit.*, p. 34.

11   This paragraph is based on chapter two of my unpublished Oxford D. Phil thesis *The House of Commons 1702–1714: a Study in Political Organization*.

12   G. Holmes, *British Politics in the Age of Anne* (1967), pp. 382–403, 421–35.

13   These paragraphs are based on W. A. Speck, *Tory and Whig: The Struggle in the Constituencies 1701–1715* (1970); W. A. Speck and W. A. Gray, 'Computer Analysis of Poll Books, an Initial Report', *Bulletin of the Institute of Historical Research* (1970), xliii, 105–112; W. A. Speck, W. A. Gray and R. Hopkinson, 'Computer Analysis of Poll Books, a Further Report', *ibid*, (1975), xlviii, 64–90.

14   J. Owen, *The Eighteenth Century* (1974), pp. xiv, 94–122.

15   R. Sedgwick, editor, *The House of Commons 1715–1754* (1970), i, ix. Dr Cruickshanks has repeated her claims in *Political Untouchables: The Tories and the '45* (1979).

16   R. Patten, *The History of the late Rebellion* (1717), pp. 93–4.

17   R. Sedgwick, *op. cit.*, ii, 46.

18   *ibid*, p. 423.

19   Stuart MSS 65/16, cited in Sedgwick, *passim*, and published in P. S. Fritz,

The English Ministers and Jacobitism (1975), 147–55.

20 Fritz, *op. cit.*, pp. 152–5.

21 The following paragraph is based on information in Sedgwick, *op. cit.*

22 *ibid*, i, 172. Linda Colley, 'The Loyal Brotherhood and the Cocoa Tree: The London Organization of the Tory Party, 1727–1760', *Historical Journal* (1977), xx, 77–95.

23 Linda Colley, 'The Tory Party 1727–60' (PhD thesis, Cambridge 1976). See Note on Further Reading.

24 B. W. Hill, *The Growth of Parliamentary Parties, 1689–1742* (1976), p. 147.

25 *ibid.*, pp. 147, 213.

26 *ibid.*, p. 227; D. Hayton and C. Jones, editors, *A Register of Parliamentary Lists 1660–1761* (1979).

27 The lists are analysed in Sedgwick, *op. cit.*, i. 86–7, 89–90, 104–5, though he classifies nearly all Court Tories as Whigs.

28 Hill, *op. cit.*, p. 191.

29 J. C. D. Clark, 'The Decline of Party, 1740–60,' *English Historical Review* (1978), xciii, 499–527.

30 J. Owen, 'The Survival of Country Attitudes in the Eighteenth-Century House of Commons,' in J. S. Bromley and E. H. Kossmann, editors, *Britain and the Netherlands* (1971), iv, 42–69.

31 Namier, *Structure*, p. x.

32 J. Brooke, *op. cit.*, p. 272.

33 Sir Richard Cocks, *A Charge Given to the Grand Jury of the County of Gloucester at the Midsummer Sessions, 1723* (1723), p. 21.

34 On Country ideology, see J. G. A. Pocock, *Politics, Language and Time* (1972), and also his *The Machiavellian Moment* (1975); H. T. Dickinson, *Liberty and Property* (1977), pp. 163–92.

35 E. Cruickshanks, *Political Untouchables*, p. 30.

36 By I. Kramnick, *Bolingbroke and His Circle* (1968).

37 Edward Wortley Montagu, 'On the State of Affairs When the King Entered,' *Correspondence of Lady Mary Wortley Montagu* (1887), i. 21.

38 Q. Skinner, 'The Principles and Practice of Opposition: the Case of Bolingbroke versus Walpole,' in N. McKendrick, editor, *Historical Perspectives: Studies in English Political Thought and Society in Honour of J. H. Plumb* (1974), p. 97.

39 P. Langford, *The Excise Crisis* (1975), p. 107.

40 cited *ibid.*, p. 107.

41 *ibid.*, pp. 114–5.

42 N. Rogers, 'Resistance to Oligarchy: the City Opposition to Walpole and his Successors,' in J. Stevenson, editor, *London in the Age of Reform* (1977), pp. 2, 5.

43 Sir Lewis Namier, 'Monarchy and the Party System,' *Personalities and Powers* (1955), p. 33.

44 Langford, *op. cit.*, pp. 116–7.

45 The seven certainties were Bristol, Kent, Liverpool, St Albans, Sussex, Wareham and Yorkshire; the five possibles were Evesham, Hampshire, Peterborough, Stamford and Worcester. See R. Sedgwick, *op. cit.*,

volume one, under these constituencies.

46   Langford, *op. cit.*, pp. 124–50.
47   See Foord, *op. cit.*, pp. 154–5.
48   Hugh Boscawen to the Prince of Wales, 12 May 1741, cited R. Sedgwick, *op. cit.*, i. 477.

Notes to colloquy 3

1   Chorus of fairies and chorus of peers from Act II of Gilbert and Sullivan's *Iolanthe*.
2   Geoffrey Holmes, 'Harley, St John and the Death of the Tory Party,' in G. Holmes, editor, *Britain after the Glorious Revolution* (1969), p. 325.

Notes to chapter 4

1   Caroline Robbins, 'Discordant Parties: a Study of the Acceptance of Party by Englishmen,' *Political Science Quarterly*, LXXIII (1955); Peter Campbell, 'An Early Defence of Party', *Political Studies* III (1955), pp. 176–7; J. A. W. Gunn, *Factions No More* (1971), p. 12.
2   John Brewer has claimed that Burke intended party to be permanent but he adduces no evidence at all to suggest that it ought to have a life longer than that of the next Rockingham administration: *Party Ideology and Popular Politics at the Accession of George III* (1976), pp. 72–4.
3   P. Langford, *The First Rockingham Administration, 1765–66* (1973), p. 283. Namier was fond of remarking that the Rockinghams were the spiritual descendants of the Tories. *England in the Age of the American Revolution* (2nd edn. 1961). pp. 185–6, 190–91.
4   Rockingham to Devonshire, 23 December 1762, Chatsworth MSS.
5   Lord Rockingham to Lord John Cavendish, 18 September 1775, R. 158–84, Wentworth Woodhouse MSS, Sheffield Public Library.
6   See L. B. Namier, *op. cit.*, pp. 185–6., 190; J. Brooke, *The Chatham Administration 1766–68* (1956), pp. 282–3.
7   As Mr Brooke suggests (*ibid.*, p. 234) and as Dr Langford at times comes dangerously near to arguing in *The First Rockingham Administration*, p. 288: 'it remodelled and redefined the party of the "Old Whigs".'
8   For these figures, see *The Rise of Party*, pp. 219–22 and Appendix One.
9   *The First Rockingham Administration, 1765–66*, p. 272.
10   Namier regarded them as the vehicles of The Rise of Party in the reign of George III: *England in the Age of the American Revolution*, pp. 415–18. See my treatment of the 'Young Friends' in *The Rise of Party*, pp. 46–66.
11   This fact is acknowledged by Dr Langford (*ibid.*, p. 271) and, surprisingly, by Dr Owen in *The Eighteenth Century, 1714–1815* (1974), p. 283.
12   M. Bateson, editor, *The Duke of Newcastle's Narrative of Changes in the Ministry, 1765–67* (1898), p. 2.
13   J. Brewer, *op. cit.*, p. 76. Namier's view of the Rockingham's Economic Reform campaign is, frankly, ridiculous. His judgement that 'the Rockinghams were out to destroy the edifice which the Pelhams had built for their

party' is nonsensical. *England in the Age of the American Revolution,* p. 190.

14 It is a charming fancy to suggest that the 'Conciliabulum' was the ancestor of the shadow cabinet. But functions within it were not sufficiently diversified to allow it to be so regarded. For examples of the meeting of the 'Conciliabula' see my *The Rise of Party,* pp. 145, 190, 385, 552 n 14.

15 The party's support in the House of Lords in 1763 had been 40–50; F. O'Gorman, *The Rise of Party,* pp. 481–2, 516 n 46. It dropped to 35 by 1770 and to 25 by 1776; A. Olson, *op. cit.,* p. 33, n 6.

16 Their list of successes includes the Nullum Tempus Act of 1769, Savile's Catholic Relief Act of 1778. Their failures include their bills to protect the rights of electors, to declare the rights of juries, to reform the Poor Law, to disqualify Contractors from sitting in the House and of revenue officers from voting. It is astonishing, therefore, that Olson can comment (*op. cit.,* p. 37): 'So little common ground had the party for discussion that many abortive bills were prepared but never even discussed'.

17 D. Ginter, *Whig Organization in the General Election of 1790* (1967), p. xlvii. Dr Colley observes that, with the Tories, whipping was left to patrons and doubts that there was a standardized format available to the whips; 'The Tory Party, 1727–60', unpublished PhD thesis, Cambridge 1976, p. 31.

18 L. Colley, *op. cit.,* pp. 32–3. Another comparison is afforded by the five divisions on the Wilkes issue for which lists survive taken between January and March 1769. Of the 56 Rockingham Whigs then in the House only one voted with the ministry, four did not vote at all. Of the remaining 51, 37 voted at least four times (72 per cent). On 9 January 1770, 39 of 52 turned out (73 per cent) and, on 25 January 1770, 40 out of 52 (78 per cent).

19 A. S. Foord, *His Majesty's Opposition, 1714–1832* (1964), p. 359.

20 Dr Brewer believes that the history of Wildman's illustrates 'the fragility of opposition organization' and 'the extent to which an opposition was dependent upon issues'. The second is a truism – when have oppositions *not* been dependent upon issues? – and the first is ambiguous. Opposition organization continued to be fragile long into the nineteenth century; J. Brewer, *op. cit.,* pp. 60–62.

21 A. S. Foord, *op. cit.,* p. 352.

22 For the navy, see J. A. Davies, 'An Enquiry into Faction among British Naval Officers during the American War of Independence', (unpublished MA dissertation, University of Liverpool, 1964). For the army, see the comments of G. H. Guttridge, *English Whiggism and the American Revolution* (1966), p. 55.

23 John Brewer, however, argues, though without citing any evidence, that 'the election of 1784 marked the almost complete destruction of the Rockinghamite edifice', but only proceeds to register the well known fact that the Fox – North coalition lost the election of 1784. It may be the case that in 1784 'aristocratic Whiggery took a terrible beating' but it had a long life ahead of it. 'Rockingham, Burke and Whig Political Argument', *Historical Journal,* XVIII (1975).

24 *ibid.,* p. 294.

25　F. O'Gorman, *The Whig Party and the French Revolution* (1967), pp. 244–9. Edmund Burke's 'An Authentic List of the Whole House of Commons' (Milton MSS, a xxxviii, f. 19, Northamptonshire County Record Office, Northampton) needs to be used much more critically than Dr Mitchell uses it in *Charles James Fox and the Disintegration of the Whig Party* (1971). p. 35. Burke's list shows that after Fox's resignation in July 1782 '84 members of the old opposition were to be found voting with Pitt by March 1784. Of these 61 were already voting with Shelburne in March 1783. . .' However, on closer examination, the 61 listed turned out to be independents and Chathamites. Only one had contact with the Rockinghams, J. Townshend, and his inclusion on the list would appear to be an error, to judge from his voting record. (Perhaps James Townsend is meant). Nevertheless, the impact of the 1784 election to judge from this list – a loss to Fox of 89 MPs – is close to my own estimate of 70–90 MPs; *The Whig Party and the French Revolution*, pp. 245–6.

26　Professor Ginter first drew attention to these developments in his article, 'The Financing of the Whig Party Organization 1783–1793', *American Historical Review*, LXXI, (1966). His full statement is contained in his Introduction to *Whig Organization*. My own general treatment of these issues may be found in *The Whig Party and the French Revolution*, pp. 12–31.

27　Professor Ginter goes on: 'Nor did they normally compete for seats where they had no personal interest. There were occasions when they did so, and there is no intention here to draw too fine a line between the 1780s and the two preceding decades.' Perish the thought. (D. Ginter, *Whig Organization*, p. xviii). John Brewer agrees with this formulation (*op. cit.*, pp. 59–60).

28　Portland had begun to attack Wigan as early as 1763. In 1768 he tried to invade Callington, Coventry, Leicester and Radnorshire. At the elections of 1774 and 1780 he intervened in London, Westminster, Buckinghamshire, Derbyshire, Lancashire and Nottinghamshire. In the electoral sense, perhaps, Portland was the heir of Newcastle and the crucial link between the old corps electoral organization in office and the institutionalization of party in the 1780s.

29　Ginter, *op. cit.*, p. xlv.

30　The revival of the Whig party in Yorkshire, for example, owed far more to Fitzwilliam than to Adam's party machine. E. A. Smith, *Whig Principles and Party Politics: Earl Fitzwilliam and the Whig Party, 1748–1833* (1975), ch. 4. Mr Smith writes, 'Nevertheless, the central organization remained dependent on the initiative and activity of local magnates, and tended merely to fill the gaps between their semi-autonomous spheres of influence.' (p. 112).

31　Ginter, *op. cit.*, pp. xlviii–xlix.

32　As is claimed by B. W. Hill: 'Fox and Burke: the Whig Party and the Question of Principles, 1784–1789', *English Historical Review*, (1974).

33　It is surely a considerable omission on Dr Hill's part to prove that anyone, other than Burke, worried lest Rockinghamite principles might be 'no longer sufficient to ensure the survival of the Whig party'. (*ibid.*, p. 24).

Further, it is sometimes assumed that the line of division in the party before 1789 was that between 'old Rockinghamites' and 'Foxite radicals'. Yet, of the 66 MPs I have judged to be Foxite Whigs in 1794, no fewer than 32 *failed* to support Parliamentary reform in May 1793. See my *The Whig Party and the French Revolution*, pp. 237–8, 253–4.

34 For the 'recovery' of the Whig Party see F. O'Gorman, *The Whig Party and the French Revolution*, pp. 51–2, 59–62; E. A. Smith, *op. cit.*, pp. 87–8, 90–93, 96, 112–3. If the Regency Crisis of 1788–89 weakened these efforts, the party was once again recovering by the election of 1790. E. A. Smith, *op. cit.*, pp. 106–12. For a rather more pessimistic view see L. G. Mitchell, *op. cit.*, pp. 99–101 but even he attributes the weakness of the party in 1784–86 to a 'tactical withdrawal' by Fox rather than to a fatal malaise.

35 These enmities are dealt with elegantly and in detail by John W. Derry, *The Regency Crisis and the Whigs, 1788–89* (1963). 'The hard work of Fitz-william and his friends to recover the ground lost in Yorkshire in 1784 was thrown away almost overnight by Fox's blunders'; E. Smith, *op. cit.*, p. 106. But there is no evidence that these divisions and disappointments had any impact on the election of 1790, for example. Referring to the quarelling sections of the party, one newspaper stated that though the 'friends may differ on the idea of French Liberty, their unanimity in the *great cause* still remains fixed to its final purpose.' *The Times*, 22 June 1790. In fact the Regency Crisis may be said to have gingered up the party's machine both in parliament and in the country. The strict party voting of the opposition during the crisis was most impressive. The crisis placed the opposition's election machine up and down the country in a state of readiness.

36 Fox to Lord Holland, 8 February 1801, in Lord John Russell, editor, *Memoirs and Correspondence of Charles James Fox*, 4 vols., (1853–57), III, p. 186.

37 L. G. Mitchell, *op. cit.*, p. 215.

38 As Dr Mitchell seems to do, stressing that 'Fox bequeathed to the nineteenth century a markedly different party than that left behind by Rockingham in 1782'. (*ibid.*, p. 269). It was also, in many ways, a markedly similar party.

39 A. Mitchell, *The Whigs in Opposition, 1815–30*, (1967), pp. 38–40.

40 M. Hinton, 'The General Elections of 1806 and 1807', (unpublished PhD thesis, Reading 1959), pp. 10–12, 36, 52–61. See also, P. C. Lipscomb, 'George Canning and the Trinidad Question', *Historical Journal* XII, (1969): 'In seeking to drive Addington from office Canning hoped to transform Pitt's connection into a large party'.

41 By 1800 there were probably only about 100 Independents left in the House of Commons. Derek Jarrett has challenged the traditional view of the Independents and has found them far from Independent. 'The Myth of Patriotism in Eighteenth Century British Politics' in J. Bromley and E. H. Kossmann, editors, *Britain and the Netherlands*, vol. v (1975).

42 A. Mitchell, *op. cit.*, p. 66; A. Aspinall and E. A. Smith, editors, *English Historical Documents, 1783–1832* (1959) p. 254.

43   J. Brooke, *The Chatham Administration*, p. 386.
44   D. Large, 'The Decline of the Party of the Crown and the Rise of Parties in the House of Lords, 1783–1837', *English Historical Review*, LXXVIII (1963).

Notes to colloquy 4

1   D. E. Ginter, *Whig Organization in the General Election of 1790* (1967).
2   A. Mitchell, *The Whigs in Opposition, 1815–1830* (1967).

Notes to chapter 5

1   W. J. Smith, editor, *Grenville Papers*, i, 223.
2   G. F. A. Best, 'The Protestant Constitution and its Supporters, 1800–1829,' *Transactions of the Royal Historical Society* (1958), 5th series, vol. 8 refers to repeal of the Test and Corporation Acts as 'the first two stages of a thoroughgoing constitutional revolution in Church and State.'
3   'Sir Robert Peel's Address to the Electors of the Borough of Tamworth', *Quarterly Review*, vol. liii, pp. 262–87.
4   *Parl. Debates*, 3rd Series, xxviii; Parkes is quoted in G. B. A. M. Finlayson, 'The Politics of Municipal Reform, 1835,' *English Historical Review* (1966), vol. lxxxi, 687.
5   See, for example, the complaint by John Wilks, a prominent dissenting MP in May 1835 that, since the repeal of the Test and Corporation Acts, not one Dissenter had been admitted to the 64-strong corporation of Liverpool; *Parl. Debates*, 3rd series, xxviii, 25.
6   'Municipal Reform,' *Quarterly Review* (1835), vol. cvii, pp. 231–49.
7   J. Brewer, *Party Ideology and Popular Politics at the Accession of George III* (1976), p. 9.; C. Bonwick, *English Radicals and the American Revolution* (1977), p. 148.
8   D. Jarrett, *The Begetters of Revolution: England's Involvement with France, 1759–89* (1973), p. 65; W. J. Shelton, *English Hunger and Industrial Disorders* (1973), p. 3.
9   *George III, Lord North and the People, 1779–80* (1949), p. vi.
10   John Cannon, editor, *The Letters of Junius* (1978), p. 408.
11   'On the Present State of Public Affairs at Home', vol. x.
12   There were of course certain boroughs, such as Sudbury and Taunton, where the Dissenting interest was powerful or even predominant, but in most corporations Dissenters were kept out.
13   Quoted John Cannon, *Parliamentary Reform, 1640–1832* (1973), pp. 53, 69.
14   *Parl. Debates*, New series, xviii, 714.
15   Something of the old hostility between Catholics and Protestant Dissenters was also diminishing. Though the tactical question of relations with the Catholics was still of great importance, fewer Dissenters were willing to put up with their disabilities lest any imprudent move on their part should play into the hands of the Papists.

16 *Parl. Debates*, New series, xviii, 731−2.

17 *ibid.*, 692.

18 Among the more obvious objections are that the division into excluded and included is too sharp: a man might have influence in certain areas and not in others.

19 This is the minimum, counting only fully committed members − see A. D. Gilbert, *Religion and Society in Industrial England*, p. 16 & note 37; C. Binfield, *So Down to Prayers: Studies in English Nonconformity, 1780−1920* (1977), p. 8; Speck, *op. cit.*, pp. 100−01 offers different figures but agrees that Dissent was in decline.

20 J. Bossy, *The English Catholic Community, 1570−1850* (1975), pp. 286−7, denies that Catholicism was actually in decline but does not argue for any vigorous advance.

21 F. R. Taylor, *Methodism and Politics* (1935), p. 98; R. Cowherd, *The Politics of English Dissent* (1959), pp. 31−2.

22 Bossy, *op. cit.*, pp. 303−16, 424.

23 *Parl. Debates*, New series, xviii, 696−7.

24 G. I. T. Machin, *The Catholic Question in English Politics, 1820−30* (1964), p. 114.

25 *Parl. Debates*, New series, xviii, 715.

26 The division list printed in *Parl. Debates*, New series, xix, 236−7 is described as on the third reading of the bill and shows several bishops opposing it. But it is clearly misplaced. The third reading was not on the 23rd but the 28th. The Bishop of Bath & Wells, shown as opposing the bill, made a speech (185) explaining why he supported it. The division must be that on Eldon's amendment to include the phrase 'I am a Protestant' in the declaration which was to replace the sacramental test.

27 *Parl. Debates*, New series, xix, 177−8.

28 See also, U. R. Q. Henriques, *Religious Toleration in England, 1787−1833* (1961); K. S. Inglis, *Churches and the Working Classes in Victorian England* (1963); W. R. Ward, *Religion and Society in England, 1790−1850* (1972); R. W. Davis, 'The Strategy of "Dissent" in the Repeal Campaign, 1820−28', *Journal of Modern History*, vol. 38 (1966), pp. 374−93.

29 *CJ*, lxxviii, 77; lxxix, 518; lxxxiii, 374.

30 *Parl. Debates*, New series, xx, 94.

31 Machin, *op. cit.*, pp. 14, 25−31, 43, 60−1, 116.

32 *The Greville Memoirs*, ed. L. Strachey & R. Fulford (1938), i, 212.

33 *Parl. Debates*, New series, xx, 15, 20, 68, 96.

34 *ibid.*, 799−800, 70.

35 *ibid.*, 3rd series, ii, 1346.

36 Robert Waithman, answering the objection in 1819 that reform would let in 'the rabble', retorted: 'Why, Sir, you have already got the rabble: it is the rabble who vote in most of the rotten boroughs, while the people of property and respectability are excluded.' *Parl. Debates*, xl, 1490. This was an ingenious attempt to turn the old argument upside down.

37 J. K. Hedges, *History of Wallingford* (1881), ii, 203; *Political Register*, 7, 14, 28 June 1806.

38 M. Bond, *Guide to the Records of Parliament*, p. 172; *Parl. Debates*,

New series, xx, 570−6.

39   *ibid.*, lxxii, 215 − 'their misery is greater than they can bear'; *Parl. Debates,* xxxvi, 21−5.

40   *ibid.*, New series, ix, 1072−3.

41   *ibid.*, New series, xx, 131.

42   John Cannon, editor, *The Letters of Junius*, p. xv.

43   G. A. Cranfield, *The Press and Society: from Caxton to Northcliffe* (1978), 93, 140; I. R. Christie, 'British Newspapers in the later Georgian age,' *Myth and Reality in Late Eighteenth-Century British politics* (1970), pp. 311−33.

44   Quoted Cranfield, *op. cit.*, pp. 81, 95.

45   Hereford City Library.

46   *The Letters of Junius*, p. 411.

47   C. Wyvill, *Political Papers, Chiefly Respecting the Attempt of the County of York. . .to Effect a Reformation of the Parliament of Great Britain* (1794−1802), ii, 95.

48   Quoted *VCH Warwickshire*, vii, 4.

49   James Ogden, *A Description of Manchester by a Native of the Town* (1783).

50   *CJ*, lxxxii, 498.

51   *ibid.*, lxxxv, 96.

52   *ibid.*, lxxxv, 405. There is also some evidence of restlessness against the local oligarchies in some boroughs with representation. The number of contested elections rose considerably in the nineteenth century: at the general election of 1818 there were at least 93 contests in England compared with only 46 in 1761. Malmesbury had been a secure corporation borough for most of the eighteenth century, but there were contests in 1796, 1802, 1806 and 1807. On the last occasion, the petitioners complained that the borough had, for many years, been represented 'to its great injury, by strangers totally unconnected with the place and its interests, and utterly unknown even to the electors themselves, who are only made acquainted with their names the instant before they are to elect them.' *CJ*, lxii, 33−4. A similar protest was maintained at Bath, where the excluded citizens complained that '22 self-appointed individuals' claimed 'the exclusive right of choosing two representatives for a city containing a population of 35,000 persons;' *CJ*, lxviii, 17). There were long-drawn-out struggles against the Exeter interest at Stamford and the Grosvenor interest at Shaftesbury in the 1820s, the latter being hailed by *The Times* in 1830 as a political landmark. There had always, of course, been revolts in some boroughs and until the volumes of the *History of Parliament* covering the period after 1790 are published, it will be difficult to say how significant the trend was. But the fact that so many of these campaigns failed meant that the dissidents had little hope save through comprehensive reform of the electoral and municipal systems.

53   *Parl. Debates*, New series, xviii, 1292.

54   *CJ*, lxxxv, 96.

55   *Bristol Journal*, 26 January 1822, quoted T. L. Crosby, *English Farmers and the Politics of Protection, 1815−52* (1977), p. 66.

56   *Parl. Debates*, New series, vii, 50.

57 Crosby, *op. cit.*, p. 74.
58 'The bad quality and high price of the article sold under the denomination of beer'. *CJ*, lxxviii, 81.
59 I do not deny that they were able to win important concessions in detail – e.g. the Chandos clause in the third Reform Bill, nor that they had important political consequences – e.g. in bringing down Wellington's government.
60 Grey to Holland, 5 January 1810, Add. MS. 51551, f. 73; see also Grey to Holland, 13 June 1809, Add. MS. 51551, ff. 27–8.
61 See E. A. Wasson, 'The Coalition of 1827 and the Crisis of Whig Leadership,' *Historical Journal* (1977), xx, 587–606.
62 W. N. Massey, *History of England During the Reign of George III* (1855), iv, 3 note c, 45 note k.
63 R. B. McDowell, editor, *The Correspondence of Edmund Burke*, vol. viii (1969), p. 345.
64 Grey to Holland, 3 April 1809 & 5 January 1810, Add. MS. 51551, ff. 7–8, 73–4.
65 E. Phipps, editor, *Memoirs of Robert Plumer Ward* (1850), ii, 17.
66 L. J. Jennings, editor, *The Correspondence and Diary of John Wilson Croker* (1884), i, 170.
67 Russell to Moore, 31 March 1828, in R. Russell, editor, *The Early Correspondence of Lord John Russell* (1913), i, 272.
68 See the comment by Patrick Colquhoun, *Treatise on the Wealth, Power and Resources of the British Empire* (2nd edn. 1818), p. 49: 'it is fair to conclude that the rapid strides which this nation has made in the course of the last and present century towards wealth and power may fairly be imputed to the form of government. . . .'
69 See Pitt's defence in February 1792, quoted in Derry's chapter on p. 127.
70 *Parl. Debates*, 3rd series, ii, 1341–3.

Notes to colloquy 5

1 *CJ*, vol. 72, pp. 55–6.
2 Asa Briggs, 'The Background of the Parliamentary Reform Movement in Three English Cities,' *Cambridge Historical Journal* (1950–52); John Money, *Experience and Identity: Birmingham and the West Midlands, 1760–1800* (1977); Donald Read, *Press and People, 1790–1850: Opinion in Three English Cities* (1961).

Notes to chapter 6

1 *Speeches of William Pitt* (London 1806) II 36.
2 *op. cit.*, II 46.
3 *Ibid.*
4 *op. cit.*, II 204.
5 *op. cit.*, II 331.
6 *op. cit.*, II 338.

7   *Hansard* XXXVI 1006.
8   *op. cit.*, XXXVI 2.
9   S. Bamford, *Passages in the Life of a Radical* (1967) 147–8.
10 C. Emsley, 'The London Insurrection of December 1792: Fact, Fiction, or Fantasy?', *Journal of British Studies*, (Spring 1978), 86.
11 *Speeches of William Pitt* II 365.
12 *op. cit.*, II 368.
13 *op. cit.*, II 373.
14 N. McCord, 'The Seaman's Strike of 1815 in North East England', *Economic History Review*, 2nd series, XXI, No. 1, 1968.
15 *Hansard* XXXVI 929.
16 *Hansard* XXXIV 272.
17 *Memoirs and Correspondence of Castlereagh* (ed. Londonderry) (1848–54) IV 394.
18 *Hansard* XVII 192.
19 Castlereagh to Cooke 4 June 1815, *Castlereagh Correspondence* X 377.
20 H. Twiss, *Life of Lord Chancellor Eldon* (1844) II 330–33.
21 *ibid.*
22 Dundas to Addington, 22 March 1803, Lord Stanhope, *Life of William Pitt* (1867) IV 24.
23 W. R. Brock, *Lord Liverpool and Liberal Toryism* (1941) 68.
24 H. van Thal, editor, *The Prime Ministers* (1974), i, 247.
25 D. Read, *Peterloo: The Massacre and Its Background* (1957) 207.
26 J. E. Cookson, *Lord Liverpool's Administration 1815–1822* (1975) 193–4.
27 *op. cit.*, 396.
28 B. Hilton, *Corn, Cash and Commerce: The Economic Policies of the Tory Governments 1815–30* (1977) 314.
29 H. Twiss, *op. cit.*, II 118.

Notes to colloquy 6

1   R. Quinault and J. Stevenson, editors, *Popular Protest and Public Order: Six Studies in British History, 1790–1920* (1975).

Notes to chapter 7

1   D. Bythell, *The Sweated Trades: Outwork in Nineteenth-Century Britain* (1978), p. 41.
2   J. H. Clapham, *An Economic History of Modern Britain: The Early Railway Age* (1930), p. 66n.
3   N. McCord & D. J. Rowe, 'Industrialization and Urban Growth in Northeast England', *International Review of Social History*, Vol. XXII (1977), Part I, p. 31.
4   Quoted by R. M. Reeve, *The Industrial Revolution 1750–1850* (1971), p. 105. This book provides a convenient survey of much of the basic information relating to economic change during this period.
5   D. J. Rowe, 'The Culleys, Northumberland Farmers', *Agricultural*

History Review Vol. 19, (1971), pp. 156–74.

S. Macdonald, 'The Role of George Culley in the Development of Northumberland Agriculture', *Archaeologia Aeliana*, 5th. Ser., Vol. III, (1975), pp. 131–141.

6 A. E. Musson, 'Industrial Motive Power in the United Kingdom, 1800–1870', *Economic History Review*, 2nd. Ser., Vol. XXIX, (1976), p. 416. This paper is of more general relevance to the argument here.

7 J. R. Wordie, 'Social Change on the Leveson-Gower Estates, 1714–1832', *Economic History Review*, 2nd series, Vol. XXVII (1974), pp. 601–2.

8 F. M. L. Thompson, 'Nineteenth-Century Horse Sense', *Economic History Review*, 2nd series, Vol. XXIX (1976), p. 79.

9 R. M. Reeve, *op. cit., passim*.

10 D. Davis, *A History of Shopping* (1966), pp. 265–6.

11 McCord & Rowe, *op. cit.*, pp. 34–5.

12 N. McCord, *The Anti-Corn Law League* (1958), p. 31.

13 For a full discussion on this point see J. T. Ward & R. G. Wilson, editors, *Land and Industry* (1971), especially the papers by D. Spring and J. T. Ward.

14 The varied interests of the Ridley family are discussed in W. R. Sullivan, *Blyth in the Eighteenth Century* (1971). F. M. L. Thompson, *English Landed Society in the Nineteenth Century* (1963) also contains a number of relevant references.

15 P. J. V. Rolo, *George Canning* (1965), pp. 167–8. Dr Robert Robson has informed me that Canning's letters contain other similar statements.

16 Quoted by A. V. Dicey, *Law and Public Opinion in England* (2nd. ed. 1962), p. 187 n. 1.

17 W. L. Burn, 'Newcastle upon Tyne in the Early Nineteenth Century', *Archaeologia Aeliana*, 4th. Ser., Vol. XXXIV, (1956), p. 8.

18 M. W. Flinn, 'Trends in Real Wages, 1750–1850', *Economic History Review*, 2nd series, Vol. XXVII (1974), pp. 412–3.

19 M. W. Flinn, *op. cit.*

20 Clapham, *op. cit.*, pp. 66–74.

21 The correspondence relating to this incident is in Public Record Office, H.O. 42/53.

22 E. Midwinter, *Social Administration in Lancashire, 1830–1860* (1969), p. 37.

23 N. Gash, *Mr Secretary Peel* (1961), p. 297.

24 H. Parris, 'A Civil Servant's Diary', *Public Administration* (Winter 1960), p. 370.

25 C. Lloyd, *Mr Barrow of the Admiralty* (1970). Barrow's career is summarized in the *Dictionary of National Biography*.

26 R. Blake, *Disraeli* (1966), p. 333.

27 Public Record Office, H.O. 87/1, documents of 11 and 31 August 1836.

28 R. Rawlinson, *Report. . .on. . .Sanitary Condition of Alnwick, etc.* (1850), p. 76.

The Hexham passage is quoted by G. Cadman, 'The Administration of the Poor Law Amendment Act, 1834, in the Hexham Poor Law Union', (M. Litt. thesis, Newcastle University, 1976), p. 390.

29 D. Owen, *English Philanthropy, 1660–1960* (1965). For a briefer account, N. McCord, 'The Poor Law and Philanthropy', in D. Fraser, editor, *The New Poor Law in the Nineteenth Century* (1976), pp. 87–110.

Note to colloquy 7

1 The many publications of J. L. and Barbara Hammond included *The Village Labourer, 1760–1832* (1911); *The Town Labourer, 1760–1832* (1917); *The Skilled Labourer, 1760–1832* (1919) and *The Age of the Chartists, 1832–54: a Study of Discontent* (1930). A late work which achieved great popularity was *The Bleak Age*, published in 1947.

Notes to chapter 8

1 L. B. Namier, *The Structure of Politics at the Accession of George III* (2nd ed. 1957), p. x. John Brewer's comments are to be found in *Party Ideology and Popular Politics at the Accession of George III* (1976).
2 See notes 22 and 23 at the end of chapter 3 on p. 203.
3 R. Walcott, *English Politics in the Early Eighteenth Century* (1956).
4 L. B. Namier and J. Brooke, *Charles Townshend* (1964).
5 *The House of Commons, 1715–54*, ed. R. R. Sedgwick (1970). The introduction to the volume was written by Dr Eveline Cruickshanks, whose views are further developed in *Political Untouchables: the Tories and the '45* (1979).
6 By 'absent friends' I meant other historians whose views were in danger of being overlooked.
7 See, for example, E. P. Thompson, *Whigs and Hunters: the Origin of the Black Act* (1975) and *Albion's Fatal Tree: Crime and Society in Eighteenth-Century England*, ed. D. Hay, P. Linebaugh and E. P. Thompson (1975). More evidence on conflict in the period is contained in J. S. Cockburn, *Crime in England, 1550–1800*, (1977).
8 See particularly E. P. Thompson on 'The Crime of Anonymity' in *Albion's Fatal Tree*.
9 P. Langford, *The Excise Crisis: Society and Politics in the Age of Walpole* (1975); T. W. Perry, *Public Opinion, Propaganda and Politics in Eighteenth-Century England* (1962); G. Rudé, *Wilkes and Liberty* (1962); Ian R. Christie, *Wilkes, Wyvill and Reform* (1962).
10 'Popular Protest in Early Hanoverian London,' *Past and Present* 79 (1978).
11 Subsequently published by the Durham County Local History Society as a pamphlet entitled *Radical Politics in the North-East of England in the Later Eighteenth Century*.
12 For Dr Colley and Dr Cruickshanks, see notes 2 and 5. J. C. D. Clark's article 'The Decline of Party, 1740–60,' is in *English Historical Review* (1978).
13 D. Ginter, *Whig Organization in the General Election of 1790* (1967).

Index

Peers are listed under their titles, thus: Bedford, John Russell, 4th Duke of